AUSTRALIA'S WELFARE WARS

DR PHILIP MENDES is a Senior Lecturer in Social Policy & Community Development in the Department of Social Work, Faculty of Medicine, Monash University. He has been a social work and social policy practitioner and educator for 15 years with particular experience in the fields of child protection, income security, and crisis counselling. He has published widely in local and international journals on the welfare state, welfare politics and welfare lobby groups.

AUSTRALIA'S WELFARE WARS

THE PLAYERS, THE POLITICS AND THE IDEOLOGIES

Philip Mendes

2003

UNSW
PRESS

A UNSW Press book

Published by
University of New South Wales Press Ltd
University of New South Wales
UNSW Sydney NSW 2052
AUSTRALIA
www.unswpress.com.au

National Library of Australia
Cataloguing-in-Publication entry:

   Mendes, Philip, 1964– .
   Australia's welfare wars: the players, the politics and the
   ideologies.

   Bibliography.
   Includes index.
   ISBN 0 86840 485 3.

   1. Public welfare — Australia. 2. Welfare state.
   3. Social policy. I. Title.

   361.60994

Cover photo Julian Kingma/The *Age*
Printer Griffin Press

CONTENTS

PREFACE

Little has been written about the impact of ideologies and interest groups on the contemporary debate surrounding the Australian welfare state. Many local texts emphasise major historical developments and key policy initiatives rather than the political debates, ideologies and interest groups which influenced these outcomes.

In contrast, this text concentrates on the role played by ideologies and lobby groups in determining welfare outcomes, with specific reference to up-to-date theories about globalisation. Students are provided with relevant case-study and source material which is used to analyse and explain contemporary policies and outcomes in the Australian welfare state, and to assist readers to predict future policy directions.

Some of the core questions examined include:

- Why do government policies increasingly focus on the alleged 'welfare dependency' of the poor and disadvantaged, rather than addressing the structural causes of poverty and unemployment?
- Why have most Western countries experienced a sharp increase in poverty and inequality?
- Does economic globalisation automatically preclude the continuation of generous national welfare states?
- Why have Australian Labor and Liberal social policies increasingly converged?
- Which interest groups — both inside and outside the social welfare sector — are most influential when it comes to social policy?
- Why do governments still fail to consult welfare consumers about welfare services and policies?

Many of the ideas in this text are drawn from my experiences as a practitioner and educator of social work and social policy over the last 15 years. During this period, I have noted with grave concern the increasing harshness of government and community attitudes towards the poor and disadvantaged, and the corresponding growth in social and economic deprivation and inequity.

This text represents an attempt to question many of the key values and assumptions that underpin contemporary social welfare policies. In particular, it is intended to be a critique and exposé of the neoliberal ideas currently dominating welfare debates locally and internationally, and an opportunity to reaffirm the continued relevance of social democratic/welfare state ideals.

ACKNOWLEDGMENTS

Particular thanks to Chris Goddard, Linda Briskman, Bob Doyle and Bob Mullaly for their consistent encouragement with this text and related projects.

Thanks also to the people in my various policy, campaign and academic networks who have encouraged me to continue blending scholarship with activism. They include most notably Susie Bunn, Gavin Dufty, Heather Fraser, Mark Furlong, Clare Griffin, Linette Hawkins, Sarah Hordern, Amanda Jones, Delia O'Donohue, Bernadette Saunders, the late Margaret Yandell and the Combined Schools of Social Work Fieldwork group. Thanks also to the numerous Monash University social work staff and students who have alternatively challenged, frustrated and inspired over the past eight years.

I am also grateful to Greg Barns, and to Bruce Duncan and Canon Ray Cleary, for kindly commenting on individual chapters pertaining to the Liberal Party and the churches respectively, and to a number of anonymous reviewers who made constructive suggestions at various stages of the manuscript. Hearty thanks to John Elliot of UNSW Press for his friendly and enthusiastic co-operation and assistance.

Above all, I would like to thank my cherished wife Tamar Lewit who has provided as always the constant and unqualified encouragement and support needed to complete the project; my darling children Miranda and Lucas for their patience and spirited enthusiasm; and my dear mother for always being there.

ABBREVIATIONS

AAP	Australian Assistance Plan
AASW	Australian Association of Social Workers
ACCI	Australian Chamber of Commerce and Industry
ACOSS	Australian Council of Social Service
ACTU	Australian Council of Trade Unions
ALP	Australian Labor Party
ANOU	Australian National Organisation for the Unemployed
ASWU	Australian Social Welfare Union
BCA	Business Council of Australia
CES	Commonwealth Employment Service
CIS	Centre for Independent Studies
CWA	Catholic Welfare Australia
DSS	Department of Social Security
EU	European Union
GDP	gross domestic product
GST	goods and services tax
ILO	International Labor Organization
IMF	International Monetary Fund
INCB	International Narcotics Control Board
IPA	Institute of Public Affairs
NGOs	non-government organisations
OECD	Organisation for Economic Cooperation and Development
SIFs	safe injecting facilities
UNDP	United Nations Development Programme
UNICEF	United Nations International Children's Emergency Fund
UWU	Unemployed Workers' Union
VCOSS	Victorian Council of Social Service

INTRODUCTION

Over the past two decades, the Australian welfare state has been a hotly contested political terrain. With the possible exception of industrial relations, welfare spending has been the foremost issue in the minds of those who wish to reduce state intervention and enhance the importance of the market place. Equally, those who wish to retain or extend the current level of state intervention identify social expenditure as central to their strategy (Burden, 1998: xii–xiii).

Yet little has been written specifically on welfare politics in this country. Much of the existing literature examines welfare policies narrowly within the context of broader debates around the Australian Labor Party/Liberal Party electoral struggle, or alternatively the economic rationalist/non-economic rationalist dichotomy. Only limited attention has been paid to the particular factors and forces which determine government social welfare agendas.

This book explicitly examines the role played by key socio-economic players and their respective ideologies in the political struggles around the welfare state.

Firstly, we draw attention to the influence of ideas and ideologies such as neoliberalism, laborism, social democracy and the Third Way, which alternatively support or reject the existence of the welfare state.

Secondly, we explore the impact of different local interest and lobby groups such as the Australian Council of Social Service (ACOSS), the Australian Council of Trade Unions (ACTU), the Business Council of Australia (BCA), the churches, the professional social work association (the Australian Association of Social

Workers), the neoliberal think-tanks, unemployed workers groups, and the media.

Thirdly, we examine the significant impact of economic globalisation, and global social policy actors and policy trends, on Australian welfare policy debates.

THE CONTESTED NATURE OF THE WELFARE STATE

In this book, we define the welfare state as state-protected minimum standards of income, health, housing, education and personal social services based on a notion of rights and entitlements, rather than on charity. Welfare provision includes both services and cash payments.

From the beginning, the welfare state has been a highly contested concept accompanied by various value-based tensions and contradictions. In particular, the welfare state has always had both social care (humanitarian) and social control (oppressive) functions. It has the potential both to liberate poor and working-class people, and to further their subordination. It represents both the gains of social and political struggle by the powerless, and the manoeuvres of powerful groups to stifle political antagonism and regulate the poor (Mullaly, 1997: 94, 127–28).

In recent years, the oppressive functions of the welfare state have come under increasing attack from Marxist, feminist and postmodern authors. Attention has been drawn to the overriding surveillance and coercion of welfare consumers, to the paternalistic and asymmetrical power relations between welfare providers and welfare recipients, and to the increasingly narrow emphasis on personal morality and the work ethic (Squires, 1990; Dean, 1991; Jordan, 1998: 161; Brown et al, 2000: 90–92).

Commentators such as Foucault, for example, have argued that the rise of the social sciences reflects the desire of government to regulate and control social order. According to this view, the main purpose of social scientists and professionals employed in bureaucracies is to categorise people into normal and abnormal categories, and to discipline the latter. Emphasis is constantly placed on the alleged deficiencies of poor and disadvantaged people, rather than the broader structural factors which contribute to social problems (Bessant and Watts, 1999: 338–46).

These criticisms of the often undemocratic and unaccountable structures of the welfare state have considerable merit. There is a strong argument for reforms that create a more bottom-up welfare system based on a genuine partnership between the state, welfare consumers and the community. At the very least, welfare services should be driven by the needs and rights of service users rather than by those of government and service providers.

However, the analysis and elaboration of such reforms are not the prime focus of this book. Rather, the emphasis is on the defence of the positive humanitarian aspects of the welfare state against neoliberal attack. On balance, we believe that the material security provided by the welfare state, despite its obvious deficits and inadequacies, still represents a significant gain for poor and working-class people in the struggle for a fair distribution of wealth and income.

In addition, there are many different forms of welfare states. States vary widely in terms of the mix of welfare provision between the state, families, the market, and other community and non-government providers including the church. Some welfare states (generally described as 'social democratic') are based primarily on public funding and service provision, others less so (Alcock, 2001: 2–3).

The Australian welfare state has always been largely a 'residual' welfare state based on the targeted direction of means-tested payments to the poor and disadvantaged (Frankel, 2001: 76). Welfare programs have generally involved a combination of public funding and private provision. Most welfare services — whether involving aged care, housing, child welfare, domestic violence, or intellectual or psychiatric disability — are delivered by non-government or community organisations. It is only income security payments that are solely managed by the Commonwealth Government (Brennan, 1998a: 130).

Advocates of residualism argue that it ensures that maximum services and benefits are received by those most in need at minimum cost to the taxpayer. However, critics argue that targeting stigmatises and marginalises the recipients, causes poverty traps, and is socially divisive (Bauman, 1998: 49–50).

The residualist model contrasts with the universalist approach prevalent in social democratic countries, whereby welfare services are provided to all citizens irrespective of income or position. Advocates of universalism argue that it enhances social solidarity and cohesiveness, reduces poverty traps, and enables the recipients to receive services and benefits without discrimination. However, critics claim that universal benefits are costly, benefit the middle class generally more than the poor specifically, and do little to affect the inequalities in society (Healy, 1998: 20–23; Pratt, 2002).

IDEOLOGICAL FRAMEWORK

This book is written from a social democratic perspective. By social democratic, I mean a commitment to substantial government intervention in the economy and a wide-ranging welfare state to alleviate market-based inequality and ensure minimum standards of support for all citizens.

This perspective interprets the historical welfare state — whether in its social liberal or social democratic model — as part of a broader project to promote income and wealth redistribution and greater equity. The welfare state is viewed as a means of extending the social rights, and bolstering the economic position, of working people. It is arguably only in recent decades that the vision of the welfare state has been narrowed to that of eliminating poverty for particular needy groups in isolation from taxation and other macro-intervention strategies (Alston and McKinnon, 2001).

Nevertheless, some readers will no doubt contest the continued relevance of social democratic and welfare state ideals. For example, some traditional Marxists and structuralists argue that the welfare state is now concerned solely with the discipline and surveillance of the poor, rather than the reduction of the inequality generated by the free market. However, I will argue that some welfare states (particularly in Europe) are more inclusive and less coercive than others, and that it is still possible for welfare states to promote greater equity.

Similarly, neoliberals (also known as 'economic rationalists') explicitly reject the welfare state's stifling of private initiative, and its commitment to equalising wealth. In contrast, they emphasise private property, the rationality of the free market, and the necessity for the size and influence of the state and government to be limited as much as possible. They believe that global social and economic changes have destroyed the political legitimacy and viability of the social democratic project.

However, I will argue that the neoliberal position is inherently deterministic and ideological, and reflects a return to discredited nineteenth-century laissez-faire ideas. The introduction of neoliberal agendas including cuts to welfare expenditure has consistently led to increased poverty, inequality and social exclusion.

The postmodern challenge to social democracy is also significant given its argument that changed historical conditions — social, cultural and economic — have undermined the universalist assumptions of the welfare state (Leonard, 1997). The postmodern perspective points to the importance of designing new localised forms of welfare intervention that reflect the increasing diversity of needs and identity. It also suggests that contemporary political struggles involve broader and more complex forces than the traditional binary contest between labour and capital. But postmodernism also has an inherent deficit: its refusal to name and critique macro-sources of wealth and power. This deficit leads postmodernism to sit on the sidelines of social conflicts, rather than promoting collective campaigns for social and economic justice (Fitzpatrick, 2002: 14).

In contrast, we believe the basic structural division in society remains that of economic inequality (Jamrozik, 2001: 12). Some groups and individuals (whether locally or internationally) have a disproportionately large share of wealth and income. Many groups have too little. The declining middle classes are increasingly being influenced towards focusing their resentment at the bottom, rather than the top. It is arguably only through the collectivist intervention of the state that the current trend towards increased inequality and injustice can be reversed.

The social democratic concern with structural inequity differs sharply from the current dominant Australian emphasis on individualistic and behavioural explanations of poverty and unemployment. This analysis assumes that people are poor or unemployed due to incompetence or immorality, and is heavily influenced by American neoliberal ideas and policies.

A particularly explicit example of this perspective was recently provided by the Commonwealth Minister for Workplace Relations, Tony Abbott. Abbott argued that poverty was the result of individual choices — people were poor because they chose to drink, gamble or use drugs — and the government could not 'stop people from making mistakes that cause them to be less well off than they might otherwise be' (quoted in Gordon and Gray, 2001). Abbott's explanation provides a justification for government policies based on motivating and disciplining welfare recipients, and re-integrating them with mainstream social values and morality.

In contrast, this book argues that Australia should give greater consideration to the social democratic ideas which remain influential in the European welfare states, and also within the new superstructure of the European Union (EU) (Emy, 2001: 16–19; Frankel, 2001: 182). Social democrats believe that structural factors such as social and economic deprivation and inequality are significant influences on the prevalence of poverty. Their definition of the causes of social problems leads to entirely different solutions to those posed by the neoliberals. For example, they would recommend that governments take action to create jobs, promote a fairer distribution of wealth and income, and generally facilitate the social and economic empowerment of the poor.

Of course, any introduction of European ideas into Australian social policy would need to take into account the vastly different political cultures. Given historical Australian attitudes towards taxation and social expenditure, European notions of social solidarity may need to be substantially re-interpreted in order to fit into the Australian setting. Nevertheless, they offer the prospect of far better outcomes on poverty and inequality than those achieved by the neoliberal doctrine of the United States (Frankel, 2001: 39–40, 183; Rundle, 2002: 23–24).

This book is divided into three major parts. In Part I, Chapter 1 explores the historical and political development of the Australian welfare state. Attention is drawn to the uniqueness of the Australian model of welfare, and its key strengths and weaknesses. This chapter clarifies that Australia has long had a very low level of social expenditure compared to the average level in Organisation for Economic Cooperation and Development (OECD) countries. Nevertheless, the Australian model enjoyed some success in preventing poverty, particularly among male wage earners.

Chapters 2, 3 and 4 explore the key ideas which are fermenting the backlash against the welfare state. Chapter 2 describes and analyses the history and nature of the neoliberal critique of the Australian welfare state. Chapter 3 explores the impact of economic globalisation and global social policy actors on welfare states. Attention is drawn to three distinct perspectives, ranging from those who believe that globalisation heralds the complete end of national welfare states, to those who believe that globalisation has relatively little impact on welfare states. The conclusion drawn is in favour of a middle-ground perspective which acknowledges the influence of globalisation on social spending, but argues that the impact varies from country to country, and is mediated by specific national factors. In support of this argument, two case studies are offered pertaining to the globalisation of Australian social policy.

Chapter 4 defends the welfare state against the agendas and forces described in Chapters 2 and 3. Attention is drawn to significant arguments in favour of the welfare state, and the continued success of the social democratic Dutch model. Nevertheless, it is acknowledged that global and economic changes render some of the structures and methods of the welfare state outdated. New strategies such as greater funding and control of service delivery by local governments and communities are recommended.

In Part II, Chapters 5 and 6 examine the impact of neoliberal ideas and other competing ideas and agendas on the welfare policies of the Federal Labor and Liberal parties. The evidence suggests an increasing policy convergence between the two parties as reflected in the case study comparison of *Working Nation* and 'work for the dole'.

The Liberal Party is judged to have been completely captured by neoliberal agendas. Its social liberal faction has been marginalised. The Australian Labor Party (ALP) has also largely abandoned any commitment to state intervention in order to secure fairer outcomes. Its principal focus appears to be on reducing welfare dependency through involvement in the labour market, rather than promoting greater equity. The current popularity of Third Way ideas within the ALP is only likely to accelerate this trend.

In Part III, Chapters 7, 8, 9 and 10 examine some of the key lobby groups involved in the welfare policy debate. Chapter 7 examines the activities of the peak non-government welfare body, ACOSS, which is the foremost defender of the Australian welfare state. Attention is drawn to both the strengths and limitations of ACOSS's lobbying activities. This analysis is further illustrated via a case study of ACOSS's role in the debate over the introduction of the goods and services tax (GST).

Chapter 8 explores the views and influence of a number of other interest groups. The business sector is depicted as generally hostile to the welfare state. Some attempt is also made to debunk the currently popular notion of 'corporate social responsibility'. Trade unions, in contrast, are philosophical supporters of the welfare state. However, in practice they are primarily passive observers of the policy debate. They continue to focus almost exclusively on the wage claims and working conditions of those in employment, and have developed only limited forms of co-operation with ACOSS and other community groups. Professional social work associations such as the Australian Association of Social Workers are also strong supporters of welfare expenditure. However, despite the close historical link between the social work profession and the welfare state, the AASW has rarely been an effective player in the welfare policy debate. Lastly, the media has played a significant role in social policy debates around welfare reform, illicit drugs, and other issues. In general, the mainstream media reinforces conservative explanations of and solutions to social problems. In contrast, local governments have begun to emerge recently as an increasingly important source of counter-ideas and initiatives to neoliberal agendas.

Chapter 9 explores the prominent role of the churches as critics of free-market agendas. Attention is drawn to the long history of church activism on social justice issues, to the central role played by churches in the provision of non-government welfare services, and to the coherent set of Christian social teachings on which their interventions are based. Counter arguments from inside and outside the churches are also explored plus the particular dilemmas posed by church involvement in the privatised Jobs Network. Whilst acknowledging the political ambivalence of much Christian teaching, the legitimacy of church social justice interventions is affirmed.

Chapter 10 examines the relative political powerlessness of contemporary unemployed people. Historically, unemployed workers groups have actively contested the political and social marginalisation of the unemployed. However, today, most unemployed groups are numerically small and insignificant. The lack of collective action by the unemployed is attributed to a number of factors, including changes in the labour market, the diversity of unemployed people, the structure of the income support system, and the general failure of ACOSS or the union movement to organise or resource the unemployed.

Lastly, Chapter 11 concludes with an assessment of the local and international political factors and forces contributing towards or against welfare retrenchment. In addition to the ideas and lobby groups described earlier, some consideration is given to the influence of public opinion. Currently, the political momentum is clearly towards further welfare retrenchment. Nevertheless, the neoliberal model may lose public support if it fails to produce more effective and fairer outcomes for all, including the poor.

part one

THE HISTORICAL, POLITICAL AND IDEOLOGICAL CONTEXT OF THE WELFARE STATE

The following chapters introduce the historical and political context of contemporary debates around the welfare state.

Chapter 1 explores the unique historical development of the Australian welfare state, and its key strengths and limitations. In particular, this chapter looks at the restructuring of the welfare state undertaken by both Labor and conservative governments since 1983.

In Chapters 2 and 3, this restructuring is attributed to the joint ideological constructs of neoliberalism and globalisation. Neoliberal ideas of small government, free markets and limited social expenditure have provided the ideological inspiration for cuts to the welfare state. Equally, pressures emanating from economic globalisation appear to be driving governments to adhere to neoliberal notions of economic competitiveness.

However, Chapter 4 challenges the neoliberal model by arguing globalisation does not preclude different paths to economic competitiveness. For example, the experience of the Netherlands suggests that a generous welfare state and economic productivity remain compatible.

1
THE HISTORICAL AND POLITICAL DEVELOPMENT OF THE AUSTRALIAN WELFARE STATE

Australia possesses one of the most selective income support systems in the Western industrialised world. Financial assistance is provided on a flat-rate basis, funded from general revenue rather than via insurance schemes. Welfare programs are mostly means tested, targeted to the poor, and low in monetary value.

The purpose of this chapter is to explain how this unique system developed, and to identify both its strengths and its limitations. The first section examines the beginnings of the Australian welfare state from the early state-based schemes in the pre-Federation period to the emergence of what Frank Castles calls the 'wage earners' welfare state'. The next section explores the introduction of the basic features of the welfare state from 1941 to 1949. It then explores the relative inaction of the Liberal Party years from 1949 to 1972; documents the social democratic initiatives of the Whitlam Government period from 1972 to 1975; and examines the Fraser Government years from 1975 to 1983. It then discusses the Hawke/Keating years from 1983 to 1996 and the major initiatives of the present Howard Government since 1996. These two later periods have been strongly influenced by the joint ideological constructs of neoliberalism and globalisation. (The social policies of these periods will be examined in greater detail in Chapters 5 and 6.) Finally, it examines the effectiveness of the Australian system in reducing poverty.

THE BEGINNINGS OF THE WELFARE STATE

Early historians regularly depicted Australia as a 'working man's paradise' in which disparities of wealth were far less prevalent than in the old world (Whiteford, 1998: 197–98). Yet, pre-Federation Australia was hardly immune to the effects of severe poverty. Research by Jill Roe suggests that 10 per cent of the Australian population lived in permanent poverty during the nineteenth and early twentieth centuries, whilst a similar proportion resided in temporary poverty. Particularly vulnerable groups included struggling farmers, unemployed labourers, the aged, and deserted and widowed mothers. There was frequent evidence of disease epidemics and high mortality rates in the inner-city slums (Garton, 1990: 3, 39–42).

The Australian states responded to these social needs with a combination of private charity and government relief for the poor. Private benevolence was minimal in order to discourage idleness, and directed only to those judged to be deserving. However, the 1890s recession and associated social and political tensions placed increasing pressure on governments to intervene. There was increasing acceptance of the notion that poverty reflected social and economic conditions, rather than individual behaviour (Garton, 1990: 43–77; O'Connor et al, 1999: 24–26).

Governments principally reacted in two ways. Firstly they introduced measures to protect the rights and conditions of workers, including women and juveniles. Secondly, they began to introduce direct payments, in preference to charity, to non-working poor groups such as the aged and infirm. These two developments earned Australia international renown as the alleged 'social laboratory' of the world (Butlin et al, 1982: 156–63; Garton, 1990: 77–85).

Following the establishment of the Commonwealth Government by Federation in 1901, the objective of decent wage levels for the working man was institutionalised via a creative class compromise between urban manufacturing interests, represented by Deakin's Liberal protectionists, and the emergent labor movement.

The three components of this alliance were compulsory arbitration, protection, and white Australia. Arbitration was enshrined in Higgins' 1907 'harvester judgement' which defined 'a fair and reasonable wage' of 7 shillings a day for adult males supporting a wife and children. Protection enabled the manufacturer to pay 'fair and reasonable wages without impairing the maintenance and extension of his industry, or its capacity to supply the local market'. The white Australia policy was justified as a defence of white workers from cheap non-white labour.

Thus in Australia a unique model of a welfare state was developed, a model which concerned itself primarily with the protection of wage levels (at least for white male breadwinners), rather than the provision of supplementary welfare benefits. Castles (1985: 102–103) calls this model a 'wage earners' welfare state' and contrasts it with both the residual model of welfare (because Australia has a minimum living wage) and the institutional model of welfare (because full inclusion in the system depends on one's status as a wage earner rather than one's status as a citizen).

In addition to wages, the Commonwealth Government introduced old age pensions in 1908, and invalid pensions in 1910. However, payments were only provided to applicants judged to be of 'good character'. Asians, some Aborigines, alcoholics, past prisoners and recent immigrants were not eligible. The Commonwealth also introduced a maternity allowance in order to promote a higher birth rate, but once again excluded Aborigines, and most Asians and Pacific Islanders. Both the pensions and the maternity allowance were funded from general revenue, rather than through contributory insurance schemes as tended to be the case in Europe. This method of financing the system through progressive taxation was viewed as uniquely redistributive (Garton, 1990: 99–101; Bryson, 2001: 73).

Nevertheless, both the wages model and the benefits system had significant flaws. The living wage granted by the harvester judgement provided an income closer to a subsistence level than one of reasonable comfort. It also failed to address the needs of large families given that the system was based on an assumption of three children, and made no formal provision for women workers. Nor was any recognition given to women's role in unpaid caring work. Overall, the model assumed that men would act as breadwinners and women as dependants (Garton, 1990: 82–83; Bryson, 2000: 48–50).

No further income security payments were introduced by the Commonwealth Government until the 1940s. Able-bodied men were expected by the state to support themselves within the labour market. Working men themselves preferred work to welfare, which was regarded as demeaning (Macintyre, 1986: 135).

Some states introduced limited new schemes. For example, the Queensland Government provided relief to assist seasonal labourers during periods of temporary unemployment, and the New South Wales Government introduced widows' pensions and child endowment. However, in general, unemployed workers and their families were forced to rely on relief from charities.

Attempts to legislate for expanded benefits were consistently frustrated by dissension between conservatives who favoured the introduction of contributory insurance schemes similar to those in Britain and Germany, and the labor movement which demanded the retention of the existing non-contributory system of funding (Watts, 1987; Roskam, 2001). Garton calls Australia's social policy record during the 1920s and 1930s 'dismal' compared to other Western countries (1990: 123).

THE GROWTH OF THE AUSTRALIAN WELFARE STATE: 1941–1949

The basic legislative and program components of the Australian welfare state were introduced between 1941 and 1945, which has been referred to as 'the heroic age in the history of the national welfare state' (Beilharz et al, 1992: 82).

A significant contributor to this development was the Joint Parliamentary Committee on Social Security set up initially by the Menzies United Australia Party Government in 1941. The committee's first interim report tabled in September 1941 reported that 'a considerable proportion of Australia's citizens are poorly housed, ill-clothed or ill-nourished — living in conditions which reflect no credit on a country such as ours'. The report recommended that social services would contribute to the war effort 'by improving the morale and willingness to work of the employees, who will feel that a regime which is prepared, even at this time of emergency, to improve their conditions is worth working and fighting for' (Shaver, 1987: 415).

The aim of the social security reforms, therefore, was to rectify the inadequacies of the earlier 'wage earners' welfare state'. Among the measures introduced during this period were child endowment (introduced in the last days of the Menzies Government), funeral benefits for deceased pensioners, a new form of maternity allowances, widows' pensions, unemployment, sickness and pharmaceutical benefits, and hospital and tuberculosis benefits. By the end of World War II, the Commonwealth had assumed responsibility for all major income security benefits and health care (Kewley, 1969: 82–95).

Labor Prime Minister Chifley argued that it was the 'duty and responsibility of the community, and particularly those more fortunately placed, to see that our less fortunate fellow citizens are protected from those shafts of fate which leave them helpless and without hope'. The labor movement would fight to ensure a future 'free from want, insecurity and misery' (Chifley, quoted in Beilharz, 1994: 63).

A BENEVOLENT WELFARE STATE?

Most commentators regard the introduction of Labor's welfare state as an expression of compassion and benevolence that marked a sharp break from the earlier periods of conservative inaction (Dickey, 1980: 167–84; Garton, 1990: 131–37). However, some left-wing critics argue that the welfare legislation also reflected pressing political and fiscal considerations.

According to this second viewpoint, there were substantial continuities in thinking on policy between the conservative governments of the 1930s and the Labor period. Much of this continuity reflected the influence of a powerful group of economists, political scientists and public servants — Coombs, Gilbin, Copland, Downing and so on — involved in the key policy-making processes. These advisers viewed welfare initiatives not solely from the vantage point of compassionate idealism, but also as a means of dealing with the demands of wartime economic, manpower and taxation policy.

Thus it is argued that Labor used its welfare measures to redefine financial obligations and to secure more revenue for the Commonwealth Government by imposing heavy taxation on low-income earners. In short, despite traditional Labor opposition to contributory funding, workers were now being asked to pay at least in part for their own welfare benefits (Watts, 1987; Beilharz et al, 1992: 83–84).

A further criticism relates to the precedence given to economic development and full employment over welfare measures. This criticism notes that the Labor Party's primary objective was to achieve full employment, which was seen as the real key to economic and social security. In the 1945 White Paper on Full Employment, for example, the essential mechanism of human welfare was defined as an efficient, fully functioning wage-labour market. Social welfare was to play a subordinate role, being seen principally as a safety net that would play a compensating part in times of economic downturn (Watts, 1987: 127).

However, a counter view holds that this critique reflects too narrow an identification of social policy with straight welfare payments, and ignores the broader Keynesian interventionist policies and objectives of the Chifley Government. Social concerns were to be directly addressed via economic planning and full employment, rather than through a narrower focus on social welfare (Smyth, 1995a: 51–52; Fenna, 1998: 288–89).

According to Smyth, 'The relatively minor importance attached to the establishment of welfare services is a sign, not that plans for post-war reconstruction were insignificant, but that other policy instruments were considered more powerful means of attaining social objectives' (1995a: 53). It was only later that the focus of social policy debate became narrowed to the relatively marginal issue of social services (1995a: 4, 175).

THE CONSERVATIVE YEARS: 1949–1972

Following the welfare initiatives of the Curtin/Chifley years, the ensuing 23 years of conservative administration were marked by considerably less innovation. Few substantial advances were made in the area of social legislation. Liberal Party policy emphasised the subsidising of existing private resources and providers, rather than the creation of new resources or the extension of Commonwealth responsibility. Social policy was characterised by cautious regulatory administration of incremental change which generally favoured the middle classes. Overall, social expenditure declined as a percentage of GDP during this period (Castles, 1985: 30; Gray, 1995: 211–212).

The only major social policy initiatives during the Liberal-Country Party coalition years were the extension of child endowment to the first child (in 1950); free pharmaceutical and medical benefits for pensioners on full pension and their dependants (1951); and a *National Health Act* based on the subsidising of private insurance expenses (1953). The Coalition also progressively liberalised the means test for pensioners, and made grants to a number of voluntary bodies in the social welfare field, including ACOSS (Kewley, 1969: 96–117; Menzies, 1970: 116–29).

The dominant philosophy of Liberal Party social policy was a commitment to individualism, incentive and self-reliance. Whilst the Liberals rejected a return to the unrestricted laissez-faire economics of the 1930s, they continued to prefer welfare provision by the family and private charities, rather than reliance on state bureaucracies. They also continued in principle to favour funding by insurance schemes rather than by general taxation, although they accepted that alternative financing methods could not be implemented within the existing political agenda (Roskam, 2001: 271).

The Liberals rejected the concept of an expanded welfare state, believing that it would undermine the combination of individual endeavour and thrift which they saw to be the basis of 'true' social security. At the same time, the Liberals endorsed the concept of a safety net to keep the needy from destitution. The net, however, was placed at a sufficiently low level to ensure that individuals retained an incentive to care for themselves (Shamsullah, 1990: 107).

Prime Minister Gorton, for example, suggested that pension rates should ensure 'at least a modest standard of living so that pensioners do not need blankets to be provided for them in winter, so that at least they have enough to eat and a roof over their head', whilst Social Services Minister William Wentworth stated that the poor, and the old and the sick were entitled to be kept in 'frugal comfort' (Gorton, cited in Tulloch, 1979: 43; Wentworth, 1969: 3).

Spending on welfare programs remained extremely low by international standards (Table 1.1). Welfare expenditure was 6.5 per cent of GDP, compared with the OECD average of 13.8 per cent. In addition, pension rates, which had been 25 per cent of average weekly earnings in 1946, had fallen to 20 per cent by 1970 (Encel, 1991: 62). Critics of Coalition policy have argued that for many Australians, income security payments were 'not so much a defence against poverty, but their first real encounter with it' (Elliott and Graycar, 1979: 91–92).

THE REDISCOVERY OF POVERTY

During the first two post-war decades, Australia was known as the 'lucky country', a term popularised by writer Donald Horne to describe the remarkably egalitarian nature of Australian life (Horne, 1964: 239). As in Britain, it was generally accepted that due to the initiatives of the welfare state and the increasing affluence of society, the problem of poverty was well on the way to eradication.

TABLE 1.1
PUBLIC SOCIAL EXPENDITURE: 1970 (% OF GDP)

Japan	5.0
Australia	6.5
Switzerland	9.1
Greece	9.4
Canada	10.5
United States	10.5
Ireland	10.9
New Zealand	11.6
Finland	13.1
Norway	14.3
Italy	14.7
United Kingdom	14.9
Belgium	15.4
France	16.9
Germany	17.8
Austria	18.4
Sweden	19.2
Denmark	20.8
Netherlands	22.6
OECD average	*13.8*

SOURCE Adapted from Arjona et al, *Growth, Inequality and Social Protection*, 2001: 67.

Even left-wing radicals and ALP activists appeared to believe that the welfare state had reduced the gross inequalities of income and wealth associated with capitalism. However, they did express some concern that the welfare state was incomplete, and that further redistribution of income and wealth should be attained via more progressive taxation and improved social services (Davies and Serle, 1954: 98–108; Mendelsohn, 1954: 316–20).

Yet, the mid-to-late 1960s saw the 'rediscovery' of poverty and the acknowledgement that the prosperity engineered by the economic growth and full employment of the Liberal years had passed many Australians by. Two young academics — James Jupp (1959) and Helen Hughes (1960) — associated with the radical journal *Outlook*, provoked some early discussion.

Hughes, writing in *Outlook* in 1960, noted that about one-third of the half million aged and invalid pensioners and widows were estimated by social workers to be 'living below subsistence'. Jupp referred to 'a submerged tenth' of the population — pensioners, slum dwellers, unemployed migrants, deserted wives, shack dwellers, Aborigines and 'no hopers' — who were not enjoying the general national prosperity. He suggested as a solution the provision of civil rights to Aborigines, slum clearance, and low-cost accommodation for migrants, pensioners and Aborigines (see Smyth, 1995a: 263–65).

Further interest in poverty was stimulated by the church-based welfare agency, the Brotherhood of St Laurence, which conducted various studies into the needs of pensioners and low-income families. Research was also undertaken by the Victorian and Australian Councils of Social Service.

Ray Brown (1963), lecturer in social administration at Adelaide University, inspired by poverty studies in Britain and America, estimated that 5 per cent of the Australian population lived in chronic poverty. Articles in the radical quarterly *Dissent* by Michael Keating, Leon Glezer and David Scott drew similar conclusions, whilst Australian National University researcher RT Appleyard (1965) argued that three groups of Australians — families with low incomes and high rents, some aged and widow pensioners, and part-Aborigines — were experiencing deprivation.

Popular awareness of poverty was extended further by the work of journalist John Stubbs. In a highly publicised book modelled on Michael Harrington's *The Other America* and evocatively titled *The Hidden People*, Stubbs (1966) estimated that half a million Australians lived in poverty.

In 1966, the Melbourne University Institute of Applied Economic and Social Research, headed by Professor Ronald Henderson, set out to measure the incidence of poverty in Melbourne. They set a poverty line of $33, close to the basic wage plus child endowment for two children. Henderson concluded that 7.7 per cent of all family units in Melbourne lived on or below the poverty line, and a further 5.2 per cent hovered dangerously close to the minimum level. The major groups in poverty were the aged, the Aboriginal population, certain migrant communities, female-headed families, rural labourers, and small farmers (Henderson, Harcourt and Harper, 1970).

In spite of Henderson's findings, the Coalition Government continued to insist that there were only 'pockets of poverty' in Australia. In 1969, in an address to a National Conference on Poverty sponsored by the Australian Institute of Political Science, Social Services Minister

William Wentworth outlined three concepts of poverty: absolute poverty, comparative poverty and personal poverty. Wentworth stated that the government was committed to the elimination of absolute poverty and to raising the threshold of acceptable comparative poverty which could not be abolished short of implementing a system of 'doctrinaire egalitarianism'. Personal poverty — described as the outcome of poor budgeting — lay outside the sphere of government and was the concern of charitable and voluntary organisations (Wentworth, 1969: 1–4).

Pressure, however, built up on the government to increase social security benefits and to undertake a systematic study of poverty throughout Australia. Calls for a public enquiry into poverty were voiced, for example, by ACOSS, the Anglican Church hierarchy and the Labor Party Opposition. Eventually, Prime Minister McMahon caved in to his critics. On 29 August 1972, he announced a Commission of Inquiry into Poverty to be conducted by Professor Ronald Henderson, the author of the earlier survey of poverty in Melbourne (Mendes, 1996: 55).

The Coalition, however, was soon to lose office.

THE WHITLAM YEARS: 1972–1975

The Whitlam Government's social welfare agenda reflected the influence of a structural model of welfare. This model emphasised the need for a broad redistribution of income from rich to poor via macroeconomic reforms, rather than social policy being limited to minor incremental changes in social security payments.

Historian Stuart Macintyre has called the Whitlam program 'the first substantial exercise of social democracy in this country' in that it involved a greatly increased role for government in promoting fairer, more egalitarian outcomes in the economy. Whitlam's commitment to large-scale government spending in the areas of health, housing, urban development and education in an attempt to improve access to these services by the disadvantaged contrasted sharply with the ALP's traditionally limited laborist emphasis on the protection of wage levels (Macintyre, 1986: 138).

In his 1972 policy speech, Whitlam declared his intention to promote equality of opportunity for all Australians. He envisaged welfare as a right available to every member of the community, rather than as charity for a stigmatised minority (Whitlam, 1985: 359–60). Whitlam's central argument was that:

> increasingly, a citizen's real standard of living, the health of himself and his family, his children's opportunity for education and self-improvement, his

access to employment opportunities, his ability to enjoy the nation's resources for recreation and cultural activity [and] his scope to participate in the decisions and actions of the community are determined not so much by his income but by the availability of services which the community alone can provide and ensure. (1985: 182–83)

The new Social Security Minister, Bill Hayden, indicated his intention to promote a redistribution of wealth and income from rich to poor in order to reduce the unacceptable degree of economic inequality in Australia. Hayden's appointment inspired the new head of the Department of Social Security, Dr Louis Wienholt to send his desk clerks out into the slums of Melbourne and Sydney to attend two-week courses organised by the Brotherhood of St Laurence — the intention being to 'sensitise' them to the problems of departmental clients (Mendes, 1996: 122).

One of the first of Labor's initiatives was the appointment of a Social Welfare Commission to investigate philosophies underlying welfare policies and to make specific recommendations to the government on policies and priorities. The commission identified three different philosophical approaches to welfare: the residual view in which government intervention occurs only when the individual or family has failed to provide basic needs; the institutional view which sees social welfare institutions as necessary for the efficient functioning of society rather than for securing the equal well-being of all members of society; and the third view which regards social welfare 'as a basic integrated institution in society ensuring not only the provision to all of primary material needs, but also genuine opportunities for social and cultural satisfaction'.

The third philosophy, which was endorsed by both the commission and the government, argued that social welfare should be:

> a positive agent for change ensuring a high level of universal services both quantitatively and qualitatively as well as selective services, positively discriminating in favour of particular disadvantaged groups. Social policy is therefore intended to bring about improvement in the standard and quality of life for all individuals and to ensure a redistribution of resources within the society. (Social Welfare Commission, 1975: 13)

SOCIAL POLICY INITIATIVES

The Whitlam years have been widely viewed as constituting an aberration in the history of Australian social policy. Whitlam shifted welfare and other social policies from the periphery onto the centre stage, and introduced a set of universalistic policy initiatives that marked a significant change from the residual incrementalism of the Liberal years (Elliott and Graycar, 1979: 94).

His government introduced a number of universalistic programs which sought to benefit the community in general as well as alleviating particular inequalities. Examples of these programs included the national health scheme Medibank which sought to supplant private health schemes, the abolition of tertiary education fees, and the Australian Assistance Plan (AAP). Well-laid plans to introduce a national superannuation scheme to cover all employees and a national compensation scheme to cover all accident-caused injuries failed to come to fruition (Elliott and Graycar, 1979: 94–95).

The AAP was a co-operative regional participatory social planning program formulated by the Social Welfare Commission and implemented by the Department of Social Security. The AAP envisaged the creation of new local governing bodies, 'Regional Councils for Social Development', to co-ordinate and advise on matters of social welfare. The AAP sought to expand the involvement of local communities, and in particular that of welfare consumers and other low-income groups, in the planning and provision of welfare services.

Yet, the evidence would suggest that participation was primarily limited to middle-class members of local voluntary agencies who were already employed in social welfare and related fields. Despite its good intentions, the AAP seems to have been of most benefit to the welfare establishment, rather than to the unaffiliated and the powerless (Graycar, 1976: 42–55).

The other highlight of the Whitlam years was the report of the Henderson Commission of Inquiry into Poverty. The Whitlam Government had broadened the original enquiry by appointing a further four commissioners to cover the areas of education and poverty; social/medical aspects; law and poverty; and selected economic issues.

The commission found that 10.2 per cent of Australians were very poor, and 7.7 per cent were rather poor. It identified poverty as the result of 'structural inequality within society' and called for 'a redistribution of income and services to increase the capacity of poor people to exercise power'. The commission endorsed the creation of a guaranteed minimum income scheme to replace the existing system of income security benefits and pensions. The scheme would ensure that everyone received an income on or above the poverty line (Henderson, 1975).

Critics of the proposed guaranteed minimum income scheme argued that it involved no significant redistribution of income from rich to poor, and failed to address existing class inequalities. However, the Minister for Social Security, Bill Hayden, gave it due consideration and various proposals for a guaranteed minimum income were mooted by the Department of Social Security's

Priorities Review staff. Eventually, the prohibitive cost of the scheme and its apparent incompatibility with work incentives frustrated moves towards implementation (Carney and Hanks, 1986: 31).

Instead, the Whitlam Government chose to raise the level of existing pensions and benefits by upgrading them to 25 per cent of average weekly earnings. Other income security changes included the introduction of a new category of benefits for single mothers (the Supporting Mothers' Benefit); the payment of Australian pensions overseas; the introduction of the Double Orphans' Pension; the Handicapped Children's Allowance; the Homeless Persons' Assistance Bill; the reduction in the differences between certain categories of benefits and pensions; the abolition of the means test for age pensions; and the establishment of Social Security Appeals Tribunals as an independent source of redress for client grievances (Whitlam, 1985: 362–63).

CRITICISMS OF THE WHITLAM GOVERNMENT'S PROGRAM

Whilst acknowledging the reformist nature of the Whitlam Government's welfare initiatives, critics have argued that the government's policies failed to come to terms with important changes in the labour market and the economy. These changes included the end of full employment with the onset of the 1974/75 recession, the decline in economic growth, and the related increase in levels of poverty as families headed by people of workforce age were forced into reliance on income security.

Professor Bettina Cass, for example, suggests that these new realities required a different type of welfare response, such as the linking of social security payments with employment creation and training, and tax reform to provide a stronger revenue base to finance adequate social security payments. These issues were not to be effectively addressed until the election of the Hawke Labor Government in 1983 (Cass, 1989: 136–37).

THE FRASER YEARS: 1975–1983

The Fraser Government's social welfare agenda reflected the influence of both individualistic and social liberal tendencies. On the one hand, government policy was based on cutting the public sector and reducing the alleged growing dependence on big government in favour of providing incentives for private expenditure. On the other hand, the government emphasised a welfarist compassion for those who were unable to support themselves.

The pragmatic compromise between these two tendencies was

typified by the rhetoric of Prime Minister Fraser. In a speech made shortly before taking office, Fraser argued strongly in favour of a secure welfare safety net. According to Fraser:

> The notion that deprivation is a necessary spur to achievement and that initiative is dulled by the provision of welfare is not only wrong, but it has no place in a philosophy that values the individual. On the contrary, the security of knowing that aid is available if needed can increase the incentives for, and reduce the costs of, achievement.

Fraser contended that 'the concept of a safety net below which no individual should fall through circumstances beyond his control' is basic to Liberal thinking (Fraser, 1975: 133). At the same time, he emphasised that welfare programs should promote independence and self-reliance, rather than encouraging a 'debilitating dependence' on the providers of social services (quoted in Ghosh, 1978: 21).

Fraser's belief in providing compassionate support to the poor and disadvantaged, whilst helping them to become independent of government assistance, was echoed by other Liberal Party ministers. Government representatives spoke of directing safety-net assistance to those genuinely in need due to involuntary economic hardship such as old age, widowhood, sickness and invalidity, whilst ensuring that recipients retained incentives for initiative and self-reliance (Mendes, 1996: 173–74).

SOCIAL POLICY INITIATIVES

In contrast to the social democratic universalism of the Whitlam years, the period under Fraser was characterised by a return to a selectivist/residual approach to welfare. Universalist programs and services — such as the Social Welfare Commission and the AAP, the enacted (but not yet proclaimed) Children's Commission, the Department of Urban and Regional Development and (through a series of measures) the Medibank health insurance scheme — were all dismantled.

The most significant social policy initiatives of the Fraser years were the introduction of the Family Allowances program in 1976 and the Family Income Supplement in the 1982/83 Budget. The Family Allowances scheme replaced the old child endowment program and income tax rebates for dependent children, and it ensured considerable redistribution to low-income families. However, the government's failure to index family allowances led to a decline in their real value. The Family Income Supplement scheme provided payments to low-income working families not eligible for social security pensions or benefits. The objective of the program was to ensure that these families would be better off in employment than claiming a social security benefit (Cass and Whiteford, 1989: 287–88).

Other initiatives included the replacement of the means test for pensions with an income test which resulted in an increase in the number eligible for some pensions; the extension of the handicapped children's allowance to include a new category for the needy and marginally handicapped; the extension of the supporting mothers' benefit to supporting fathers; the provision of automatic changes in the rates of pensions in accordance with changes in the consumer price index; and the assumption of financial responsibility for sole parents in the first six months of eligibility, which had previously been a state function.

The government also introduced a series of support schemes for the young unemployed known as Community Youth Support Schemes; provided increased real support for handicapped, aged and homeless persons' facilities and migrant integration services; and set up a Social Welfare Research Centre (later renamed the Social Policy Research Centre) to undertake and sponsor research in important aspects of social welfare (Ironmonger, 1980; Carney and Hanks, 1986: 32).

These initiatives were accompanied by a series of attacks by the Fraser Government on the welfare state in general and welfare recipients in particular. For example, the government promoted animosity towards welfare recipients by suggesting that they were abusing or defrauding the social security system. The government waged a particularly vigorous campaign against alleged dole fraud. Large numbers of field officers were employed to apprehend persons illegally receiving social security payments. Critics of the government alleged that the dole fraud campaign sought to detract attention from the high rate of unemployment and constituted 'political persecution' of the unemployed (Windschuttle, 1979: 180–220).

Unemployment continued to rise throughout the Fraser years. But despite the large increase in the number of unemployment beneficiaries, the government presided over an erosion of real benefit levels — largely through abolition or dilution of indexation. The unemployment benefit for persons aged 16 and 17 years was increased only once between 1975 and 1983, whilst indexation for single people over 18 years was withdrawn in 1978 (Ironmonger, 1980: 34–35).

The Fraser Government also tightened the eligibility criteria for unemployment benefits; denied payments to people who moved to areas of low employment opportunity or who were stood down as a result of strikes; and increased the waiting periods for school leavers and people who voluntarily left their jobs. In addition, the government introduced a crackdown on the eligibility criteria for invalid pensions, changing the interpretation of the relevant Act so that in judging whether or not a person was 85 per cent incapacitated for work no account was taken of the state of the job market. Under

pressure from the media, the state of the job market was reintro-
duced into eligibility consideration (Elliott, 1982: 128–33).

WELFARE EXPENDITURE AND THE NEW RIGHT

In spite of the government's concern about rising welfare expenditure and its commitment to reducing welfare costs, the level of welfare spending during this period fell only slightly, from 15.7 per cent
of GDP in 1975/76 to 13.6 per cent in 1981/82, and from 50.8
per cent of total Budget outlays to 46.2 per cent. This was primarily because increased numbers of people became reliant on social
security benefits as a result of the recessions of 1977/78 and
1982/83. In particular, the number of recipients of unemployment
benefits increased from 160 700 to 390 700, or from 4.6 per cent
to approximately 10 per cent. There was also a significant growth in
the number of sole parents (Cass and Whiteford, 1989: 277).

The failure of the Fraser Government to match its neoliberal
rhetoric with results and reduce the welfare state angered advocates
of small government, and created the context for the emergence of
the anti-welfare New Right in Australia (Garton, 1990: 168–69).
We discuss this political development in greater detail in Chapter 2.

LABOR TARGETING: 1983–1996

The Hawke/Keating Governments were characterised by a persistent philosophical tension between an economic policy dominated
by free-market objectives, and a social policy based at least in principle on the promotion of social justice.

On the one hand, the ALP carefully conformed to an economic
rationalist agenda based on lowering taxes, and decreasing social
expenditure. This strategy led inevitably to increased inequality. Yet
at the same time, it maintained a genuine commitment to lifting the
incomes of particular groups in poverty. The framework used to promote social justice was that of targeted welfare, whereby greater
assistance was provided to those welfare recipients who were most in
need, rather than through across-the-board increases in universally
paid benefits. Thus the ALP introduced means tests on previously
universal payments, such as old age pensions and family allowances.

Targeting enabled Labor to provide substantial increases in real
incomes to most social security beneficiaries, particularly age pensioners and low-income families with children. The Family Package
of 1987 was especially generous. Other initiatives included the Jobs,
Education and Training scheme for single parents, the Child
Support Scheme, Medicare, and the Better Cities Program.

At the same time, the ALP pursued vigorous anti-welfare fraud campaigns, and introduced compulsory training schemes for the long-term unemployed. Often the initiatives that benefited low-income earners were coupled with attacks on the rights and living standards of other disadvantaged groups.

Overall, the emphasis continued to be on ameliorating the economic and social consequences of free-market policies — such as poverty and unemployment — rather than intervening directly in the market place to promote job creation and a fairer distribution of income. In short, admirable social policy objectives were consistently subordinated to the unjust outcomes of the free market.

LIBERAL RETRENCHMENT: 1996–2002

The social welfare policies of the Howard Liberal-National Coalition Government have been dominated by two ideological tendencies: the neoliberal concern to reduce government interference with free-market outcomes by restricting access to social security payments; and the social conservative concern to reinforce traditional institutions such as the family.

However, these objectives have been moderated by Howard's cautious pragmatism, and his commitment to meet, at least in part, his election-time promise to maintain the social welfare safety net. Thus, his government has chosen to save money through incremental changes based on the concept of mutual obligation which tighten eligibility to some existing benefits, but do not at this stage directly challenge any fundamental entitlement.

For example, the government has introduced a number of measures to eliminate alleged incentives to welfare dependency. These initiatives have included a review of the Young Homeless Allowance; the tightening of access to unemployment benefits; and the introduction of massive spending cuts on services used principally by the poor and disadvantaged such as the Commonwealth Dental Health Program, labour market programs and public housing.

In addition, the government has employed a number of measures to discipline those welfare beneficiaries who are perceived to be undeserving of assistance. These measures have included the introduction of a work for the dole scheme which emphasises the elimination of the individual 'flaws' of jobseekers rather than measures to address the absence of sufficient jobs; constant crackdowns on alleged welfare fraud including the introduction of a 'dob in a dole bludger' hotline; and massive penalties for breaches of welfare requirements.

Similar assumptions underlie the 2000 welfare reform review

which recommended that principles of mutual obligation be extended to unemployed people aged 35–64 years and recipients of parenting payment whose youngest child was aged six years or above.

NEOLIBERALISM AND GLOBALISATION

Much of the policy debate since 1983 has been influenced by perceived policy constraints arising from the joint ideological constructs of neoliberalism and globalisation. Both Labor and Liberal governments have assumed that Australia has no choice but to undertake a particular form of neoliberal restructuring in order to remain competitive in a global world. This form of restructuring has generally followed the policy parameters set by the United States, and ignored the alternative paths followed by most European countries.

The following three chapters will contest many of the assumptions underlying this neoliberal policy agenda. To be sure, we acknowledge that immense global social and economic changes have fundamentally altered the operating structure of the welfare state. Nevertheless, we will argue that Australia retains significant political choices about how to respond to these changes.

THE UNIQUENESS OF THE AUSTRALIAN WELFARE STATE MODEL: MEAN OR EFFECTIVE?

International commentators such as the Swedish theorist Esping-Andersen have often described the Australian welfare state as a 'residual' or liberal welfare state typified by low levels of welfare spending and minimum interference with the free market. Overall, the Australian welfare state was rated in 1980 as having the lowest level of 'decommodification' — meaning that few social rights are guaranteed independently of the market — in the OECD (Esping-Andersen, 1990: 50–52, 74–77). Esping-Andersen's overall typology is discussed in greater detail in Chapter 4.

However, local commentators such as Castles and Mitchell have contested the assumed link between greater social expenditure and income redistribution. They argue that the Australian model is both effective and egalitarian. It is effective because its careful targeting of benefits to particular needy groups maximises the reduction in poverty attained by any given expenditure. For example, unemployment benefits are available irrespective of the duration of unemployment, and without any insurance contribution. It is egalitarian because its historical focus on the rights of wage earners and full employment has ensured a relatively low level of 'working poor' (Castles and Mitchell, 1992).

In response, Esping-Andersen argues that the liberalisation of the Australian economy over the last two decades has eroded the 'social democratic' features of the Australian welfare state. In particular, the large increases in unemployment and sole-parent families accompanied by greater wage inequality have undermined the traditional emphasis on egalitarian outcomes (Esping-Andersen, 1999: 89–90).

There is no doubt that the Australian model now faces far greater fiscal and political challenges than in the past. For example, by 1997/98, 20 per cent of income units with a head of working age were dependent on welfare payments as their principal source of income. This compares with less than 3 per cent in 1970. By June 1999, 17.4 per cent of all dependent children were growing up in jobless families (Borland et al, 2001: 2).

A recent study of egalitarianism found that Australia ranked higher in terms of inequality of income distribution than 9 out of 13 other OECD countries (Sheehan, 2001: 42). However, there remains some evidence to the contrary. As we shall see in Chapters 5 and 6, Australia continues to have a small welfare state with relatively low government spending on middle-class welfare in areas such as retirement incomes, health and education (Cox, 2001: 35).

Nevertheless, recent Australian governments have introduced more generous benefits for particular groups such as low-income families with children in an attempt to address these structural changes. At the very least, it would appear that Australian income security payments continue to be effective in improving the relative position of low-income earners, and in offsetting the effects of market-based inequality. But it is debatable whether they are adequate to prevent poverty (Whiteford, 1998: 211–213; Harding, 1999).

CONCLUSION

The Australian welfare system has long been characterised by a low level of targeted benefits accompanied by a strong focus on the work ethic. This system worked reasonably well during the period of full employment from 1945 to 1975, although even then certain groups were vulnerable to poverty. The rise of high unemployment since that time has placed new stresses on the system. In particular, the increase in long-term jobless families with dependent children has raised demands for more adequate payments, and more effective labour market schemes.

There are a number of possible policy responses to this situation. One option which we will discuss in Chapter 4 is to reform the welfare state in a manner that empowers welfare recipients, and loosens the bond between income security payments and formal participation in the paid workforce. However, the most influential response (as we will discuss in Chapter 2) has been the neoliberal drive to blame the existence of welfare programs per se for poverty and disadvantage. This agenda seeks to restore the unemployed to the workforce at whatever wage rate the free market determines, irrespective of the impact on poverty and inequality.

Questions for consideration

1 Why did the Australian welfare state emphasise the protection of wage levels for male workers, rather than welfare payments for those not in the workforce, as tended to be the case in most European countries?
2 Has the Australian system focused primarily on preventing poverty and reducing inequality, or rather on promoting self-help amongst the poor?
3 Is the Australian welfare state equally a creation of Labor and conservative governments, or has the Labor Party been mainly responsible for its achievements?

Exercise

Examine the following statements on welfare policy made by various Australian political leaders. Imagine you are a member of the opposing political party espousing a different political ideology. Write a critique of the policy statement pinpointing differences in underlying philosophy and values.

1 But if the motto is to be that each citizen is entitled, whatever his own effort or deserts, to a maintenance which will suffice without labour; in other words, that utter security in the economic sense is our divinely allotted portion; all incentive to effort will vanish and we shall become a race ready for the destroyer ...

   We are threatened by the dry-rot of social and political doctrines which encourage the citizen to lean on the State, which discourage thrift, which despise as reactionary those qualities of self-reliance which pioneered Australia. (Sir Robert Menzies, Liberal leader in Opposition, 1942)
2 In my electorate, I witnessed the freedom that was enjoyed by 2000 men who congregated outside the gates of a factory in an attempt to secure the one job that was offering. I was able to study the freedom to starve, and to live on a dole of 8 [shillings and] 9 [pence] a week. Those were the fruits of freedom of private enterprise and the exercise of economic individualism, under which everybody had the right to go his own way, without disturbance ...

   All this sort of talk about freedom is sheer, utter hypocrisy ... If regimentation be necessary in order to secure to everyone a decent standard of living, freedom from economic insecurity, proper housing and requisite food and clothing, I say quite frankly that I should prefer it to the economic individualism that we had under the old order. (Ben Chifley, ALP Treasurer, 1944)

3 We are a Government committed not just to the protection of the weak, the handicapped, the disadvantaged, but also to bringing about a change in the structure of our society. Thus, although there are large areas of social welfare programmes which would be common to all the major political parties in Australia, the Labor Government goes much further than any other government would do in considering the purpose of a welfare programme to be of bringing about a redistribution of wealth and income from rich to poor, and indeed, from the richest groups to the rest of the community, whether poor or not. (Bill Hayden, ALP Minister for Social Security, 1974)

4 There can be no doubt that one of the greatest drains on the public purse in recent times has been the welfare apparatus built around the multitude of Whitlam programs ... The dramatic expansion of welfare programs over recent years is a very important, if not the principal, reason why such a heavy burden has been placed on Australian taxpayers. One of the most damaging aspects of dependence is its effect on self-respect. (Phillip Lynch, Coalition Government Treasurer, 1977)

5 The central objective of the Government's social justice strategy is to develop a fairer, more prosperous and more just society for every Australian. The strategy is directed at expanding choices and opportunities for people so that they are able to participate fully as citizens in economic, social and political life ...

The capacity to make such choices is constrained for many people, however, because of factors such as inadequate income, gender, race, location or disability. The social justice strategy addresses the disadvantages that often result from these factors ... so that all in society can have a decent standard of living. (Bob Hawke, ALP Prime Minister, 1991)

6 Before the election, many in the Labor Party said that there was no room for improvement, that most of the waste in social security was due to departmental error rather than deliberate 'rorting' of the system. I hope that you are now convinced that the Labor Party rhetoric was wrong ...

Some may accuse us of heartlessness, but by restoring the integrity of the system we have not only made huge savings, but are trying to rebuild the image of social security for those who are genuinely entitled and who, of course, do not want to be regarded as cheats or bludgers by their neighbours. (Senator Jocelyn Newman, Coalition Minister for Social Security, 1997)

LEADING THE BACKLASH: THE NEOLIBERAL CRITIQUE OF THE WELFARE STATE

This chapter examines the ideological backlash against the Australian welfare state, from its beginnings in 1973 to the present day. It begins by looking at the early manifestations of the backlash, such as the attacks on the unemployed during the Whitlam Government years, the formation of the Workers Party, and the media campaign against the welfare state. It then explores the views of the Liberal free-marketeers group and their ideological influences, such as Friedrich Hayek and Milton Friedman. The next section examines the growth of the New Right following the defeat of the Fraser Liberal-National Coalition Government in 1983. Some consideration is given to the political role played by free-market think-tanks.

In a more extensive study, this chapter then examines the neoliberal critique of the Australian welfare state. A five-point framework is introduced which examines the alleged capture by interest groups of the welfare state; the need for deregulation of the labour market; the alleged relationship between a generous welfare state and welfare dependency; the distinction between the deserving and undeserving poor; and the potential role of private charitable welfare. Lastly, we briefly discuss why the neoliberal drive has been so successful.

THE BEGINNINGS OF THE BACKLASH: 1973–1983

The ideological backlash against the Australian welfare state began as early as 1973, when South Australian Liberal parliamentarian Bert Kelly responded to the Whitlam Government's liberalisation of unemployment benefits by coining the term 'dole bludger' to describe those unemployed persons who he alleged were 'work-shy' (Windschuttle, 1979: 156–57).

Kelly's comments mirrored those of Liberal Party front-bencher Phillip Lynch. Lynch claimed that the changes in entitlement to unemployment benefits 'displayed reckless regard for taxpayers' funds', would undermine 'the philosophy of the work ethic', and 'disturb economically desirable employment patterns in our society' (Lynch, 1973). Similar concerns were also expressed by Labor Minister for Social Security Clyde Cameron (Windschuttle, 1979: 157–58).

Right-wing *Bulletin* columnist Peter Samuel went even further, depicting a class struggle between supporters of income redistribution via the welfare state, and the business community. Samuel argued that 'Welfarism involved a rapid growth in job opportunities and incomes of social workers, nurses, teachers and public servants of all kinds ... at the expense of business, industrial workers and the underprivileged themselves' (Samuel, 1973).

Two years later, advertising magnate John Singleton formed the Workers Party to promote Friedmanite economic principles and libertarian political philosophy. The Workers Party called for the dismantling of the welfare state. Singleton claimed that the welfare state provided a negative incentive for all people to work and produce; created welfare recipients by killing independence and self-respect; and contributed to the growing burden of taxation and inflation which fell most heavily on precisely those people who welfare is supposed to help. The Workers Party advocated the replacement of guarantees of assistance with temporary assistance only at a level of bare necessity, and help from private charities and the network of family, friends and neighbours (Singleton, 1977: 267–73).

Reflecting growing trends in the United States and elsewhere, the anti-welfare cause was soon taken up by senior Liberal-National Coalition Government ministers such as Treasurer Phillip Lynch, who blamed the welfare state and welfare recipients for Australia's economic problems. Similarly, Bert Kelly, writing in the *Financial Review*, attacked welfare spending for the growing burden it was placing on taxpayers (Kelly, 1981: 136–38).

The backlash was further inspired by the Murdoch Press. Writing in the *Australian*, for example, feature contributor Maxwell Newton blamed the welfare state for everything from union demands to high taxation, and from inflation to family breakdown. According to Newton:

> The welfare state has turned out to be a divisive and destructive thing, whose cost is seen in wild wage demands, bitterness and frustration,

disillusion and community hatred ... The welfare state has left family goals deeply confused and has generated confusion and resentment among male family heads ... There will be no end to today's great age of inflation until the welfare state is dismantled. (Newton, 1980)

LIBERAL FREE-MARKETEERS AND CLASSICAL LIBERALISM

The backlash became more organised in the early 1980s with the formation of the Liberal free-market group. Following the 1980 federal election victory, a group of Liberal Party backbenchers, led by John Hyde, Jim Carlton, Murray Sainsbury and Peter Shack, rebelled against the established agenda of the Fraser Government. The backbenchers campaigned for free-market ideas in a number of policy areas, calling for smaller government, low inflation, lower protection, lower taxation, an attack on trade union privileges, the sale of public enterprises, and welfare cuts. They advocated the 'direction of welfare towards the truly needy' as opposed to what they called 'middle-class welfare' (Kelly, 1992: 34–39).

The Liberal free-marketeers based their ideas on the classical liberal doctrines of eighteenth-century anti-collectivist philosopher and economist Adam Smith, the Austrian theorist Friedrich Hayek and the American economist Milton Friedman. These doctrines have more recently been described as 'neoliberalism' or 'economic rationalism', or in North America as 'neo-conservatism'.

Hayek, for example, argued in *The Road to Serfdom* that economic inequality produced by the free operation of the market — where distribution depends partly on the ability and enterprise of the people concerned and partly on unforeseeable circumstances (as opposed to inequality which is deliberately imposed by totalitarian authority) — was the engine of economic and social progress. Egalitarianism would only lead to coercive policies and the breakdown of social cohesion. According to Hayek, when states act to conceal or soften the impact of failure via the redistribution of incomes and the promotion of abstract values like social justice, they encourage laziness and other forms of unproductive behaviour, and ultimately threaten the societies which they govern with stagnation, decline, political oppression and totalitarianism (Hayek, 1944: 72–88).

Similarly, Friedman argued that the main impulse for economic growth comes from a tiny minority of entrepreneurial leaders who take big risks for the chance of large profits. According to Friedman, government policies for equality and for progressive taxation interfere with this natural struggle for self-enrichment. The pursuit of egalitarian policies is incompatible with freedom. Left to themselves, market forces will in fact lead to constantly rising minimum incomes, and to less inequality than alternative systems of organisation (Friedman, 1962: 161–95).

In contrast to 'welfare' or 'social liberals', who believe in the concept of positive liberty — that is the duty of the state to intervene in society in order to ensure that the poor or disadvantaged, who are unable to compete in the market, have sufficient material resources to make their formal rights a reality — Hayek and the classical liberals preferred the idea of negative liberty. Freedom was identified as the absence of restraints or coercion. Taxation involved confiscation of private income. Poverty did not imply a lack of freedom. Individual freedom consisted in being able to do what the law did not actually forbid (Green, 1991: 24–39; Fabian Society, 2000: 83–85).

Critics of classical liberal ideology argue that it is 'social Darwinist' in intent, that it threatens all those unable to compete effectively in the market, and serves to increase and legitimise social and economic inequalities (Sherraden, 1991: 79).

THE EMERGENCE OF THE NEW RIGHT

Following the defeat of the Fraser Liberal Government in 1983, the Liberal free-marketeers extended their influence, forming informal links with a variety of supporters based in the media, academia, Commonwealth public service and business, and gradually secured control of the political agenda of the Liberal Party. The views expressed by the free-marketeers mirrored those espoused by the Thatcher and Reagan governments, and came to be referred to (often pejoratively) as the ideas of the 'New Right'.

The emergence of the New Right reflected the changing social and economic conditions of the early 1970s. In particular, the oil shock of 1973 led to slower rates of economic growth, government deficits, excessive unemployment, inflation and high interest rates. This was accompanied by changing social patterns, including the decline of the traditional nuclear family. There was also a shift from Fordist practices of semi-automated mass production to a more automated mode based on microelectronics and computer applications.

The Keynesian economic philosophy which had underpinned the growth of the welfare state over the two previous decades was discredited. Welfare states in the United States, the United Kingdom,

Canada and elsewhere became subject to ongoing cutbacks and restructuring (Mishra, 1984; Mullaly, 1997: 3–12).

The New Right sought to undo the post-war Keynesian consensus on state intervention in the economy, including a centralised arbitration system and high public expenditure on welfare, in favour of reducing government spending, lowering taxation and deregulating the economy — especially the labour market. There was nothing inherently new about the ideas of the New Right or its advocates, rather (as already noted), they represented a revival of the classical liberal ideas espoused by Hayek, Friedman and Smith — that is, the belief in the perfectibility of the market (Moore, 1995: 126–27).

Nevertheless, the ideas of the New Right did reflect a different social and economic context to that of earlier conservative ideologies. In addition, they involved a politically sophisticated strategy to reconstruct and revitalise conservative ideas by combining traditional conservative social values such as family, authority and self-help with the free-market principles of classical liberalism (Mullaly, 1997: 42).

NEOLIBERAL THINK-TANKS

Following the Great Depression and World War II, collectivist/ Keynesian ideas urging government intervention to manage the economy became dominant. Hayek and the classical liberals were effectively marginalised. However, over the last 25 years, classical liberal ideas have enjoyed a remarkable international revival to the point where they can reasonably be described as constituting a new political orthodoxy (George, 1997: 47–48). Their revival has been greatly assisted by an international conglomerate of neoliberal think-tanks generously funded by corporate resources. The term 'think-tanks' refers to institutes engaged in the scholarly research of public policy independently of government or political parties (Stone, 1991: 200).

The neoliberal think-tanks trace their origins to the relatively obscure Mont Pelerin Society founded by Friedrich Hayek in 1947 as an international forum for classical liberal ideas. As noted by Cockett (1994: 4–5), the think-tanks largely mirror the earlier successes and methods of the left-wing Fabian Society in their commitment to converting a generation of 'opinion formers' and politicians to a new set of ideas.

Neoliberal think-tanks have been particularly prominent and influential in the Anglo-Saxon countries, for example major US think-tanks include the Heritage Foundation and the Cato Institute. The Heritage Foundation has a budget of over $25 million per year, of which almost 90 per cent is raised from more than 6000 private donors. Both organisations exerted considerable impact on the Reagan Government's policy agenda from 1980 to 1988. Similarly, in Britain, the Institute of Economic Affairs and the Centre for Policy Studies appear to have been significant influences on the Thatcher Government from 1979 to 1990, although some writers contest the extent of their direct impact (Denham and Garnett, 1996). Numerous think-tanks also exist in Europe, Canada and Latin America (Beder, 1997: 78–81; Balanya et al, 2000: 17–18).

In Australia, a group of academic-style think-tanks was established and/or revived as a part of a broader economic rationalist coalition in the late 1970s and early 1980s. This group included most prominently the Tasman Institute, the Australian Institute for Public Policy, the Institute of Public Affairs (IPA) and the Centre for Independent Studies (CIS). Leading figures included Des Moore, former head of Treasury and former National Party Senator John Stone, Mike Nahan, Michael James, and former Federal Liberal parliamentarian John Hyde. Some of these think-tanks were directly modelled on similar institutions overseas, and consequently described by critics as mere derivatives or clones (Pusey, 1991: 227; Beder, 1997: 82).

Yet, the transposing of Anglo-American ideas onto the Australian policy agenda proved highly successful. Australian think-tanks vigorously promoted neoliberal ideas concerning economic liberalisation, privatisation, competition reform, labour market deregulation, reduced government spending, and lower taxation. These ideas rapidly succeeded in achieving hegemony over the political agendas of both Labor and conservative governments (Pusey, 1991: 228; Marsh, 1995: 79). This was particularly the case in the state of Victoria where the Tasman Institute and IPA provided policy blueprints for the Kennett Liberal-National Party Government from 1992 to 1999.

Think-tanks have arguably been able to not only shape the policies of individual governments, but have also succeeded in moving the whole policy debate to the right. According to Beder (1997), the free-market ideas promoted by the think-tanks have become hegemonic not only amongst conservative parties, but even within traditionally social democratic groupings. They have become publicly accepted as self-evident truths against which there is no other alternative.

The Australian neoliberal think-tanks have considerable resources at their disposal. According to Alex Carey, the annual budget of right-wing Australian think-tanks in 1986 was between $6 and

$8 million — about eight times the entire ACTU publicity fund levied on union affiliates three years later (Carey, 1987: 41). In 1987, for example, the Centre of Policy Studies think-tank at Monash University published *Spending and Taxing: Australian Reform Options* at a cost of $500 000 to various employer groups associated with the New Right (Murphy, 1987: 180). A more recent estimate by Ian Marsh (2000) suggests a combined income of approximately $4–5 million in 1998. In addition, the BCA has an annual income of $5 million, whilst the equally conservative National Farmers' Federation has a budget of around $2.3 million.

The IPA enjoys annual funding of approximately $1 million, about one third of which is raised from large mining and manufacturing companies (Beder, 1997: 82). It enjoys considerable influence in the media through regular columns in major newspapers. Similarly, the CIS enjoys an annual income of approximately $1.6 million including substantial corporate donations. The CIS also maintains a high media profile with many of its visiting speakers and publications attracting regular coverage in state-based and national newspapers.

The think-tanks claim to be politically independent, and to be offering impartial and disinterested expertise. They insist that their intellectual integrity and hence credibility is protected by their diverse sources of income (Stone, 1996: 117). However, critics such as Carey (1987) and Beder (1997: 75–77) argue that they are generally partisan, motivated by political and ideological bias, practise the art of directed conclusions, and have more in common with vested-interest groups or pressure groups concerned with political activism and propaganda than with genuinely academic or scholarly institutions.

A FRAMEWORK FOR THE NEOLIBERAL CRITIQUE OF THE WELFARE STATE

The Australian neoliberals generally advocate the partial withering of the welfare state, rather than its outright abolition. As a sample of neoliberal criticisms, Nahan and Warby (1998) argue that the welfare state undermines savings and investment, and traditional family life. Sullivan (2000) attacks the welfare state for encouraging dependency and contributing to large increases in sole-parenthood, youth homelessness, drug abuse and youth suicide. And Saunders (2002) claims that welfare lobby groups make misleading claims in order to promote an egalitarian political agenda. The common recommendation is to place limits on the growth of welfare spending. More extreme, Kasper (2000) writes that the welfare state fails on moral, fiscal, economic and social grounds; and he recommends the abolition of the entire welfare system within 25 years, replacing it with private, family and voluntary provision.

In general, however, neoliberal critics accept a minimal safety net, but reject any linkage with social justice outcomes. Most recognise, for example, that government does have a responsibility to pick up people in dire straits, and to ensure that those unable to provide for themselves have access to adequate food, shelter, heat, clothing, health care and education. The qualification is that this support should be minimal and not comfortable, so as not to reduce the incentive to work (Theophanous, 1993: 66).

The neoliberals do, however, mount a significant critique of the existing welfare state. This comprises the following five concerns:

I THE CAPTURE OF THE WELFARE STATE BY INTEREST GROUPS

According to neoliberal theory, the process of democratic government is frequently captured by 'public interest' pressure groups, which then allegedly manipulate the redistributive process to their own advantage (James, 1989). Thus, the welfare state and its services supposedly operate in the interest of the well-paid social workers who administer them, rather than in the interest of the disadvantaged consumers whom they are intended to serve. These producers of the welfare services (it is argued) have a vested interest in maintaining and expanding welfare programs that has little to do with alleviating poverty and far more to do with enriching themselves (Bennett and Di Lorenzo, 1985: 6, 182).

This argument is based on the economic doctrine known as 'public choice theory'. Public choice theory is an economic methodology that evolved from the work of US theorists such as James Buchanan, William Niskanen and Gordon Tullock. Although there is no intrinsic connection between public choice methods and neoliberal perspectives, most adherents firmly support the primacy of the free market, and oppose government welfare programs (see Dullard and Hayward, 1998: 16–20).

Public choice theory argues that all individuals, whether in the public or private sector, act in their own self-interest. The only constraint on this pursuit of self-interest is the market, which constrains the pursuit of the interests of pressure groups for the benefit of the consumer (Pierson, 1991: 45–47). Consequently, public choice theorists favour private rather than public provision of goods whenever possible. They believe in a slimmer, allegedly impartial state which will be unconstrained by the demands of obstructive interest groups.

Arguments for efficiency should take precedence over alternative concepts such as equality of opportunity and social cohesion (Self, 1993: 59–61).

Thus, neoliberal theorists refute the case for government intervention and welfare spending, not by an analysis of the actual workings of the welfare state, but rather by arguing that income redistribution and welfare spending is inspired by powerful interest groups (Davidson, 1991). The broad implication of this argument is that groups concerned with welfare spending (often pejoratively labelled the 'compassion industry') should be excluded as far as possible from public policy debates.

The assumptions of public choice theory exerted a particularly significant influence on the former Victorian Liberal-National Coalition Government's delivery of human services, including the notion of compulsory competitive tendering. Some of the key features of the Kennett Government's public sector model during the 1992–1999 period included:

- the notion of governments steering (making policy decisions), but not rowing (direct service delivery) as popularised by the American writers David Osborne and Ted Gaebler in their 1993 book *Reinventing Government*. According to Osborne and Gaebler, governments should not directly deliver services, but rather should contract private providers to do so in the most effective and efficient manner. *Reinventing Government* explicitly reflects public choice assumptions about the role, scope and proper working of government including the importance of minimising government bureaucracy (Alford et al, 1994: 13–15).

- the associated purchaser/provider split, based on funding designated outputs or outcomes rather than labour or service inputs. This aims to prevent the capture of government decision-making and resources by producer and beneficiary interest groups (Alford et al, 1994: 17). The inevitable conclusion to be drawn from such policies is that community participation is no longer considered a legitimate part of government decision-making processes.

- the empowering of welfare consumers — however disadvantaged, disabled or isolated — as self-interested individuals whose freedom of choice is to be maximised by output-based service delivery. Consumer choices are to be judged by market research surveys and opinion polls, rather than by representative collective structures or consultations which may pose an unacceptable challenge to government policy agendas (Ernst and Webber, 1996: 132).

Public choice theory also reflects the neoliberal obsession with what its adherents call the 'new class'. The term refers to the alleged takeover of the welfare state and the public sector by middle-class professionals, environmentalists, feminists and New Left Marxists who claim they are acting in the interests of the poor and under-privileged, but are (according to the neoliberals) actually pursuing a hidden and highly political agenda aimed at radical social change (Browning, 1990: 3–4, 15–16).

However, as Boris Frankel has noted, the neoliberal concept of 'new class' is not a real class, 'but only a loose category conveniently linking together all those who happen (for a wide variety of reasons) to oppose their views'. According to Frankel, it is not whether a person is employed in the public or private sector which determines his/her membership of the 'new class', but rather adherence to anti-free market views (Frankel, 1992: 150).

In line with public choice theory, neoliberals have constantly criticised the activities of ACOSS and the welfare lobby, calling them unelected and unrepresentative, and suggesting that their main concern is their own professional advancement, rather than the relief of poverty (quoted in Mendes, 2001e). For example, according to former National Party Senator and current IPA research fellow, John Stone:

> ACOSS contains a significant number of denizens of the New Class who have parlayed their volubly expressed compassion into various forms of personal advancement, increased income, more comfortable life-styles and so on. Their chief activity is not directed to, for example, the relief of poverty, but to devising various more or less complex programmes which they or their industry colleagues then administer, to the greater good of the smaller number. (Stone 1991)

Similarly, former ALP minister and current IPA senior fellow Gary Johns suggests that ACOSS represents its own vested interests, rather than the poor. He accuses ACOSS and other welfare lobby groups of receiving more than $3 million of government funding per year under false pretences. Johns suggests that information about ACOSS's real activities is denied to the public (Johns, 2002).

Critics of public choice theory reject the notion that private markets are inherently superior to public enterprises, or that there can or should be a strict boundary between the two modes of production. Instead, they emphasise the interdependence of the public and private sectors, and the importance of production for a wide range of purposes beyond individual financial gain (Stretton and Orchard, 1994: 184–219). They also reject as simplistic the concept of public sector welfare producers exploiting the poor and disadvantaged for their own benefit, noting that human service employees are actually among the worst-paid members of the workforce (Brennan, 1998: 134). Concern is expressed that the intended exclusion of interest groups from policy debates may be an infringement of democratic processes (Quiggin, 1991: 53).

Another criticism is that advocates of economic rationalism *also* represent vested interests, and that these interests are likely to gain directly from any withering or rolling back of the welfare state. As noted by Head:

> Changing the rules always benefits some groups ... the market-liberal agenda for deregulation would most benefit transnational corporations and the speculative sectors of capital ... protection of wage earners' and welfare clients' interests would at best be accidental under conditions of generalised deregulation. (Head, 1989: 501)

Similarly, Emy argues that calls for 'radical cuts to welfare, major cuts in taxation, even replacing the progressive tax scale by flat taxes, appeared to be arguments which favoured the rich and powerful at the expense of the poor' (Emy and Hughes, 1991: 197).

In fact, the evidence from Victoria's experience during the Kennett Government years suggests that neoliberal think-tanks not only possess an increasingly privileged access to government via membership of Commissions of Audit and so on, but are also arguably able to benefit financially from the policy outcomes such as privatisation of these processes through acting as commercial advisors on the privatisation of public utilities (Dullard and Hayward, 1998: 25, 41).

Overall the public choice critique of the welfare state appears more concerned with legitimising the 'self-interest' of the powerful and the wealthy and delegitimising the agendas of those groups who seek increased government spending, than with genuinely reducing the privileges of special interest groups.

2 LABOUR MARKET DEREGULATION

Neoliberals argue that laws preserving minimum wages deny the less skilled and more disadvantaged workers access to jobs. They emphasise the need for a more flexible labour market without awards and minimum wages (Mendes, 1993: 6). For example, Des Moore (1998), director of the Institute for Public Enterprise, argues that wage regulation has adverse effects on employment, and is an inefficient method of trying to reduce income inequality. He also says it is better to have 'working poor' than 'unemployed poor'.

Critics of labour market deregulation argue that there is no evidence to prove that it would lower unemployment. Moreover, even if successful in reducing unemployment it may cause new problems such as wages below poverty level and the likelihood of increased inequality (Ramia, 1995: 44).

As former Victorian Council of Social Service director, Rob Hudson, has noted, the absence of adequate minimum wages in the United States means that many employed people are unable to afford housing and are forced to live on the street. Hudson has also expressed concern 'that a downward pressure on wages, especially at the lower end, will allow governments to justify cutting social security payments because of the smaller gap between them and low wages', thus leading to an increased demand for emergency relief (Hudson, quoted in Milburn, 1993).

3 WELFARE DEPENDENCY

Neoliberals also maintain that government programs encourage 'welfare dependency' and anti-social behaviour, and the development of a feckless underclass typified by high rates of unemployment, illegitimacy and lawlessness; that they devalue the family; and do little to encourage self-reliance and desirable behaviour.

Further, they allege that the high income-tax burdens imposed on those in the workforce, in order to pay for the high costs of social welfare programs, undermine the productive private sector of the economy and the incentives of those who bear the tax burden to work and to save. In addition, too much welfare spending is allegedly going to middle-class families via government expenditure on health, education, superannuation and child-care, rather than being targeted to the poor (Mendes, 1993: 7).

The general argument here is that welfare programs have a 'perverse' effect: that is they produce poverty instead of relieving it. As noted by Hirschman (1991: 27–35), this 'perversity thesis' dates from the time of the Poor Laws in England when critics of social assistance argued that it promoted idleness and mendicancy instead of relieving distress.

One of the strongest contemporary critics of the benefit dependency culture has been influential American neo-conservative political scientist Charles Murray. Murray argues that the welfare state, by providing automatic support for the disadvantaged, has undermined individual responsibility and made it profitable for the poor to become dependent on welfare. Murray claims that the solution to the problem is to scrap the entire US federal welfare and income-support structure for working-aged persons and force individuals to rely on their own resources and those of family and friends (Murray, 1984).

In Australia, various neoliberal authors have argued separately that many teenage girls have children in order to qualify for the sole-parent pension, which pays more than the single rate of unemployment benefit; that the availability of unemployment benefits increases the duration of unemployment by providing an incentive to spend longer looking for the 'right' job; and that the availability of the young homeless allowance may fuel a growth in the number of young homeless people (Mendes, 1996: 490). High-profile public commentators such as Bettina Arndt and Padraic McGuiness have also levelled continual attacks on sole parents.

In order to eliminate this alleged incentive to welfare dependency, neoliberals advocate the introduction of a six-month qualifying period for the Sole Parent Pension and a shorter period of eligibility. After a prescribed period, parenthood would be treated in the same way as other contingencies preventing workforce participation and sole parents would be expected to claim unemployment benefits.

Neoliberals also recommend that Australia follow other countries such as the United States and Japan in requiring previous work experience to establish eligibility for unemployment benefits, a longer waiting period, a much stricter work test and a restricted duration of the period over which full benefit is payable to approximately six months, with the payment dropping to 75 per cent of the full rate after this time. Such proposals, it is claimed, will end the supposed current incentive for individuals to choose welfare rather than employment (Mendes, 1996: 490–91).

Critics of neoliberalism argue that welfare spending in Australia is relatively low compared to other OECD countries, as is the level of taxation (see Table 2.1, page 44), and that there is no evidence to support the view that increased spending on social welfare has hindered saving, investment and economic growth. They also present evidence to refute the suggestion that the availability of social security benefits is responsible for the rise in welfare dependence (Emy and Hughes, 1991: 196; Lambert, 1994).

TABLE 2.1
TOTAL TAX REVENUE AND PUBLIC SOCIAL SPENDING: 1998
(% GDP)

	Social expenditure	Tax revenue
Korea	4.8	21
Mexico	7.9	16
Turkey	10.0	29
Japan	14.4	28
United States	16.0	29
Canada	16.6	37
Australia	17.4	30
Ireland	17.9	32
Iceland	18.0	34
Portugal	18.7	34
Czech Republic	19.4	38
New Zealand	20.7	35
Spain	20.9	34
United Kingdom	21.1	37
Greece	22.2	34
Switzerland	22.4	35
Luxembourg	23.9	41
Poland	24.5	38
Netherlands	25.1	41
Norway	25.1	44
Hungary	25.3	39
Austria	25.4	44
Germany	26.6	37
Italy	26.9	43
Belgium	27.2	46
Finland	28.7	46
France	29.4	45
Denmark	30.8	50
Sweden	33.3	52
OECD average	*21.3*	*37*
European Union average	*25.2*	*41*

NOTE The expenditure figure for Hungary is for 1993 (Deacon et al, 1997).
SOURCE Adapted from OECD, *Taxing Wages*, 2001: 346; Arjona et al, *Growth, Inequality and Social Protection*, 2001: 67.

In addition, critics reject the attack on so-called 'middle-class welfare', arguing that whilst the stated intention of this strategy is to save money and better target services to those who most need them, the real objective is to erode public support for government services. Provision of services on a targeted, rather than universal, basis is likely to reduce support for the welfare state per se.

Further, they maintain that neoliberal proposals are repressive and intended to blame and punish the victim, rather than attacking the structural causes of dependency and poverty. Antcliff, for example, argues that reducing the rate of benefits for the long-term unemployed will only serve to impose extreme hardship on a particularly vulnerable group 'who have minimal resources with which to protect themselves or climb out of the deep poverty traps such an approach would create' (Antcliff, 1988: 69). And the savings from such measures are likely to be outweighed by the increased social costs — from homelessness, illness and crime — that will inevitably follow when benefits are withdrawn. Moreover, the use of the term 'dependency' is in itself ideological and pejorative, and intended to focus attention on the assumed flaws of the poor person, rather than the causes of their poverty (Fraser and Gordon, 1994).

Of greater concern is the negative impact that the intended abolition of the welfare safety net is likely to exert on the bargaining position of working people seeking employment. As noted by Block et al (1987: xv) 'Without a safety net, low-paid workers would face the choice of acquiescence to employer demands or the risk of joblessness and its traditional consequence — hunger'. The neoliberal proposals to promote work incentives are likely, particularly when combined as intended with the abolition of minimum wages, to lead to a dramatic increase in exploitation and inequality.

4 THE 'DESERVING POOR' AND THE 'UNDESERVING POOR'

According to neoliberalism, current welfare programs encourage people who do not genuinely need or deserve it to seek help.

Distinctions between the deserving and undeserving poor reflect the influence of the 1834 amendment to the English *Poor Laws Act*. The Poor Laws were based on the 'less eligibility' principle: that unemployment payments for the able-bodied poor must never exceed the level of wages able to be earned by the lowest paid labourers in the land, so as to maintain work incentives (Beilharz et al, 1992: 59–60).

The deserving poor — those who had become briefly dependent on relief through no fault of their own, and who with some assistance could return to independence — are to be cared for. The undeserving poor (more recently labelled the underclass) whose poverty is viewed as the result of individual anti-social behaviour or moral defects — laziness, profligacy, reckless family planning and so on — are to be disciplined (Conley, 1982: 281–82). Thus various coercive measures of 'tough love' will be used to promote their re-integration with main-stream morality and values (Jordan and Jordan, 2000: 25–30).

An extension of this argument is that the welfare state is too 'permissive in character' and emphasises the claims, needs and entitlements of welfare recipients without expecting any obligations in return. Advocates of this 'workfare' school, such as the American philosopher Laurence Mead (1997), believe that welfare recipients have an obligation to work for their support.

Critics of the deserving/undeserving distinction argue that poverty is not equivalent to laziness or moral failure. They view the distinction as an attempt to isolate one group of poor people from the rest, and to stigmatise them. The intention is to force the poor to work for low wages (Gans, 1995).

5 PRIVATE CHARITABLE WELFARE

The neoliberals argue that the welfare state has reduced the sphere of individual freedom through state monopolisation of welfare services. Instead, welfare programs should be provided by churches, families and the charitable voluntary sector. A 1990 publication from the CIS for example, proposed that taxpayers be permitted to switch at least some of their welfare dollars from government departments to voluntary welfare agencies of their own choice. According to this argument, the growth of public expenditure on social security and welfare has stifled or 'crowded out' private donations to voluntary organisations which are more likely to be motivated by 'compassion' than are the payments of compulsory state taxes which fund state welfare.

Nicholas and Goodman (1990) claim that voluntary organisations are better at delivering welfare programs. This is said to be due to a discretionary approach which allows for a case-by-case assessment. Voluntary agencies are said to discourage dependency, and to encourage behavioural change. Government programs, in contrast, are said to encourage dependency and to go to those least in need.

Critics of welfare privatisation argue that the distribution of the welfare budget by voluntary agencies would destroy the integrity and accountability of the system. Agencies would have to make decisions about discretionary payments without consistent national standards. Inequities would be common and difficult to identify. Social security recipients could also be required to divulge personal details to a welfare agency which lacks a legal commitment to confidentiality or formal constraints on the use of such information (Richardson, 1991).

Charities are also renowned for emphasising the moral, rather than structural, causes of poverty. Historically, groups such as the Charity Organisation Society Movement of the late nineteenth and early twentieth century eschewed solutions to poverty and inequality based on social action or income redistribution, and instead concentrated on the regeneration of moral character (Wagner, 2000). For example, the US branch of the movement viewed poverty as the outcome of personal deviations from middle-class values such as thrift, temperance, hard work and family cohesiveness. The solution was the re-introduction of the work ethic and the concept of self-reliance into working-class neighbourhoods. Charity was used as an explicit method of social control (Lubove, 1972: 1–17). Even today, charitable agencies frequently use moral judgements to categorise deserving and less deserving clients (Wearing, 1998: 81).

Further, studies of the American experience of privatisation demonstrate that cuts in government expenditure are rarely matched by proportionate compensating increases in private donations to non-government agencies. In fact, non-profit organisations are left with little choice but to shift the focus of their work to target those able to pay the new or higher fees that they are forced to impose. Overall, agencies with a history of advocacy on behalf of the disadvantaged may have to restructure their core focus and activities as they become more dependent on business funding. Low-income earners are the big losers (Hudson, 1992).

Critics also suggest that arguments in favour of private philanthropy replacing state welfare programs are merely ideological justifications for reducing the taxes of the well-off. Privatisation is about individual rights and duties rather than collective values, and therefore spurns the redistribution of income to the disadvantaged groups.

WHY HAS THE NEOLIBERAL AGENDA BEEN SO SUCCESSFUL?

Few politicians in Australia would publicly admit to favouring neoliberalism's real agenda which appears to be to redistribute income from the poorest to the most affluent, from the most needy in society to the least needy (Mishra, 1989: 178). So why is the neoliberal agenda winning the debate? Some possible explanations include the greater resources of the wealthy; the political apathy and marginalisation of the poor and unemployed; the global domination of free-market policies; the highly targeted nature of our welfare state; and public hostility to 'dole bludgers'.

The first and most obvious explanation is that those who represent the interests of the rich and powerful enjoy greater resources
than those who don't. We have already noted that the principal free-
market lobby groups enjoy generous funding. In contrast, supporters of the welfare state have generally failed to create or adequately
fund similar structures. Most Australian left-wing research centres
such as the Evatt Foundation, Fabian Society or Australia Institute
are relatively small, and operate on shoe-string budgets. The prominent Australian sociologist Michael Pusey speaks of a 'structured
inequality in interest group representation in Canberra and hence a
ready-made mobilisation of bias in the context in which any particular scheme or initiative is raised' (Pusey, 1991: 143).

But the wealthy have always enjoyed greater resources. Yet in the
past, they often promoted schemes such as the welfare state which
involved a surrender of some of their assets to working-class interests in return for social peace and harmony. One important reason
why they are no longer doing this is that the working-class, and particularly the poor and unemployed, are perceived to be politically
apathetic (Mendes, 1997a: 48–49). As we will note in Chapter 10,
the centralised and bureaucratic nature of the welfare state appears
to have blunted the potential of the working class and poor to challenge the system. Equally as we will discuss in Chapter 3, the globalisation of trade seems to have weakened the interventionist power
of governments, and strengthened the influence of financial markets.
The affluent now feel sufficiently secure to not only preserve, but
also extend, the existing inequalities.

An associated factor is that Australian neoliberals seem to have
engaged more effectively than their critics with global influences and
trends. Neoliberal think-tanks such as the IPA and the CIS have regularly utilised their international connections in order to promote
particular neoliberal versions of globalisation in Australia. In contrast, the Left has generally failed to offer alternative interpretations
of global policy trends and agendas. For example, few if any prominent guests have been invited from Europe to extol the virtues of
social democratic welfare regimes.

A further explanation arguably involves the failure of our highly
means-tested welfare state to benefit anyone but the poor and disadvantaged. This is particularly the case since the last two universalistic benefits — the age pension and the family allowance payment
— were means tested by the Hawke Government. This exclusion of
the middle classes from the welfare state appears to produce 'downwards envy' towards those below them who are entitled to payments
(Cox, 1995: 51, 74).

In addition, the high unemployment of the last two decades has produced a widespread perception among employed Australians that the unemployed are scroungers who do not want to work. The structure of the welfare state means that the unemployed quickly become alienated and isolated from mainstream society. This in turn promotes and perpetuates mainstream stereotypes of their character-istics. These stereotypes are then exploited by neoliberal govern-ments in order to justify the introduction of work for the dole and other 'mutual obligation' schemes. In contrast, defenders of the wel-fare state have failed to create effective alternative models that would promote, but not force, the re-integration of the unemployed with mainstream society (Mendes, 1997a: 49–50)

CONCLUSION

In summary, neoliberal ideas of small government, free markets and a reduction in the welfare state have exerted a substantial impact on the Australian policy agenda in recent years. Well-funded think-tanks have promoted antipathy towards the welfare state, welfare produc-ers and welfare beneficiaries. The neoliberal critique of the welfare state has been adopted in part by the former Hawke/Keating Labor governments, and in far greater measure by the current Howard Liberal-National Coalition Government.

The success of the neoliberal agenda reflects a number of factors including the decline of alternative policy ideas such as Keynesianism, and the emergence of economic globalisation. For many, globalisation seems to provide objective evidence for the assumed link between neoliberal policies and economic competitive-ness. However, as we shall see in Chapter 3, there are many differ-ent interpretations of the nature of the impact of global trade and finance on nation states, and globalisation does not in itself preclude the continued presence of generous welfare states.

Questions for consideration

1 Why has the neoliberal agenda been so successful in influencing political parties and public opinion?
2 Which groups in society are most supportive of neoliberal ideas?
3 Is there any evidence at either the local or global level that neoliberal policies have helped poor and disadvantaged people?

Exercise

Here are a number of fictional quotes from neoliberals. How might a social welfare activist respond to these quotes?

1   Social workers advocate greater government spending on welfare programs not in order to relieve poverty, but rather to further their own career opportunities.

2   If only we abolished the minimum wage, all the young unemployed would be able to find work.

3   More and more teenage girls are deliberately having children so as to qualify for the sole-parent pension which pays more than the unemployment benefit.

4   Long-term welfare recipients are members of an anti-social underclass characterised by early dropping out of school, laziness, reckless family planning and crime (especially in the drug industry).

5   Voluntary charities are better at delivering welfare payments. This is due to a discretionary approach which allows for a case-by-case assessment. Recipients only receive assistance if they change their behaviour. Government programs, in contrast, define assistance as a 'right' and encourage welfare dependency.

3

DRIVING THE BACKLASH? THE IMPACT OF GLOBALISATION ON WELFARE STATES

In recent years, welfare states have been the subject of increasing political and ideological debate over their effects and effectiveness. Most advanced Western states appear committed to reducing social expenditure, and to introducing measures such as labour market deregulation and lowered tax rates. These facilitate greater economic competitiveness, but impact adversely on rates of poverty and inequality.

These economic and political initiatives have coincided with a period of intense economic globalisation. The growing significance of international trade, investment, production and financial flows appears to be curtailing the autonomy of individual nation states. In particular, globalisation appears to be encouraging, if not demanding, a decline in social spending and standards.

This chapter examines the impact of globalisation on welfare states, with some specific reference to the Australian situation. First, we examine a number of different views of globalisation, and conclude that while globalisation has imposed new policy constraints, social democratic interventions remain possible. The next section explores the influence of global social policy actors and institutions. The following section considers the particular relationship between globalisation and the Australian welfare state. We then introduce two case studies of the globalisation of Australian social policy pertaining to welfare reform and illicit drugs.

DIFFERENT VIEWS OF GLOBALISATION

Economic globalisation appears to have been fuelled by the collapse of communism, and the absence of any serious alternative to the free market (Mishra, 1999: ix). The term refers to a shift in the scale of social and economic relations from the regional or national to the global. Factors such as hi-tech communications, lower transport costs and unrestricted trade are perceived to be transforming the world into one single market (Bessant and Watts, 1999: 229).

'Globalisation' remains a highly contested term with significant political implications. One divide exists between those who view globalisation as a social as well as economic phenomenon, and those who argue that recent changes to social and family relations have developed independently of globalisation. Another divide centres around whether globalisation is inherently linked to neoliberal interests and agendas, or alternatively whether more democratic and participatory forms of globalisation can be developed. An overriding debate considers whether or not globalisation has fundamentally undermined the autonomy of national policy-makers (Callinicos, 2001: 15–19; Ife, 2002: 141–47).

International studies suggest roughly three distinct perspectives on globalisation and the welfare state. Firstly, there is what may be called the 'hyperglobalist' or 'convergence thesis'. This rather deterministic perspective views globalisation as systematically transferring power from national governments to uncontrollable market forces and new economic actors such as transnational corporations, international banks and other financial institutions.

Globalisation is seen in this interpretation as an all-powerful phenomenon which increasingly pushes national states towards a common model of highly deregulated, privatised and liberalised capitalism. States are forced to offer lower and lower taxes in order to compete for footloose private investment. Numerous commentators call this 'a race to the bottom' based on cutting social costs to promote national economic competitiveness. Social dumping is employed by replacing high-cost producers with low-cost producers, and relocating firms to low-cost countries (Alber and Standing, 2000: 99–101; Martin and Schumann, 1997; Yeates, 2001: 21–26).

Consequently, globalisation leads inevitably to the decline of the welfare state through the vetoing of initiatives towards greater social expenditure and full employment by international financial markets (Held et al, 1999: 3–4; Gray, 1998). To the extent that welfare states continue, they increasingly focus not on helping people or reducing inequality, but rather on control, surveillance, compulsion and correction (Jordan, 1998; Jamrozik, 2001).

However, this perspective arguably ignores the continued impact of national political and ideological pressures, and lobby groups on policy outcomes. It also fails to acknowledge the significant existing and continuing differences between welfare states (discussed in greater detail in Chapter 4) which in turn reflect differing national economic and social systems (Cochrane et al, 2001: 267, 284).

Moreover, the empirical evidence suggests that the increased mobility of capital has not resulted in reduced business tax burdens. To the extent that tax rates are cut, states tend to protect revenue levels by reducing traditional business investment credits and allowances (Swank, 1998). Taxation levels also continue to vary widely from the higher rates prevalent in European countries to the lower rates of the United States.

A second perspective, which may be called the 'sceptical thesis', holds that globalisation has relatively little impact on welfare states (Weiss, 1998). For instance, Hirst and Thompson (1999) argue that hyperglobalist conceptions are largely a myth. This perspective suggests that the level of contemporary global trade is no greater than that which existed at the beginning of the twentieth century, that most multinational companies remain wedded to a major national location, and that national governments retain considerable sovereignty and autonomy (Held et al, 1999: 5–7; Palier and Sykes, 2001: 5–8). However, this perspective arguably neglects the significant political and ideological influence of globalisation and global policy actors on domestic policy debates.

A third perspective, which may be called the 'mediation' or 'divergent thesis', acknowledges that globalisation is impacting upon welfare states, but argues (eg Turner, 2001) that the impact varies from country to country, and in turn is mediated by specific national factors. The mediation thesis does accept that global economic competition has reduced the autonomy of individual nation states, and contributed to greater inequality. There is evidence, for example, of an increasing policy convergence between social democratic and right-wing parties towards welfare retrenchment. There is also evidence of a general trend towards welfare cutbacks in order to attract mobile capital (George, 1998; Shin, 2000).

Nevertheless, there is no evidence of widespread dismantling of welfare programs. Even in Anglo-Saxon countries, a substantial part of the structure of social provision remains in place. In addition, social expenditure as a percentage of GDP has not decreased in most countries, and most European states are still involved in combating poverty and social exclusion. The dominant trend appears to be one of adaptation and resilience, rather than movement towards radical reform.

This thesis also suggests that globalisation is as much a political and ideological phenomenon as it is economic. Thus national social policy responses to globalisation are not uniform, and continue to reflect the ideological and political traditions of individual states, and their positions in the global political economy (Yeates, 2001: 142–47). For example, social standards appear to have declined more in those English-speaking countries strongly influenced by neoliberal ideas than in continental Europe and Japan. Similarly, Ireland takes a far more generous approach to social expenditure than Britain. In addition, there was considerable variation in state responses to the Asian financial crisis (Gough, 2001). Some countries such as Thailand and South Korea substantially *increased* social expenditure (Ginsburg, 2001; Yeates, 2001: 86–87).

In short, the influence of globalisation on welfare spending appears to be determined at least in part by internal political choice as much as by externally imposed economic imperatives (Alcock, 2001: 11–13; Palier and Sykes, 2001: 5–13).

This text views the mediation thesis as reflecting most accurately the complexity of the relationship between the local and the global. As we shall see in the Australian debate, competing local policy forces consistently refer to different global policy discourses in order to legitimate their own political and ideological solutions.

GLOBAL SOCIAL POLICY ACTORS AND INSTITUTIONS

The debate about the effects of economic globalisation is complicated by the increasing influence of international organisations and institutions on national social policies. These include global institutions such as the World Bank, the International Monetary Fund (IMF), the International Labor Organization (ILO), the United Nations International Children's Emergency Fund (UNICEF), and supranational bodies such as the OECD and the European Commission.

According to Deacon and his colleagues (1997: 2–3), globalisation has raised social policy issues to a supranational level. They define the scope of global social policy as including social redistribution between countries; global social regulation of the terms of trade and the operation of firms in the interests of social protection and welfare objectives; and social welfare at a level above that of national government (eg the United Nations High Commission for Refugees).

Some powerful international institutions have regularly inspired welfare retrenchment. The IMF, for example, was originally formed at the 1944 Bretton Woods Conference to ensure monetary stability in an open economy, as a substitute for the gold standard, which had fulfilled this function successfully until World War I. Its key purpose was to discourage individual nations which faced external balance-of-payments difficulties from taking steps such as currency and import restrictions, or devaluations, that would negatively affect other countries.

The IMF has long been regarded as an unrepentant advocate of neoliberal ideas. Since 1980, its structural adjustment programs in the Third World and former Soviet Bloc countries have been based on rigid loan conditions including trade liberalisation, reduced imports, reduced public expenditure, cuts in progressive taxation, privatisation of state-owned firms, increased interest rates, non-inflationary monetary policy, and an overall reduction in national sovereignty (Deacon et al, 1997: 61–65; Koivusalo and Ollila, 1997: 83–85). According to its many critics, these policies have lead to further indebtedness and impoverishment. For example, Chossudovsky (1999) refers to declining spending on health and education, leading to millions of children being denied access to primary education, and a growth in infectious diseases. A report by Oxfam (1999) identifies major declines in social indicators in countries involved with IMF programs in East Asia, sub-Saharan Africa, and Latin America.

The IMF has less direct influence on industrialised Western nations. However, it has actively encouraged European welfare states to adopt neoliberal models based on the reduction of social assistance, and the maximisation of labour market flexibility and competitiveness (Mishra, 1999: 8–9). According to Deacon (et al, 1997), the IMF has begun to acknowledge the detrimental social impact of some of its structural adjustment programs. In addition, it does support a short-term social safety net to support the poor during periods of economic reform. Deacon describes, for example, the application of such policies in post-communist Hungary. However, overall, the IMF appears to still prioritise the interests of commercial banks at the expense of people living in poverty.

The World Bank was also formed in 1944, and has focused principally on making loans to Third World governments to pay for investments in large basic infrastructure projects such as dams, power plants and roads. In contrast to the IMF, the World Bank has responded to earlier criticisms of its policies and practice in developing countries by initiating anti-poverty programs, and forming alliances with non-government organisations (NGOs) such as Oxfam. According to Deacon, this emphasis has led to some softening of the earlier structural adjustment policies in Africa and Latin

America. There are also divisions within the organisation between those who have been influenced by the social guarantees of former communist states into supporting more collectivised, social solidaristic forms of policy and provision, and those who still subscribe to fundamentalist neoliberalism. Overall, Deacon and his colleagues argue that the World Bank appears to stand for social safety nets for the poor, but against organised labour or European corporatist social security structures (Deacon et al, 1997: 65–70; Koivusalo and Illila, 1997: 23–45).

Other commentators are more sceptical about ideological changes within the bank. Chossudovsky (1999), for example, argues that its emphasis on poverty alleviation fails to effectively challenge the dominant neoliberal macroeconomic agenda. He speaks of a token targeting of funds to the poor, alongside the dismantling of state social expenditure.

The OECD is another highly influential global policy institution. Founded in 1961, it is comprised of 29 leading industrialised countries, including Australia, and broadly functions as a research centre for finance ministers of the member nations. The OECD aims to promote high economic growth, employment and living standards amongst its member countries. Its 1981 report on the welfare state in crisis was used by many countries as an argument for reducing social expenditure. A number of subsequent OECD reports have described welfare spending as an obstacle to economic growth. Similarly, the OECD's 1994 Jobs Study has been interpreted as an endorsement of the United States' low-wage model (Mishra, 1999: 8–11).

Deacon argues that recent OECD publications have recognised the need for increased social protection to accompany global economic restructuring (Deacon et al, 1997: 70–73). However, the OECD still seems to prioritise work incentives and the promotion of independence and individual responsibilities over the prevention of hardship (Rodger, 2000: 6).

Other international instruments, including regional trade agreements such as the North American Free Trade Agreement, have also played a role in reducing existing social welfare and labour market rights and conditions. Similarly, the World Trade Organisation appears predisposed to defending the rights of the world's largest corporations at the expense of social justice, health and labour considerations. In addition, international credit rating agencies such as Moody's and Standard & Poor have pressured governments into cutting social expenditure (Deacon et al, 1997: 81; Mishra, 1999: 38–39).

In summary, international organisations such as the IMF, the World Bank and the OECD are important players in the globalisation debate. They generally promote a neoliberal version of globalisation based on cutting social protection in order to facilitate economic competitiveness. Their influence on governments — both in Third World and Western countries — appears to be significant (Yeates, 2001: 29).

GLOBAL AND REGIONAL CRITICS OF NEOLIBERALISM

In contrast, a number of international forces campaign for a different version of globalisation based on the retention or expansion of social protection. For example, a group of social reformist agencies exist under the auspices of the United Nations Economic and Social Council. Perhaps the best known is UNICEF, which was established in 1946 as a temporary body to meet the emergency needs of children in post-war Europe. More recently, UNICEF has focused its attention on the development of child health and welfare services to prevent malnutrition in the Third World.

UNICEF has been a persistent critic of the anti-social policies of the IMF and World Bank, and the negative consequences of structural adjustment policies for children. It has consequently had an important influence on the World Bank's adoption of anti-poverty programs (Deacon et al, 1997: 84–85; Koivusalo and Ollila, 1997: 46–61). The work of UNICEF has been reinforced by the activities of the United Nations Development Programme (UNDP). The UNDP was established in 1965 as the central funding and co-ordinating organisation for United Nations technical assistance to developing countries. It recently created a new measure of social progress, the 'human development index', which combines longevity with education attainment and a modified measure of income and poverty to rank countries on a scale somewhat differently to, for instance, narrow classifications based on GDP. A further associated agency is the semi-autonomous United Nations Research Institute for Social Development. The institute has explored the socially disintegrative aspects of globalisation, and the notion of citizenship at a global level.

The UN Economic and Social Committee was responsible for the much publicised 1995 World Social Development Summit which aimed to tackle issues of poverty, social exclusion and social development. The summit concluded with commitments to the eradication of poverty, the promotion of full employment, gender equality, quality health care and education, and the fostering of social integration (Deacon et al, 1997: 84–89; Koivusalo and Ollila, 1997: 62–70).

The ILO aims to set and maintain common international labour and social standards. It has established a number of conventions which, if ratified, provide for an efficient system of social insurance, social support and social assistance. Currently, the ILO has more than 172 conventions on its books with 5500 ratifications by member countries, and it has achieved some success in securing compliance with ratified conventions. However, overall the efficacy of ILO conventions appears to be weakened by the principally voluntary nature of ratification and compliance (Deacon et al, 1997: 73–77).

At a regional level, the EU has included a social dimension via its Charter of the Fundamental Social Rights of Workers of the European Union. This comprises free movement of workers and social security for migrant workers, equal pay for men and women, health and safety standards, and the requirement that the EU establish a social dialogue with both employers and employees.

According to Deacon (1997: 79–81), the EU has laid the basis for a regional social policy and forms of social protection, although some touted initiatives have been frustrated by the existence of global economic competition, the non-binding status of the charter, and political constraints such as the Maastricht Treaty which limit fiscal expansion. Whilst the EU does not endorse traditional social democratic policies of high taxation and income redistribution, its dominant social-liberal orientation also rejects the claims of neoliberalism.

In recent years, we have also seen the growth of what Brecher and Costello (1994: 8) call 'globalisation from below', which is a form of globalisation involving actions by ordinary people, grassroots movements and those concerned for the goals of social justice, human rights and environmental sustainability. Technological advances such as the Internet have opened up opportunities for not only the powerful, but also the disadvantaged, to act more quickly and effectively on an international basis.

Global political actions take a number of forms including market-based strategies based on consumer boycotts of transnational companies in order to bring about improved standards for groups of workers in particular industries; campaigns against powerful international institutions such as the OECD, the IMF and the World Bank; and campaigns to defend social rights in particular states (Yeates, 2002: 78–86).

One remarkably effective campaign has been that of Jubilee 2000, an international coalition of religious groups, trade unions and aid agencies which sought the cancellation of the unpayable debt of the world's poorest countries by the end of the year 2000. Over 22 million signatures were gathered in support of the campaign including 382 000 from Australia, and during a Global Week of Action about one million people took part in demonstrations around the world. In 1999, US President Bill Clinton agreed to cancel 100 per cent of the $5.7 billion owed by the poorest countries to the United States. Overall, about $108 billion worth of debt relief has been promised by the G8 — the world's leading industrialised countries (Jubilee 2000, website).

Another remarkably successful campaign has been the international movement against the signing of the Multilateral Agreement on Investment. Activists worldwide led by over 600 NGOs from 67 countries demanded that any agreement must incorporate high labour and environmental standards (Goodman, 2000). Similarly, the 1999 meeting of the WTO in Seattle was confronted with massive protests of 50–80 000 people organised by a coalition of unionists, conservationists, clerics and consumer groups. Protesters demanded that the WTO incorporate labour and environmental standards into its rulings. A significant anti-globalisation movement based on various progressive groups and alliances has also developed in Australia (Hastings, 2001: 53–60).

The broad concern of these activities and campaigns by NGOs and social movements is to create a counterweight to the neoliberal or corporate version of globalisation described above. Their aim is to limit the power of global capital, and to force international institutions and governments to make concessions to concerns around social and economic equity. In short, they seek to resist and/or reverse a process which appears to have created some big winners including powerful Western countries and associated multinational companies, and many big losers including mass peasant movements, exploited workers and public employees (Hopkinson, 2001: 69–70). They appear to have enjoyed at least some success not only in moderating the policies of international institutions such as the World Bank, but also in influencing national governments to critically examine neoliberal agendas (Yeates, 2001: 147–63).

Nevertheless, these counter-movements still lack a formal institutional presence at the global level. There is no effective international organisation which represents the interests of workers or peasants as opposed to those of the corporate sector. Many commentators believe that initiatives in global social policy are required to offset the power of global capital and its neoliberal sympathisers.

Thus they argue for the creation of international social policy institutions which have the power to promote and implement binding social rights at a global level. Specific recommendations, for example, have included the introduction of the oft-proposed 'Tobin Tax' to reduce financial speculation and instability, the formation of regional trade unions, and the establishment of international social standards linked to the economic standard and capacity of individual nations (Teeple, 2000: 195–200; Kerr, 2001: 134–59).

GLOBALISATION AND THE AUSTRALIAN WELFARE STATE

In recent years, Australian social policy programs and initiatives have increasingly been guided by global agendas, actors and evidence. However, the impact of globalisation has also been modified by local political and ideological pressures and lobby groups. Australian governments have been active participants in the globalisation process. For example, they have used global economic pressures and sympathetic international commentators and organisations as a means of justifying economic rationalist policies including tariff reduction, financial deregulation and labour market deregulation (Watts, 2000a: 147; Conley, 2001).

In addition, numerous business leaders and commentators have argued that Australia must reduce social expenditure in order to be internationally competitive. As noted by Wiseman (1998: 69), there has been a gradual narrowing of the discussion of alternatives to neoliberal policies due to a belief that such ideas would be effectively vetoed by the international financial markets. Both Labor and particularly Liberal governments have followed the general international trend of introducing measures which tighten eligibility criteria and controls for unemployment benefits and increase incentives to become self-reliant.

OECD prescriptions first made their mark in the early 1990s, when the Labor Government responded to concerns about passive income support measures by introducing new unemployment assistance schemes known as the Job Search Allowance and the NewStart Allowance. These programs explicitly reflected the OECD's preference for an 'active society' approach to unemployment based on obligations as well as rights (Kalisch, 1991).

More recently, members of the Howard Liberal-National Coalition Government have emphasised the connection between global economic pressures, national economic competitiveness and acceptable rates of social expenditure. For example, Treasurer Peter Costello has spoken of the need to more closely align Australia's tax rates and social spending levels with those of Australia's Asian trading neighbours (Costello, 1997: 336). The IMF has specifically praised government initiatives in welfare reform designed to promote greater labour market participation and reduced welfare spending (IMF, 2001: 24–26).

THE CRISIS OF AN AGEING POPULATION

The discussion around the fiscal effects of increased life expectancy (the so-called 'demographic' or 'ageing crisis') on social expenditure is particularly indicative of this narrow political trend.

International organisations such as the World Bank and the OECD suggest a doubling or tripling of health and pension expenditure and other forms of care for the aged by the year 2040 (Carey, 1999). Similarly, the Australian Commission of Audit suggested that future increased expenditure on Australia's ageing population would cause a massive budget deficit unless action was taken to reduce social expenditure (Officer, 1996: xv, 123–46). Consequently, the Howard Government has taken a number of measures particularly through the 1997 *Aged Care Act* to promote greater self-reliance. These measures include encouraging individuals to save for their retirement through private superannuation funds, greater use of private health insurance, and the funding of nursing home care by family contributions (Ozanne, 2000: 192–96).

The 2002 Federal Budget featured an Intergenerational Report which warned that the pressures of an ageing population would require increases of $87 billion in health and aged care expenditure (approximately 5 per cent of GDP) by 2041/42. The report claimed that Australia would be forced to reduce social spending, or face higher taxes, in order to meet these demands (Costello, 2002).

Yet other local authors argue that there is no reason why a reversal of policies towards early retirement and overall increased labour force participation cannot offset the costs of increasing numbers of older people. Compared to other OECD countries, Australia is well placed to cope with future pressure on pensions. Pensions expenditure in Australia is projected to increase only modestly from 3 per cent of GDP in 2000 to 4.5 per cent of GDP in 2040, a figure well below that of the OECD average (Table 3.1).

TABLE 3.1
PENSION OUTLAYS IN AUSTRALIA: 1998–2050 (% GDP)

Year	Percentage of GDP
1998/99	3.0
2010/11	3.1
2020/21	3.5
2030/31	4.1
2040/41	4.5
2049/50	4.5

SOURCE Adapted from Kinnear, *Population Ageing: Crisis or Transition?* 2001: 29.

Critics of the 'ageing crisis' suggest importantly that this debate has been hijacked by neoliberals who see demographic change and associated global pressures as an opportunity to reduce social protection (Mitchell, 1997: 55–56; Kinnear, 2001).

TWO CASE STUDIES OF THE GLOBALISATION OF AUSTRALIAN SOCIAL POLICY

The following case studies outline the impact and influence of globalisation on two areas of social policy in Australia: The Howard Government's welfare reform review; and the Victorian 'Safe Injecting Facilities' scheme.

CASE ONE
THE HOWARD GOVERNMENT'S WELFARE REFORM REVIEW

In September 1999, the Howard Coalition Government announced a review of the Australian welfare system, the outcome of which came to be known as the McClure Report. The specific political context and result of the welfare reform debate are discussed in greater detail in Chapter 5; what is important here is the extent to which the welfare reform process reflected the increasing influence of globalisation on Australian policy.

In particular, the government consistently used global policy trends as a means of legitimising its own neoliberal agenda. Reflecting the increasingly important role of what has been called 'policy transfer' (Alcock, 2001: 4–5), the case for Australian welfare reform was made with reference both to OECD recommendations, and specific policy developments in Britain and the United States. The influence of a guru of US welfare reform, Lawrence Mead, was also particularly significant. Alternatively, critics of government policy offered different interpretations of overseas trends and agendas.

The government referred positively to OECD statements addressing the question of increased dependence on income support. For example, the OECD has consistently recommended tighter administration of welfare payments and a stricter balance between rights and obligations in order to reduce the number of jobless households and maximise opportunities for paid employment (FACS, 2000; Newman, 2000).

Substantial public debate also took place around developments in Britain and the United States. According to the government, the US *Personal Responsibility and Work Opportunity Reconciliation Act* and the British 'New Deal' have a common three-pronged approach focused on improved financial incentives to take up work; increased obligations on jobseekers; and expanded services to help jobseekers get a greater share of available jobs. Thus the government argued that its expectation of increased social and economic participation by income security recipients 'was consistent with views emerging internationally' (Newman, 2000).

However, the government's argument conveniently ignored the fact that there are significant differences between the British and US schemes, reflecting variations in political philosophy and culture. For example, the US scheme is highly punitive, and involves time-limited payments, compulsory participation in workfare programs, and the right to deny benefits to unmarried teenage mothers and assign them to the care of government-appointed guardians. The scheme assumes that recipients lack work motivation, and its sole purpose appears to be to push recipients off welfare rolls.

In contrast, the British scheme seems to be based more on a carrot rather than stick approach. Lone parents are not obliged to work, and there is a stronger focus on job creation, wage subsidies, and the provision of education and training. The scheme appears to recognise structural as well as individual barriers to joblessness, and assumes that business and government have a responsibility to actively promote employment opportunities for disadvantaged jobseekers (Mendes, 2000b: 34).

Significantly, a number of commentators have argued that the existing Australian work for the dole project far more closely approximates the US rather than the British scheme, in that it appears to involve a punitive and one-sided approach based on a negative view of welfare recipients (Curtain, 2000; Ferguson, 2000).

During the welfare reform debate, the government also brought Lawrence Mead to Australia to extol the virtues of US-style reform. Mead was the keynote speaker at the annual conference of the quasi-independent research body, the Australian Institute of Family Studies. The institute, then under the research direction of British neoliberal academic Peter Saunders (now with the CIS), lauded the views of Mead and their relevance to the Australian situation (Saunders, 1999: 4).

The government and its supporters persistently praised the US welfare reform scheme, arguing that the numbers of people on welfare had fallen by 40 to 50 per cent over recent years. They also denied that these reforms have caused any undue harm to the poor. However, they ignored contrary evidence suggesting that US welfare reform has moved large numbers of families including children into increased poverty, dependence on emergency relief and temporary foster care, and even homelessness (Link et al, 2000; Midgley, 2001).

The example of welfare reform, therefore, suggests that the interaction between local policy debates and global policy trends reflects complex political motives and influences. In this case, global intervention was principally the result of political and ideological manoeuvres by an autonomous national government, rather than a direct response to external economic pressures. The outcome appears to be an increasing ideological convergence of US and Australian welfare reform agendas (O'Connor, 2001: 230–32).

CASE TWO
THE VICTORIAN SAFE INJECTING FACILITIES SCHEME

In April 2000, the Victorian Labor Government announced its intention to introduce safe injecting facilities (SIFs) in five Melbourne municipalities on a controlled trial basis. SIFs are legal facilities where heroin users can inject in relative safety.

An intense public and political debate followed over the next six months. Opinion was divided between 'harm minimisers', who define drug use as a public health issue, and prohibitionists, who view drug use narrowly in criminal and moral terms. Harm minimisers strongly favoured SIFs, whilst prohibitionists were vigorously opposed. Eventually, the SIF legislation was blocked by the conservative majority in the Victorian Legislative Council. Consequently the trial was not able to proceed.

During the debate, both supporters and opponents of SIFs consistently referred to evidence concerning the efficacy of existing SIFs in Europe. Supporters of the SIF trial, including the Victorian Government, sympathetic local councils, welfare groups and some newspaper journalists, generally interpreted overseas outcomes optimistically and argued they could be successfully transferred to the Australian setting. In contrast, opponents of SIFs claimed that overseas evidence was at best equivocal and inconclusive (Mendes, 2002a).

In addition, the debate was directly influenced by a number of international organisations. For example, the conservative Australian Prime Minister John Howard, who strongly opposed the proposed SIF trial, brandished a report by the International Narcotics Control Board (INCB) condemning SIFs. The INCB, which is responsible for monitoring compliance with international drug control treaties, is well known for its hard-line prohibitionist views, and has often been described as a conservative mouthpiece of the US State Department.

The INCB suggested that the proposed facilities contravened international drug control treaties by encouraging illicit drug trafficking (INCB, 1999: 26–27, 62). Howard then indicated he would seek legal advice on whether the Federal Government could use the INCB report to invoke its external powers to stop the planned facilities. However, Howard eventually conceded that the Federal Government could not interfere in the decisions of the states regarding injecting facilities.

Prime Minister Howard also sought support from hard-line prohibitionists in the United States. In August 1999, he met with the director of the US Office of National Drug Policy, General Barry McCaffrey. McCaffrey, known as a crusader for prohibition policies, strongly rejected the proposed SIFs, comparing 'legal injecting rooms' to 'pouring alcohol into an alcoholic'. At the invitation of Howard, McCaffrey subsequently visited Australia in November to help ensure a 'drug-free Sydney Olympics'. He also confirmed his continued strong opposition to SIFs.

The intervention of the Vatican provided another example of the internationalisation of the SIF debate. This occurred principally in relation to a similar situation in New South Wales, where the Sisters of Charity Health Service had agreed to supervise a proposed injecting facility. This initiative had provoked considerable contention and division within the Catholic Church. Following an approach from the Archbishop of Sydney, the Vatican ordered the Sisters of Charity to withdraw from the program on the grounds that their involvement in the New South Wales trial or any other SIF trial would be perceived as condoning drug abuse, and involve co-operation with 'grave evil'. Subsequently, the Uniting Church agreed to administer the New South Wales injecting room, which opened for business in May 2001 (Mendes, 2002a).

The SIFs controversy confirms the increasing influence of global policy actors and evidence on Australian debates on social policy. It also suggests that the impact of globalisation is significantly mediated by the activities and agendas of local political and ideological pressures and lobby groups.

CONCLUSION

This chapter suggests that the relationship between globalisation and welfare states reflects complex and mostly indirect processes, rather than a direct and universal correlation.

On the one hand, the increasing power of international financial markets does appear to limit the autonomy of individual nation states, and particularly their ability to implement traditional social democratic agendas. Globalisation does provide some ideological reinforcement for neoliberal ideas and agendas.

On the other hand, there is little evidence that globalisation is driving a consistent and uniform decline of social standards. On the contrary, the impact of globalisation continues to be modified by disparate national structures, and policy and political agendas. Global economic trends are not forcing governments to cut welfare expenditure in order to enhance national competitiveness.

To the extent that the neoliberal agenda is leading the way, this is not because there is no policy alternatives, but rather because many national governments have expressed a preference for this agenda. As we will demonstrate in the next chapter, there are other policy directions, including those of substantial social protection which are arguably also compatible with open, globalised economies.

Questions for consideration

1 Is globalisation primarily an economic, or ideological, phenomenon?
2 Does increased global trade and competition necessarily mean the end of the welfare state? Is there likely to be a direct linkage between international tax cuts and welfare retrenchment?
3 Compare recent social policy developments in two OECD countries, such as Australia and Canada? What are the common trends and what are the differences? To what extent can these similarities and differences be attributed either to globalisation or to internal political and ideological traditions?

Exercise

Compare the following quotes in terms of their differing views about the influence of globalisation on the welfare state:

1 'The model of the European welfare state has outlived its usefulness ... From Sweden through Austria to Spain, there is essentially the same programme of reducing public expenditure, cutting real wages, and eliminating social services. And everywhere protest ends in resignation ... At a world level, more than 40 000 transnational corporations play off their own employees as well as different nation states against one another.' (Martin & Schumann 1997:6)
2 'Events around the world demonstrate that strong compaigns can still be mounted against the state to defend welfare rights and entitlements ... For both developed and developing countries, the fate of globalisation is often decided locally rather than globally, is mediated by class struggle, and is dependent on the national balance of power.' (Yeates 2001:141–42)

4

DEFENDING AND REFORMING THE WELFARE STATE

This chapter argues that the existing welfare state should be defended against neoliberal agendas and forces. However, it acknowledges that widespread social and economic changes have undermined some of the original assumptions and structures of the welfare state, and that new methods are required for promoting greater equity in society.

The first part examines moral, political and historical arguments in favour of the welfare state. A contrast is drawn with the demonstrated negative social consequences of neoliberal policies and arguments. The next section suggests strategies for reconstructing the welfare state in order to reflect global changes in society, families and labour markets. In particular, control and delivery of community services should be devolved to the local community groups that make up our civil society. Finally, it considers the alleged trade-off between equity and efficiency, and suggests that welfare states are compatible with globalisation. Attention is drawn to the successful reconstruction of the social democratic welfare state in the Netherlands in order to show that generous welfare states can produce positive social and economic outcomes.

ARGUMENTS FOR THE WELFARE STATE

Modern welfare states began to emerge in late nineteenth-century Europe. However, most of these initiatives were limited to the establishment of insurance schemes for occupational injuries. Some countries also offered minimal old age and sickness insurance. For example, the German Chancellor Bismarck introduced social insurance systems in the 1880s to protect workers from sickness, industrial injury and in old age. These reforms were designed at least in part to offset the growing popularity of the socialist movement (Leisering, 2001: 162).

More advanced welfare states were introduced in the 1930s and 1940s to alleviate the immense social injustices existing within free-market capitalist systems. These inequities were typified by the mass poverty and unemployment of the Great Depression. Many drew the conclusion that modern industrial society required new methods beyond traditional institutions such as the family, churches and charity in order to provide adequately for those in need. The state would take collective responsibility for addressing the vagaries of social risk (Kuhne and Alestalo, 2000: 3).

Beveridge, the father of the British welfare state, wrote of the five 'giant social evils' which had bedevilled British society before the war. They were ignorance, disease, idleness, squalor and want. The post-war British Labor Government subsequently introduced free education up to age 15 to combat ignorance; a free national health service to combat disease; full employment to combat idleness; public housing to combat squalor; and national insurance benefits to combat want (Alcock and Craig, 2001: 126–27).

Yet, the major consolidation of welfare states took place in the 1960s and 1970s. During this period, total public expenditure in OECD countries (as a percentage of GDP) increased by an average of 30 per cent, mostly as a result of social expenditure growth. All welfare states acted to increase levels of payments and promote greater equality. However, the late 1970s and early 1980s saw the beginnings of the neoliberal backlash (Esping-Andersen, 1999: 2–3).

The welfare state is based on the notion, espoused by social theorists such as Marshall and Titmuss, that people require social rights (social and economic resources, opportunities and powers) in order to also exercise their formal political and legal rights. Alternatively, if left to the market, the inequitable distribution of resources would restrict the freedom of those worst off (Lister, 1997: 15–17).

Advanced welfare states vary both in terms of their levels of de-commodification (the extent to which social rights such as health care, education, housing and income security are guaranteed equally to all independent of the labour market), and social stratification (the extent to which the welfare state serves to structure the quality of social citizenship). The famous comparative study of welfare states by the Swedish theorist, Esping-Andersen (1990), identified three principal welfare regimes:

1 liberal welfare states, based on selective, residual benefits and market provision of services in which de-commodification is low, and where liberal principles of stratification are dominant. The liberal welfare world consists of Australia, the United States, the United Kingdom, New Zealand, Canada and Ireland.
2 corporate welfare states, composed of nations such as Austria, France, Germany and Italy with moderate de-commodification and conservative stratification. Social rights are based on class and status linked to occupation and employment, and redistribution of income is negligible.
3 social democratic states such as Holland, Denmark, Norway and Sweden, where de-commodification is high, and there is considerable stratification based on universal benefits and a high degree of benefit equality.

Goodin and his co-writers (1999) summarise Esping-Anderson's framework with reference to the social and economic goals pursued. They argue that liberal regimes attach relatively more importance to economic efficiency than do other welfare regimes; social democratic regimes attach greater importance to equality than do other welfare regimes; and corporatists attach a higher value to social integration and social stability than do other welfare regimes.

Some authors have criticised Esping-Andersen for narrowly assuming that increased social expenditure is the only means of promoting greater income redistribution. They argue for the classification of a fourth 'radical' or 'laborite' welfare world (pertaining to Australia, New Zealand and the United Kingdom) in which progressive taxation, and increased expenditure on the poorest groups whilst excluding the affluent, lead to enhanced poverty amelioration and income equality (Castles and Mitchell, 1992; Hill, 1996: 46–49).

Feminist authors have also criticised Esping-Andersen for failing to identify whether women are entitled to benefits as individuals, or whether their welfare is tied to their position in families. They argue for an extension of Esping-Andersen's typology to take into account family welfare orientation (based upon the strength of family support policies), female work desirability (based upon the extent of female access to work opportunities comparable to those for men), and which parent receives benefits for children (Hill, 1996: 43–45).

Numerous factors appear to have contributed to the above cross-national variations, including the nature of working-class mobilisation and the size and activity of trade unions; the existence of strong social democratic or labor governments; the extent of resistance by right-wing parties; and the structure of political and class coalitions (Castles, 1998).

Welfare states confronted some early criticism from right-wingers concerned that increased public spending would under-mine the free market. However, in general, there was a mainstream consensus in favour of greater social protection. In Britain, this consensus was called Butskellism to reflect the increasing policy convergence between the parties, represented by Labour Treasurer Gaitskell and his Conservative successor Butler (Deakin, 1987: 46–53).

Later in the 1960s and 1970s, the welfare state came under attack from progressive sources. Marxists criticised its contribution to reinforcing the institutions and values of capitalist society, and its failure to resolve significant social inequalities. They claimed that welfare services acted to stifle and reduce working-class antagonism to the existing social order, and that social justice could only be attained by the abolition of capitalism. Nevertheless, they acknowl-edged that the welfare state also represents a gain for the working class in its struggle against exploitation (Mullaly, 1997: 88–96; Esping-Andersen, 1999: 2–3).

Similarly, feminists criticised the welfare state for its patriarchal nature and reinforcement of traditional gender inequities (Leonard, 1997: 3–5). The late 1970s and early 1980s saw the challenge of the New Right which we have examined in Chapter 2, and a newer challenge from movements of welfare consumers. These groups had vastly different agendas, but both emphasised greater opportunities for welfare users' participation and choice (Beresford, 2002: 96).

Nevertheless, the welfare state has retained substantial public support, and continues to be underpinned by a number of power-ful moral and political arguments. Firstly, the welfare state serves to promote the personal autonomy and freedom of those without alternative sources of income, and to protect the poor from overt exploitation. In particular, the welfare state is positively distin-guished from voluntary charities by its focus on non-discretionary welfare provision. The rights or entitlements of the claimant are determined by legislatively mandated rules and regulations, rather than being subject to the values or whims of the individual bene-factor (Goodin, 1988: 11–12).

Further, unemployment payments can reasonably be viewed as compensation for those whose involuntary exclusion from the labour market during a period of structural unemployment explic-itly benefits the working majority (Goodin and Schmidtz, 1998: 184–89).

In addition, the welfare state does promote greater equity. A number of commentators argue that the welfare state has been successful in preventing destitution, and reducing poverty among particularly vulnerable groups such as the sick, the aged, sole parents and the unemployed. Overall, the welfare state appears to have been effective in alleviating the worst extremes of market-based inequalities, in promoting some degree of redistribution of income and life chances, and in facilitating social cohesiveness and inclusion rather than social exclusion (Brennan, 1998b; Mishra, 1999: 29).

For example, the Australian welfare state has been particularly successful in reducing poverty amongst the elderly and children. The higher old age pensions introduced since the 1975 Henderson Inquiry into Poverty have assisted the elderly, whilst the higher parenting payments and child support scheme introduced in the 1980s have substantially reduced child poverty (O'Donnell, 1999: 130–32; Harding and Szukalska, 2000: 6). Similarly, research has demonstrated the important role played by government benefits in the United States, Britain and Holland in reducing aged and child poverty. Overall, the more generous social democratic welfare states have been most successful in reducing poverty (Goodin et al, 1999: 34, 54–62; Taylor-Gooby, 2001b: 8–10).

On the other hand, there is evidence that welfare states have generally failed to effect a significant overall redistribution of income and wealth in favour of greater equality. In particular, universal services such as health care, education, housing and transport seem to favour the better off, rather than the poor (Le Grand, 1982; Teeple, 2000: 41–45).

Another concern raised (which we will discuss further below) is that the contemporary welfare state has failed to respond to global social and economic changes. One response to these changes has been the increasing implementation of the neoliberal agenda since the late 1970s. Yet, policies involving cuts to welfare services and programs have consistently led to greater inequality both within Western countries, and between developed and developing countries. This trend is particularly prevalent in countries which have reduced social expenditure, but less so where welfare supports have been retained (Paul Pierson, 2001: 438). Table 4.1 (page 72) shows the extent to which inequality increased during the 1980s. There were relatively lower increases in inequality in disposable income (earnings after tax and transfers) than in market income (earnings from wages), due to progressive taxation and income security transfers.

TABLE 4.1
WORSENING INEQUALITY IN OECD COUNTRIES: 1980s

	Period	Market income	Disposable income
Australia	1980–90	C	C
Belgium	1985–92	C	C
Canada	1980–92	C	D
Denmark	1981–90	C	C
Finland	1981–92	B	D
France	1979–89	D	D
Germany	1983–90	C	D
Ireland	1980–87	C	D
Israel	1979–92	C	D
Italy	1977–91	E	E
Japan	1981–90	C	C
Netherlands	1981–89	C	C
New Zealand	1981–89	C	C
Norway	1982–89	C	C
Portugal	1980–90	D	D
Spain	1980–90	n/a	D
Sweden	1980–93	B	B
UK	1981–91	B	A
USA	1980–93	B	B

NOTES A Extremely large increase (>30%); B Large increase (16–29%); C Small increase (5–10%); D Negligible (-4 to +4%); E Small decline (–5% or more).

SOURCE Adapted from United Nations Development Programme, *Human Development Report*, 1999: 39.

For example, the gap between the rich and poor in the United States is now larger than at any time in the past 20 years. Similar trends are prevalent in Britain and New Zealand. Britain and the United States also have the highest poverty rates in developed countries (Mishra, 1999: 29–32). In Australia, the differences in the distribution of income between the highest and lowest income earners have increased from a ratio of 3.70:1 in 1973/74, to 6.14:1 in 1995/96. Even after allowing for variables of tax, welfare benefits and family size, high-income households now have on average more than four times as much to spend as those on low incomes (Jamrozik, 2001: 97).

Not only that, a United Nations *Human Development Report* states that the gap between the wealthiest 20 per cent and the world's poorest 20 per cent grew from 60:1 to 74:1 in the seven years from 1990 to 1997. By the late 1990s, the fifth of the world's population living in the wealthiest countries held 86 per cent of world GDP, whilst the bottom fifth held just 1 per cent. In addition, the assets of the 200 richest people in the world were greater than the combined income of more than 41 per cent of the world's population (UNDP, 1999: 3, 38; Kerr, 2001: 25–33).

However, advocates of neoliberalism generally ignore the social costs of their policies. Instead, they advocate more of the same remedy. To critics, they appear to be zealots determined to sacrifice a whole generation of poor and disadvantaged people as part of a social experiment that may potentially benefit future generations (Allan, 1997: 4).

RESPONDING TO GLOBAL SOCIAL AND ECONOMIC CHANGES

The welfare states which emerged in the 1940s were based on the assumption of stable families and efficient, full-employment labour markets. Social assistance focused principally on the elderly. Income support for the able-bodied young was designed to compensate for temporary income loss, not to provide long-term benefits. However, since the mid-1970s, advanced welfare states have confronted new social and economic challenges and pressures including:

- labour market changes characterised by persistently high levels of unemployment, including significant numbers of long-term unemployed, and increased participation of women in employment
- the associated decline in blue-collar manufacturing jobs, and the recent emergence of the 'knowledge' economy based on technological innovation
- changes in family structures characterised by increases in divorce and sole-parent families
- the rise of individualism at the expense of tradition and post-war collectivism
- the projected ageing of populations, leaving more elderly citizens dependent on government support for longer periods and a corresponding decline in fertility rates leading potentially to an increasing fiscal burden. (Giddens, 2001: 3–5; Alcock, 2001: 14–15)

These changes have influenced (along with neoliberal ideas and economic globalisation) an international trend away from collective and universal principles of social solidarity towards greater individual, family and community responsibility for welfare.

Thus, several commentators speak of a mixed economy of welfare, based on a new concept of risk management which goes beyond the old framework of collective pooling of risks against unforeseen hardship through universalistic state services. That framework assumed a relatively homogeneous industrial male working class. Instead, it is argued that the new diversity of social risks (growing insecurity of employment, the need for frequent retraining or reskilling, and demonstrated lower child poverty rates amongst two-earner households) demands a renegotiation of risk management responsibilities between individuals, families, the market and the state. This may include strategies which recognise the positive sides of risk, such as opportunity and economic mobility, as well as the need to protect against disadvantage (Esping-Andersen, 1999: 148–68; Mitchell, 2001; Rodger, 2000).

Nevertheless, this text explicitly rejects the notion that the universalist welfare state is doomed, or that other institutions such as the family, the market or the community can effectively take over social protection from the state (see also Goodin, 2000: 60–61). It also views as highly simplistic the neoliberal attempt to blame the welfare state for problems such as increased dependence on income security payments which arguably lay beyond its control. Rather, these problems can be attributed primarily to market failure and associated changes in the labour market (Whitfield, 2001: 131).

However, it does accept that many of the criticisms of the existing welfare state are valid. In particular, there is little doubt that many poor and disadvantaged people are disempowered by current welfare services. The dependence and subordination of women continues to be reinforced. Many large, centralised welfare bureaucracies are paternalistic, inflexible and insensitive to the needs of service users. Too often, welfare consumers are the passive and powerless recipients of services, and are denied the opportunity to participate in the identification of their own needs and possible solutions (Brown et al, 2000: 92; Ife, 2002: 6, 18–20).

In addition, whilst the welfare state has arguably succeeded in relieving financial poverty, it has been less successful in preventing the wider social exclusion of poor and disadvantaged people. (By 'social exclusion', we mean people or communities being denied the opportunity to participate in mainstream social, economic, political and cultural systems.) It assumes exclusion from informal social networks, as well as from formal institutions such as work and education (Room, 1999).

A reformed welfare state does need to find ways and means of including disadvantaged groups within the social and economic mainstream. However, it is important that social inclusion not be based solely on pathways to paid employment, but rather on broadly defined opportunities for social participation. These could include a variety of social, cultural, educational and caring activities including, for example, participation in local exchange and trading schemes (Fitzpatrick, 1999: 166; Vandenbroucke, 2001: 142–43).

To be sure, the redirection of passive income maintenance towards active labour market programs may help to reintegrate some people into the mainstream. However, given the current high level of unemployment in Australia, it is highly likely that a significant section of the population will remain outside the workforce.

Therefore it is argued that whilst government should continue to provide central funding of welfare payments, it should consider introducing community development principles to the delivery of welfare services. This could mean handing over control of the resourcing and provision of welfare support services to local communities. Such devolution may contribute to the strengthening of social capital in these communities which refers to processes of social trust and co-operation. ('Social capital' depends on the formation of neighbourhood relationships and networks, and a sense of belonging to and having some stake in the common good: Edgar, 2001: xv, 102.)

Thus the notion of 'place management' could be utilised whereby funding is targeted at social problems identified and prioritised by local experts (Latham, 2001a: 127–29). Services should if possible be delivered by local community members who understand the problems of the area, rather than by disinterested strangers (Ife, 2002: 15–19, 92–93). Relevant consumer groups should be invited to actively contribute to the planning and delivery of services with the potential in the longer term for transforming welfare programs into user-controlled co-operatives (Botsman, 2001: 177–83; Beresford, 2002: 96–98).

A particularly innovative strategy for developing local community control called 'associationalism' is suggested by the British academic Paul Hirst. Hirst proposes the establishment of voluntary self-governing organisations based on partnerships between service users and providers. These organisations would prioritise the empowerment of citizens through maximising consumer choice and control, and preferably operate in tandem with a guaranteed minimum income scheme. The state would continue to provide most of the funding for welfare services, but civil society would take much greater responsibility for the design and delivery of services (Hirst, 1994; 1997).

Hirst's proposal is appealing in that it offers the potential for welfare consumers to become genuine players in the service delivery and policy development process. This contrasts with the present situation whereby consumers are virtually excluded from decision-making processes. For example, no representatives of service users were included in the Federal Government's Welfare Reform Reference Group. As we will note in Chapter 11, the absence of any viable framework for the collective political representation of welfare recipients is one of the key factors contributing to welfare retrenchment.

In recommending that greater local community participation in and control of service delivery be considered, we are nevertheless mindful that local communities are not united and homogeneous groups. Rather, they are often divided by class, ethnicity, race and other significant social, economic and attitudinal barriers. Recent policy debates in Victoria, for example, suggest that some local communities and community groups are just as likely, for example, to exclude, rather than include, marginalised groups such as welfare recipients, drug users and street prostitutes (Edgar, 2001: xiii–xiv; Mendes, 2001c). It is also possible that some local communities will be dominated by traditional charity networks concerned with judging and moralising service users, rather than with empowering them.

It is therefore crucial to ensure that local initiatives are based on the community development principles of social inclusion, diversity, empowerment and participation. Social inclusion refers to the notion that processes should always seek to include rather than to exclude; that all members of a community should be valued even if they hold conflicting views; and that we should respect and value others even when we disagree with their ideas, values and politics. Similarly, diversity emphasises the celebration of differences within the community. Particular care should be taken to encourage and validate groups traditionally excluded such as gays and lesbians, people with disabilities, and racial or ethnic minorities (Ife, 2002: 203, 223). Empowerment involves providing people with the skills and resources necessary to increase their capacity to determine their own future, and to effectively participate in the life of their community. Participation refers to the right of community members to directly participate in the identification of social problems, and in determining strategies for their resolution. It is important to ensure that all sections of a community including potentially marginalised groups such as drug users are able to participate (Ife, 2002: 208–209, 219–20).

Another concern is the evidence of declining public support for the system of progressive taxation and associated public spending.

Research by the British Fabian Society suggests a need to reconnect specific taxes with specific social services. For example, a certain percentage of income tax or consumption tax could be specifically earmarked to fund health care, public education, unemployment training programs or particular income security payments (Fabian Society, 2000). In Australia, the existing Medicare levy could be extended to other social services.

We also need to find some way of empowering poor and disadvantaged groups which goes beyond mere protection from destitution. This is not likely to occur via the increasing use of the welfare state to control and police disadvantaged groups, and bully them into the already over-crowded labour market (Kerr, 2001: 60–67; Jamrozik, 2001: 8–9). Rather, we need to develop strategies that use the welfare state to signify a renewed commitment to equitable outcomes. In particular, governments need to consider:

- the need for additional taxation to fund social investment and full employment
- taking greater responsibility for the provision of training and employment opportunities for those unable to access employment in the private sector
- an expansion of universalistic services such as health and education which promote social solidarity, rather than the narrow and divisive targeting of services only to the poor. (Cass, 1998)

TRADING EQUITY FOR EFFICIENCY?

As we noted in Chapter 3, some commentators (particularly but not exclusively those associated with the hyperglobalist thesis) argue that globalisation has contributed to a limiting of domestic policy choices. An extension of this argument is that welfare states today face a fundamental trade-off between employment growth and efficiency on the one hand, and egalitarian social protection on the other.

The first model — strongly recommended by the 1994 OECD Jobs Study — suggests achieving growth through welfare retrenchment. Lower wages, less job security and lower taxation are introduced as a means of facilitating greater economic growth. Social protection is provided largely through the labour market, and only a minimal safety net is provided for those outside the workforce. The result tends to be higher levels of employment, but also greater inequality (McBride and Williams, 2001: 287–89).

The alternative model is based on the pursuit of growth through a high-skilled, high-wage and socially cohesive society. A generous welfare state remains to reduce inequality through the use of progressive taxation measures and universal welfare payments (Alcock, 2001: 10–11).

A specific dichotomy is often suggested between the high employment but rising poverty and inequality prevalent in the United States, and the high unemployment but relative egalitarianism of most European countries. In short, the American road is depicted as more likely to facilitate national competitiveness within the global economy (Esping-Andersen, 1996; 1999).

There are a number of problems with this argument. Firstly, levels of unemployment in Europe have fallen from an average of 10.7 per cent in 1997 to 8.4 per cent in 2000, and are projected to fall further. Moreover, a number of European countries including Holland, Denmark, Austria, Sweden and Portugal all have unemployment rates similar to, if not lower than, US levels. There does not appear to be any consistent relationship between social security and unemployment in either a positive or negative direction (see Table 4.2).

TABLE 4.2
UNEMPLOYMENT AND SOCIAL SECURITY EXPENDITURE IN 16 OECD COUNTRIES

	Unemployment 1974–92 (%)	Social security 1970s–80s (% GDP)
Switzerland	0.6	13.0
Japan	2.3	9.9
Sweden	2.4	17.3
Austria	2.7	19.1
Norway	2.9	14.8
Germany	4.9	16.7
Finland	5.2	9.6
USA	6.9	10.8
Australia	7.0	8.9
France	7.7	19.6
Netherlands	7.8	25.7
Denmark	8.0	15.7
UK	8.2	12.2
Italy	8.7	16.0
Canada	8.7	10.9
Belgium	8.8	20.7
OECD average	6.5	15.1

SOURCE Adapted from Boreham, Dow and Leet, *Room to Manoeuvre: Political Aspects of Full Employment*, 1999: 126.

Turner argues that the gap between some European countries and the United States can in fact be explained by lower levels of service-sector employment in areas such as wholesaling, retailing and human services, rather than by the vagaries of global competition (Turner, 2001: 152–54).

The specific efficacy of the US low-wage model has also been questioned. For example, the United States has by far the largest proportion of the adult male population in incarceration of any developed country. This includes 1.5 million men in prison, and a further 3.5 million on parole. If this prison population were included in the unemployment figures, it is likely that the official rate would be almost 2 percentage points higher. This is without counting a further 1 million Americans who appear to be homeless (Clarke, 2001: 147–48).

In addition, the US model does not appear to be replicable. Countries such as Britain and New Zealand that have followed the US direction have experienced only modest employment growth offset by large increases in poverty and inequality (Huber and Stephens, 2001: 142–43).

Finally, there is some evidence of a positive relationship between increased integration into global markets and welfare spending. Research suggests that the welfare state may actually enhance rather than corrode economic competitiveness (Hay, 2001). Many countries appear to use expanded social protection programs as an alternative to traditional protectionism in order to compensate those groups unable to compete in global markets. Social expenditure also arguably contributes to economic and political stability, facilitates the availability of skilled and productive employees, and reduces social costs such as crime and ill-health.

Such positives may act as an investment incentive, rather than disincentive, to owners of mobile capital. Alternatively countries which attempt to use global pressures as a means of legitimating welfare cutbacks may find public opinion turning against free trade and economic integration (Garrett, 1998; Pierson, 2001: 463–65).

THE DUTCH ALTERNATIVE

During the 1980s, the welfare state in the Netherlands was regarded as economically unsustainable. The system was based on benefits for full-time male breadwinners, with high social insurance costs per employee. Unemployment rose to almost 14 per cent, and another 13 per cent of workers exited the labour market through access to training schemes, disability benefits or early retirement. A fiscal crisis ensued. Critical observers described the

Dutch system as representing the prime example of a 'welfare without work' society.

Yet, today the same commentators speak of the Dutch employment 'miracle'. Unemployment has been reduced to 2.3 per cent by a range of policies including wage moderation, labour market flexibility, reform of social security entitlements to discourage the use of sick leave and disability schemes, and measures to redistribute employment. These measures were aimed both at increasing participation in employment, and reducing the demands of disability and sickness payments on public finances.

This has led to a massive increase in part-time jobs, particularly in the services sector, a huge entry of women into the labour force, and the replacement of older workers by younger, cheaper and possibly more flexible and skilled workers. Yet, some problems remain particularly in relation to the low labour force participation rate of older males, and the high unemployment rates for low-skilled workers (Visser and Hemerijck, 1997; Hemerijck and Visser, 2001: 191–92).

However, compared to the United States, employment growth has been less associated with a rise in earnings inequality. The Netherlands remains one of the most internationalised economies in the world, but there has been no reduction in the real wages of unskilled workers, and little evidence of working poverty. In fact after Belgium, the Netherlands has the lowest poverty rates in the OECD. The Dutch continue to spend a relatively high 31.6 per cent of their GDP on social protection (Hirst and Thompson, 1999: 175–80; Rhodes, 2001: 181–84).

Thus the Netherlands seem to be successful in pursuing both social and economic goals. A recent international study, for example, compared the social democratic regime in the Netherlands with the corporatist German regime and the neoliberal US regime across a range of economic and social indicators. The study found significantly that the Netherlands equalled or exceeded the performance of the alternative regimes in all areas including economic growth and efficiency, poverty and inequality, social integration and social autonomy (Goodin et al, 1999).

This study appears to confirm the conclusion of Chapter 3 that globalisation does not preclude different paths to national competitiveness. The Dutch experience suggests (contrary to the neoliberal model discussed in Chapter 2) that generous welfare states and economic productivity remain compatible.

CONCLUSION

With varying degrees of success, welfare states have contributed to greater equity and the alleviation of poverty. However, widespread social and economic changes have undermined their effectiveness, and led to demands for new methods of social policy intervention.

Some potential new models of welfare service delivery, based on localist and consumer control, and employment of community development principles, have been suggested. In addition, the alleged effectiveness of the harsh neoliberal US welfare model is challenged by pointing to the success of other more equitable models in European countries such as the Netherlands.

Questions for consideration

1 The Australian welfare state seems to be under attack from all sides. Yet it remains largely intact. Why?
2 Has the welfare state been successful in promoting a more equitable society? If not, why not?
3 Has Australia been too willing to borrow from the latest fashions in the United States? Are there other welfare state models we could follow?

Exercise

Most existing welfare services are paternalistic and driven by the political and policy agendas of government and service providers. What structural changes would need to occur in order to transform this system into a democratic welfare model whereby consumers were able to control the planning and delivery of services?

part two

THE POLITICAL PARTIES AND CONTEMPORARY WELFARE POLICY DEBATES: TOWARDS IDEOLOGICAL CONVERGENCE

The following chapters consider the impact of neoliberal ideas, and other competing ideas and agendas, on the welfare policies of the Labor and Liberal parties. In Chapter 3, we noted that globalisation has influenced an increasing policy convergence between social democratic and right-wing parties towards welfare retrenchment. This pattern appears to be particularly prevalent in Anglo-Saxon countries, including Australia. Alternatives to neoliberalism have been marginalised. Today, both major parties favour the free market, low taxes and limited social expenditure. Both Labor and Liberal governments emphasise the targeting of safety net benefits to the most needy groups, rather than expanded universalistic programs and services.

This does not mean that the Liberal and Labor parties hold identical attitudes to social welfare. The Liberal Party continues to pursue a greater preference for private provision, whilst the ALP remains more sympathetic to public sector solutions. In addition, the Liberal Party remains reluctant to interfere with market allocations of income and wealth, whilst the ALP retains at least a rhetorical commitment to greater equity. Nevertheless, in practice, the difference today is arguably one of emphasis rather than principle (Smith, 1994: 60–62).

5

LIBERAL PARTY POLICY: FROM THE 'FORGOTTEN PEOPLE' TO 'MUTUAL OBLIGATION'

This chapter examines the federal Liberal Party's approach to social welfare policy. The Liberal Party has traditionally been a party of pragmatic conservatism blending three disparate ideological tendencies. The social liberal tendency favoured state intervention to protect the social and economic rights of the underprivileged. This tradition stands in stark contrast to the now-dominant neoliberal tendency which emphasises individual rights, the rationality of the free market and self-help. A rather less organised tendency, broadly defined as social conservatism, remains influential — but mainly with respect to defending traditional institutions such as the monarchy and nuclear family (Jaensch, 1994: 157–58; Norton, 2000: 22–26).

However, since 1983, the federal Liberal Party has arguably become dominated by neoliberal ideas of small government and individualism. Under the influence of the New Right, the Liberal Party has mounted a significant critique of the welfare state. The party's espousal and implementation of these ideas has, however, been moderated on occasions by broader political and electoral considerations.

This chapter begins by briefly exploring the ideological fluidity of the Menzies and Fraser periods. It then examines the neoliberal takeover of the Liberal Party. The third section uses the analytic framework introduced in Chapter 2 to explore the principal themes of the Liberal Party's critique of the welfare state. The final sections discuss firstly the re-alignment of Liberal thinking in response to electoral defeat in 1993, and the particular policy initiatives of the Howard Liberal-National Coalition while in government since 1996.

No specific reference is made in this chapter to the social welfare policies of the National Party. This is because the Nationals have traditionally deferred to their senior coalition partner on social welfare policy. Former National Party leader Ian Sinclair remains the only National to hold the social welfare portfolio in a Federal Coalition Government, back in the mid-1960s, although another National leader, Charles Blunt, was briefly Opposition spokesman on social security in the mid-1980s. Some National Party figures, including most prominently former senator John Stone, have spoken out on social welfare policies from time to time. But in general, the National Party shares and replicates the views of the Liberal Party on this issue.

IDEOLOGICAL DIVERSITY UP TO 1983

Keynesian economic theory, which emphasises the importance to economic growth of full employment and social security, was highly influential in the immediate post-war decades (Brett, 1994). Keynesianism allowed the Liberals to develop a compromise between the full-scale planning of 'extreme' socialism — which they despised — and the inhumane laissez-faire economics which had been discredited by the mass unemployment and poverty of the 1930s (Smyth, 1995a: 90–96).

This pragmatic compromise between individual and market freedom on the one hand, and welfarist compassion for the poor on the other, was typified by the rhetoric of the founder of the Liberal Party, Sir Robert Menzies. In his famous 'Forgotten People' speeches of 1942, Menzies specifically rejected 'a return to the old and selfish notions of laissez-faire' in which the state merely maintained 'the ring within which the competitors would fight'. Instead, Menzies argued in favour of government assistance to, and protection of, underprivileged groups:

> The country has great and imperative obligations to the weak, the sick and the unfortunate. It must give to them all the sustenance and support it can. We look forward to social and unemployment insurances, to improved health services ... to a better distribution of wealth, to a keener sense of social justice and social responsibility. (Menzies, 1942a: 25)

At the same time, Menzies warned against the false benevolence of the 'all-powerful State' that would undermine the individual initiative and self-reliance which Liberals valued. Menzies opposed policies 'designed to discourage or penalise thrift, to encourage dependence on the State, to bring about a dull equality on the fantastic idea that all men are equal in mind and needs and deserts: to level down by taking the mountains out of the landscape' (Menzies, 1942b: 20).

In practice, Menzies forged a limited welfare state which provided a safety net sufficient to keep the needy from destitution, whilst ensuring that the net was low enough to encourage self-reliance rather than dependence. Social services were to be used only to supplement personal savings and insurance, and help from private charity organisations (Tiver, 1979: 318; Shamsullah, 1990: 107).

The Fraser era was marked by a similar compromise between competing ideas. The Liberals of the mid- to late 1970s advocated compassionate support to the poor and disadvantaged whilst ensuring that the recipients retained adequate incentives for self-reliance. A typical Liberal Party statement of this period emphasised the 'provision of effective assistance to people who are in ill-health, disadvantaged or in need, in ways which enhance their dignity and independence' (Liberal Party, 1977: 358).

THE NEOLIBERAL TAKEOVER AND THE MARGINALISATION OF THE SOCIAL LIBERALS

Since 1983, the Liberal Party has increasingly embraced radical libertarian positions favouring reliance on private charitable welfare in place of government welfare provision. This movement towards neoliberal ideas of small government reflects the takeover of the Liberal Party by the free-market faction, and the virtual marginalisation of the social liberal faction. It also arguably reflects a complete break with previous Liberal Party tradition which emphasised a central (albeit limited) role for the state in both intervening in the free market and protecting the poor (Stokes, 1994: 17).

The Liberal Party's shift to laissez faire can be attributed to a number of interacting local and international factors. The first and perhaps most important influence was the world-wide crisis of the welfare state accompanied by a backlash against public expenditure, the taxation system and welfare recipients, which led to a loss of confidence in traditional Keynesian methods of state intervention (Mishra, 1984; see also Chapter 2).

The second influence was the corresponding international revival of the classical liberal doctrines of Adam Smith, Friedrich Hayek and Milton Friedman. The success of the Thatcher and Reagan governments in Britain and the United States suggested an association of these ideas with electoral popularity.

A third influence was the political re-positioning of the governing Labor Party, which moved to the political centre and adopted many traditional Liberal Party policies, including greater restraint in public and social expenditure (Gruen and Grattan, 1993: 192–93). In response, the Liberal Party identified a need to move further to the right in order to properly distinguish its political views and ideology from those of the Labor Party.

Finally, there was considerable disappointment within the Liberal Party at the failure of the Fraser Government to cut public spending — despite much rhetoric in that direction. The neoliberals regarded these years as a period of lost opportunities. Right-wing commentator Gerard Henderson (who was sympathetic to the neoliberal agenda) epitomised their frustration when he described Prime Minister Fraser as 'really a bit of a bleeding heart' (Henderson, 1983: 36).

Following the 1980 federal election, a group of neoliberals began to campaign for free-market ideas in the Liberal Party. As discussed in Chapter 2, these neoliberals were assisted by other influential free-marketeers in academia, media, business, the public service and private think-tanks. Over time, they were able to secure control of the political agenda of the Liberal Party (Kelly, 1992: 34–35, 38–39).

The neoliberal takeover of the Liberal Party was signified by the 1983 adoption of the individualist, free market-oriented Valder Report (Liberal Party, 1983). The Valder Report attributed Australia's economic problems to the increased government spending in the 1970s. According to the report, Australia suffered from a welfare mentality in both corporate and individual terms. The report called for welfare benefits to be concentrated on 'those in need', and for the privatisation of some welfare services (Kelly, 1992: 105–106).

The social liberals responded to the economic rationalist takeover by forming the Liberal Forum group in February 1985 to promote a continuing social liberal agenda within the party. The social liberals emphasised that individuals have obligations to others as well as rights. They rejected the laissez-faire position that placed the highest value on personal liberty at the expense of other values such as opportunity and equality. They believed that government should intervene to limit the rights of individuals (or groups of individuals) when this is deemed necessary to protect the rights of other individuals or groups (Davidson, 1988).

The free-marketeers responded with vigorous attacks on the remaining social liberals. They were accused of being ignorant of the real causes of poverty and homelessness, which the neoliberals attributed to unnecessary government intervention. Leading social liberals, such as Ian MacPhee, Peter Baume and Chris Puplick, were manoeuvred out of the party. The free-market doctrine became hegemonic (Mendes, 1998a: 69).

THE NEOLIBERALS AND THE LIBERAL PARTY
SOCIAL WELFARE AGENDA: 1983–1993

As noted in Chapter 2, the free-market critique of the welfare state comprises five related themes which have all been reflected in Liberal Party policy:

INTEREST GROUP CAPTURE

The Liberal Party has consistently attacked 'vested interest' pressure groups such as the welfare lobby for allegedly manipulating the redistributive process to their own advantage. As early as 1986, for example, Liberal Party leader John Howard attacked welfare professionals for allegedly 'making ever increasing demands on the taxpayer' in order to finance their own career structures (Howard, 1986: 10). The attack on welfare interest groups was taken up with even greater fervour by another Liberal Party leader, John Hewson. In a speech to the ACOSS Congress of 1991, Hewson claimed that ACOSS was more interested in obtaining more money for the welfare sector and in building large bureaucracies than in helping the poor (Hewson, 1991). Hewson subsequently threatened in 1992 to cut ACOSS's government funding, querying whether its policies actually served the interests of its constituency.

LABOUR MARKET DEREGULATION

The Liberal Party has long argued for a more flexible labour market without award and minimum wage provisions. The 1992 Liberal Party 'Jobsback' policy incorporated these views, recommending a training wage of $3 an hour for 18 year olds, and $3.50 an hour for 18–20 year olds.

WELFARE DEPENDENCY

The Liberal Party has consistently argued that current welfare programs encourage long-term dependency on government and do little to encourage personal independence and self-reliance. As early as 1983, for example, the Liberal Party leader Andrew Peacock emphasised the need to 'avoid creating needless and unproductive dependence on welfare' (Peacock, 1983).

Subsequent Liberal Party manifestoes recommended the termination of unemployment benefits after nine months, and the termination of the sole-parent pension when the youngest child turns 12 (rather than the current 16). The aim of these reforms was to end incentives to welfare dependency, and promote a transfer of responsibility for welfare from the government to families and the individual (Mendes, 1998a: 71).

THE DESERVING POOR AND THE UNDESERVING POOR

The Liberal Party has consistently distinguished between the 'genuinely needy' (the deserving poor) who are entitled to assistance, and those who can look after themselves (the undeserving poor). In his 1986 Alfred Deakin Lecture, for example, Liberal Party leader John Howard advocated compassion and assistance to the 'deserving needy'. However, this compassion needed to be balanced by an attack on those who were not deserving — social security recipients who attained payments by fraud. Howard also proposed that unemployment beneficiaries should be required to work in return for their payments (Howard, 1986: 10). Subsequent Liberal Party policy statements also distinguished between the genuinely needy and the alleged rorters and welfare cheats.

PRIVATISATION OF WELFARE

The Liberal Party has consistently advocated a return to private charitable welfare as the vehicle of choice for assistance to the needy. As early as 1985, the Liberal Party leader, John Howard, called for the privatisation of welfare programs (quoted in Steketee, 1985).

The next Liberal Party leader, John Hewson, went even further, suggesting that the Department of Social Security be abolished, and the delivery of all welfare services be contracted out to community-based organisations. Hewson explained that the Liberals preferred voluntary to government welfare because voluntary agency assistance 'was often conditional on the beneficiary undertaking some form of self help', whereas government assistance encouraged welfare dependency (Hewson, 1992: 335).

THE LIBERALS RESPOND TO UNEXPECTED ELECTORAL DEFEAT: 1993–1996

Following their unexpected electoral defeat in 1993, the Liberal Party was urged by a number of commentators to modify its free-market views, and re-instate the long-discarded social liberal element.

The Liberals displayed some signs of listening to their critics. Successive party leaders John Hewson, Alexander Downer and John Howard, for example, re-affirmed the Liberal Party's traditional commitment to a decent social security safety net. Howard also made strenuous attempts to restore relations with the welfare lobby (Mendes, 1998a: 73–74).

Nevertheless, the Liberals continued to be strongly influenced by the neoliberal agenda. In an address to the National Press Club, for example, Alexander Downer launched no less than five separate attacks on unnamed 'special interest groups' which were allegedly granted 'special deals' by the ALP Government at the expense of ordinary Australians (Downer, 1994). It is highly unlikely that ACOSS would have been exempted from this list of supposedly disreputable groups.

In addition, the Liberals continued to condemn the alleged increased welfare spending under Labor, and the associated increase in welfare dependency. Under the Liberals, they claimed, beneficiaries would be given increased incentives for self-reliance, and the unemployed forced to work for the dole. They also emphasised that support would only be provided to those who were 'genuinely needy and disadvantaged'. Stringent measures would be taken to protect the system from potential abuse or exploitation.

Overall, the emphasis continued to be on the need to restrict the eligibility to benefits in order to encourage greater self-reliance, rather than the social liberal alternative of expanding help and support for disadvantaged groups in order to assist them to attain greater independence (Mendes, 1998a: 74).

NEOLIBERALISM VERSUS PRAGMATISM: THE HOWARD GOVERNMENT 1996–2002

The social welfare policies of the Howard Government have been dominated by two ideological tendencies: the neoliberal concern to reduce government interference with free-market outcomes by restricting access to social security payments; and the social conservative concern to reinforce traditional institutions such as the family.

A key moderating influence on government policies, however, has been John Howard's cautious pragmatism, and his commitment to meet at least in part his electoral commitment to maintain the social welfare safety net. Thus, instead of implementing the more radical proposals of the earlier *Fightback* package, such as the cessation of unemployment benefits after nine months and the reduction in the eligibility period for sole-parent pension, his government has chosen instead to make incremental changes which do tighten eligibility to some existing benefits, but do not at this stage overtly challenge any fundamental entitlement.

Moreover, those cuts which have been made to existing safety-net programs have been justified so far principally (and some would argue deceptively) on the basis of economic necessities, such as reducing the Budget deficit, rather than for the purpose of achieving broader ideological objectives.

The current balancing act between pragmatism and ideology can best be understood by examining the Howard Government's social welfare policies according to the five-point breakdown of Chapter 2.

INTEREST GROUP CAPTURE

The Howard Coalition Government has largely abandoned the Liberal Party's earlier hostility to the welfare lobby. Whilst Howard has continued to criticise the influence of 'special interests' and remains suspicious of advocacy groups, he, the treasurer, the Social Security minister and other leading ministers have all engaged in regular consultation with ACOSS. By including ACOSS in policy deliberations, the government has hoped pragmatically to influence the previously hostile body towards adopting a more sympathetic viewpoint on issues such as welfare reform and taxation (Mendes, 1998a: 75–76). However, the government has withdrawn its funding from other advocacy groups such as the Australian Youth Policy and Action Coalition (now defunct); the housing lobby group National Shelter; and the Australian Pensioners' and Superannuants' Federation.

LABOUR MARKET DEREGULATION

Prime Minister Howard has stated a clear preference for lower minimum wage rates on the basis that this would allegedly produce greater employment of young and unskilled workers. The government also commissioned (without formally endorsing) a report by neoliberal ideologue Des Moore, which called for the abolition of minimum wages and industrial awards (Moore, 1998).

However, when faced with criticism that labour market deregulation could potentially lead to greater poverty and inequality, and be electorally unpopular, the prime minister elected not to press ahead with his preferred objective. The outcome reflected the government's concern to balance their ideological objectives with political and electoral realities (Mendes, 1998a: 76).

WELFARE DEPENDENCY

The government has introduced a number of measures to eliminate alleged incentives to welfare dependency. Most of these initiatives have so far involved the incremental tightening of access to benefits, rather than wholesale changes to entitlement criteria. In September 1999, for example, the government announced a review of the welfare system designed to prevent and reduce welfare dependency. A Reference Group on Welfare Reform consisting of representatives of the business, academic, government and the community sectors was appointed to conduct the review.

The then minister for Family and Community Services, Senator

Jocelyn Newman, argued in an accompanying discussion paper that dependency on social security payments had increased from around 10 per cent of workforce-age Australians in 1978 to 18 per cent in 1998, totalling some 2.6 million people. Her paper described 'long-term welfare dependency' as having major social and economic consequences including intergenerational welfare reliance. Newman called for a shift from long-term welfare support to greater self-reliance so that people can move off welfare more quickly (Newman, 1999).

The Reference Group report subsequently recommended the extension of 'mutual obligation' requirements to new categories of welfare recipients. The report argued that income security payments should not only provide an adequate safety net, but also maximise people's opportunities for economic and social participation (Reference Group on Welfare Reform, 2000).

In addition, the government strongly tightened the criteria and level of payments for unemployment benefits, by toughening the 'activity test' and associated penalties for non-compliance, reducing rent assistance for single people who share accommodation, extending the liquid assets waiting period, introducing a means-tested common youth allowance, and imposing a two-year waiting period for new immigrants.

The government has also imposed massive spending cuts on services used principally by the poor and disadvantaged, such as the Commonwealth Dental Health Program, labour market programs and public housing (Mendes, 1998a: 77). Most recently, the 2002 Budget introduced tighter eligibility rules for the disability support pension in order to force thousands of recipients with a limited work capacity onto unemployment benefits.

THE UNDESERVING POOR: MUTUAL OBLIGATION

The Howard Government has employed a number of measures to discipline those welfare beneficiaries who it perceives as undeserving of assistance. Many of these measures have been based on the concept of mutual obligation developed by the neoliberal American philosopher, Lawrence Mead.

Mead argues that the permissiveness of the welfare state is the key to understanding the growth in unemployment and welfare dependency. Welfare programs have given benefits to their recipients, but have not asked for anything in return. He believes that the welfare state should be based on the concept of 'new paternalism' which emphasises contractual duties and obligations as well as needs and rights. People should be offered a combination of 'help and hassle' to end the cycle of welfare dependency, and drive them into self-reliance. The principal and mandatory obligation should be to work for welfare benefits (Mead, 1997).

In Australia, this philosophy has inspired the introduction of the work for the dole scheme, which emphasises the elimination of the individual flaws of jobseekers, rather than measures which address the absence of sufficient jobs. According to the prime minister, the unemployed have an obligation to give something back to society in return for the dole.

Critics of the scheme suggest that it could lead to the displacement of existing workers in the regular labour force; that it may deter people from applying for unemployment benefits; that it is likely to reduce the bargaining power of the unemployed and so depress wages in unskilled labour markets; and that it is designed to discipline, punish and control the victims of unemployment (Mendes, 1997c).

Similar assumptions underpinned the welfare reform review. The review recommended that mutual obligation principles be extended to unemployed people aged 35–64 years and recipients of parenting payments whose youngest child was aged over six years. Whilst voluntary compliance was the preferred option, the report suggested that compulsion would be necessary for a minority of income support recipients. In contrast, the government decided pragmatically that recipients of the disability support pension would be assisted, but not coerced, to increase their level of social and economic participation (Mendes, 2000b).

The philosophy of mutual obligation has also been associated with a generally punitive approach to the unemployed reflected in both policy (for instance a massive increase in the number of payment 'breaches' and fines) and rhetoric (ACOSS, 2001b).

Critics of mutual obligation argue that it lacks reciprocity, in that there is no corresponding obligation on government to improve the employment prospects of welfare recipients. Nor are similar obligations imposed on affluent groups in society such as the business community. Furthermore, the social contract between government and welfare recipients is based on coercion rather than consent, in that recipients have no choice but to agree in order to retain their sole source of livelihood.

Overall, mutual obligation measures seem to be designed to shift responsibility for the poor in the community from government onto the private and community sector — particularly through increased demand for emergency relief — and so reduce public expenditure (Kinnear, 2000).

Another government initiative concerned with disciplining the undeserving poor was the 'dob in a dole bludger' hotline. The former minister, Jocelyn Newman, suggested that convicted dole cheats should be 'publicly outed' by the media in order to dissuade others from undertaking similar misdemeanours (quoted in Bull, 1996). Whilst the government claimed that its anti-fraud campaign was a great success, the former minister's own statistics demonstrate that less than 10 per cent of social security overpayments involve deliberate fraud that can be prosecuted (Department of Social Security, 1997). During 1999/2000, for example, there were 2881 convictions for social security fraud. This number constituted only 0.04 per cent of the 6.4 million recipients of income support (ACOSS, 2001b: 10).

One of the consequences of the government's anti-fraud campaign, however, is that the legitimacy of all welfare beneficiaries comes under question. This is hardly unexpected when one considers some of the language used by the minister in relation to alleged welfare fraud. For example, a report published on Social Security compliance makes constant references to 'welfare cheats', 'the greedy' and 'rorters'. Whilst the report does re-affirm that 'those in genuine need will continue to receive assistance', the overall suggestion is that welfare fraud is rampant among social security beneficiaries (Department of Social Security, 1997).

The emphasis placed by the current government on the undeserving nature of many welfare claimants almost certainly serves to undermine public support for the current entitlements of the income security system, and to provide a potential rationale for any further spending cuts being contemplated.

PRIVATISATION OF WELFARE

At the time of writing, no specific recommendations have been made by the government for the involvement of community organisations in the actual delivery of income security payments. However, the introduction of the privatised Jobs Network suggests at least some movement in that direction (Considine, 2001: 117–43).

As we discuss in Chapter 8, the government has also strongly urged the business sector to take a more active role in the funding and provision of welfare services. In addition, Howard has stated on a number of occasions his personal admiration for traditional charities such as the Salvation Army and St Vincent De Paul, and his preference for greater private welfare provision (Mendes, 2000c: 37–40).

Nevertheless, the likely consequence of government cuts to various social welfare programs and payments is that more and more poor and disadvantaged Australians will be forced to turn to non-government charities for emergency relief support, irrespective of whether government funding or private sector donations are sufficient to meet the ensuing level of demand (ACOSS, 2001b: 22–23).

CONCLUSION

This chapter has argued that the Liberal Party has traditionally been a party of three disparate ideological tendencies: social liberalism, classical liberalism and social conservatism. These three tendencies were all present to a lesser or greater degree in the social welfare policies of the Menzies and Fraser governments. However, since 1983, the Liberal Party has been captured by the neoliberal agenda of the New Right which seeks, in conjunction with complementary social conservative ideas, to substantially retrench the existing welfare state. The party's social liberal agenda has been virtually marginalised. No longer does the Liberal Party articulate any state obligation to defend the rights of the poor and disadvantaged.

The social welfare policies of the Howard Coalition Government have been strongly influenced by this neoliberal agenda, albeit tempered by pragmatic political and electoral considerations. Some neoliberal objectives such as work for the dole, the discipline of the undeserving poor, and a gradual redirection of responsibility for the disadvantaged from government to individuals and families, have been implemented. Others such as a lower minimum wage and fundamental changes to welfare payments criteria have not.

Nevertheless, the proposals of the Welfare Reform review suggests a fundamental ideological shift from income support as a means of poverty alleviation to income support as a 'participation' payment (Roskam, 2001: 268). The major themes of this shift are that poverty is behavioural not structural; that unemployment is an individual rather than societal responsibility; that welfare should be transformed from an entitlement to a conditional payment dependent on prescribed activities; and that the older unemployed and sole parents should be potentially subject to the same sanctions currently experienced by younger jobseekers.

The increasing conditionality of welfare payments is a worldwide phenomenon. Even in the Netherlands, for example, there has been an increased use of sanctions in order to persuade job seekers to comply with their labour market obligations (Considine, 2001: 54–57, 106–109). Yet, the particular ideological assumptions underlying Australian welfare reform appear destined to produce a harsher income security system more akin to that of the United States. This system would comprise lower levels of income support; reduced access to income support; more people being pushed into part-time; casual and otherwise low-paying work; and increased dependence on families and charities (Mendes, 2000b: 36).

The predicted retirement of Prime Minister Howard and his replacement as Liberal Party leader by Peter Costello are likely, if anything, to further these ideological trends (Mendes, 2001a).

Questions for consideration

1 Why do you think the social liberals have been marginalised within the Liberal Party?
2 What is currently the major difference between the Liberal Party and the Labor Party in their approaches to the welfare state?
3 What is likely to be the Liberal Party's long-term objective concerning the welfare state?

Exercise

Identify which ideological tendency or tendencies is present in these quotes from prominent Liberal Party figures:

1 The purpose of all measures of social security is not only to provide citizens with some reasonable protection against misfortune, but also to reconcile that provision with their proud independence and dignity as democratic citizens. The time has gone when social justice should even appear to take the form of social charity. (Liberal Party leader Robert Menzies, 1945)
2 A key priority is to look after children in need, the old, the disabled, the sick and the poor, and to encourage families to help their own members. Our objective is to have a more caring community in which the family, neighbours, friends and non-government welfare organisations share their important responsibilities. (Liberal Party leader John Howard, 1988)
3 They have seen government welfare spending become the fastest growing area of the Hawke Government's spending over recent years, and a continuing drift to greater dependence on government welfare ... We want to ensure that the sick, the old and those genuinely in need receive the assistance they deserve, but we want to put an end to the rorts and abuses of such assistance by people who can, and should, provide for themselves. (Liberal Party leader John Hewson, 1991)
4 The Coalition supports the maintenance and improvement of the welfare system so as to care for those in society who are genuinely needy and disadvantaged ... We support a social security system that is fair and equitable and provides genuine support for those in need. At the same time, we support a social welfare

system that does not result in welfare dependency. (Liberal Party leader Alexander Downer, 1994)

5 For people on unemployment benefits, the government is to abolish long-term idleness at taxpayers' expense. (Minister for Employment, Workplace Relations and Small Business, Tony Abbott, 1999)

6

LABOR PARTY POLICY: FROM THE WAGE EARNERS' WELFARE STATE TO TARGETED WELFARE

This chapter examines the Federal Labor Party's approach to social welfare policy. Traditionally, the ALP has been a laborist party committed to a fairer distribution of income through the achievement of improved wages and conditions for the working class. Whilst social security and welfare initiatives generally played a minor role in this plan, they were still viewed as an integral part of a broader egalitarian agenda.

However, since 1983 the ALP has devised welfare policy in isolation from broader social and economic structures. The laborist plan for a fairer and more egalitarian society has largely been abandoned in favour of the virtues of the free market. In its place, we are left with welfare policies which target the poverty of particular needy or deserving groups, rather than attacking structural inequities.

This chapter briefly explores the laborism of the pre-1983 period, and then examines the policies of the Hawke/Keating ALP governments from 1983 to 1996, and the ALP in Opposition from 1996 onwards. It presents a case study involving a comparison of the two major unemployment initiatives of the last decade: the Keating Government's *Working Nation* program and the Howard Government's work for the dole scheme. Finally, it examines the recent influence of 'Third Way' ideas on social democratic parties including the ALP.

THE ALP AND LABORISM BEFORE 1983

The Labor Party has traditionally been a party of pragmatic laborism which has been willing to incorporate a number of varied and sometimes disparate ideological tendencies. Whilst these tendencies ranged from social democracy to even the margins of classical liberalism, the dominant ALP tradition prior to 1983 was arguably that of government intervention on behalf of the less-privileged groups to achieve a more egalitarian society. The ALP never aimed to abolish capitalism, but rather favoured state intervention in the free market via progressive taxation and public sector investment to promote full employment, support for the disadvantaged, and greater income inequality (Maddox and Battin, 1991; Scalmer, 1997: 306–308).

The key laborist program has been to seek fair or higher wages through direct state intervention in the market to determine wage levels. As we noted in Chapter 1, the laborist emphasis on high wages led to a relatively high level of equality in the market place, but it also led to the neglect of those who were unable to participate in the workforce. Herein, classical liberal views of the undeserving poor exerted some influence (Castles, 1991: 10–14).

However, other ideological influences have also been present. For example, the ALP governments of Curtin and Chifley from 1941 to 1949 were strongly influenced by a Keynesian social liberal tradition. This emphasised the integration of social and economic policy via a combination of free markets and government economic planning to ensure continuous economic growth and full employment, and protection of the social and economic rights of the underprivileged (Pixley, 1996: 48–49).

At the same time, the ALP's social liberal concern to provide a minimum income for all citizens was balanced by a classical liberal concern not to promote welfare dependency by providing social security 'on a scale that would eliminate personal incentive or a proper measure of self-help' (Chifley, quoted in Mendelsohn, 1954: 156).

During the long period in Opposition from 1949 to 1972, the ALP consistently called for an expanded welfare state as part of a broader program to promote a fairer distribution of wealth and income. All commentators emphasised the need for a Labor government to intervene in the free market via taxation and other measures in order to ensure a minimum income for all (Calwell, 1963: 72–73; Whitlam, 1967: 4–9; Hayden, 1972).

In the late 1960s and early 1970s, the ALP came under the influence of Fabian and social democratic ideas, which emphasised extensive state intervention in the economy in order to attack the structural causes of poverty and inequality (Beilharz, 1994: 118). These ideas were a dominant influence on the Whitlam Government. Following the dismissal of the Whitlam Government, the party continued to advocate social democratic and social liberal ideas designed to promote a fairer distribution of income (Grimes, 1980).

However, the early 1980s saw the ALP retreat from policies emphasising substantial government intervention and wealth redistribution. The ALP's pragmatic shift away from its traditional principles was influenced by its three successive election defeats of 1975, 1977 and 1980. In addition, polls suggested that Labor policies designed to promote a fairer distribution of income were electorally unpopular. Instead, the ALP adopted the economic rationalist agenda of wealth creation, market forces, reduced taxation, and only limited social expenditure (Smith, 1994: 70–71).

THE HAWKE/KEATING GOVERNMENTS: 1983–1996

The ALP governments between 1983 and 1996 were influenced by a number of different ideological perspectives, including traditional laborist and social liberal/social democratic concerns about equity, and newer economic rationalist concerns around private sector growth and wealth creation. Not surprisingly, conflicting perspectives exist regarding the overall social impact of ALP social policies.

The ALP and its supporters portray the Hawke/Keating governments as traditional laborist regimes which attempted to implement social justice policies and protect the interests of the most vulnerable at a time of economic hardship when the political emphasis was on reducing government expenditure (Whiteford, 1994: 251–54; Castles, 1996). In contrast, critics of the ALP (particularly on the Left) portray these governments as economic rationalist regimes which pursued globally driven free-market policies that undermined the interests of traditional Labor supporters, and produced greater inequality (Wiseman, 1996; Stilwell, 2000: 142–52).

The evidence suggests that there is a bit of truth in both perspectives. On the one hand, ALP governments did adopt significant elements of the economic rationalist, free-market agenda — lower taxes, smaller government, privatisation of government assets, deregulation of banking, the floating of the dollar, the freeing up of the industrial bargaining system, and the abolition of tariffs (Kerr, 2001: 2–3). The inevitable outcome of this free-market strategy was increased inequality. According to research by the Social Policy Research Centre at the University of New South Wales, the top 20 per cent of income earners' share of market income increased from 48 per cent to 53 per cent between 1981/82 and 1989/90, whilst the share of the bottom 40 per cent fell from 8 per cent to 6 per cent (Raskall, 1993).

On the other hand, the ALP did maintain a genuine commitment to socially just outcomes for the less fortunate. Most social security beneficiaries, particularly old-age pensioners and low-income families with children, received substantial increases in their real incomes (Grattan and Gruen, 1993: 192–93).

Nevertheless on balance, the ALP appears to have granted priority to the economic imperatives of the free market over social objectives. ALP welfare policies involved a redistribution of income from one disadvantaged group to another, rather than a structural redistribution from the rich to the poor. The emphasis was on tackling poverty rather than inequality. The subordination of social policy to the ALP's economic rationalist agenda led in fact to greater inequality within Australian society (Mendes, 1999b: 34–35) and, as discussed in Chapter 5, pushed the Coalition Opposition to even greater conservatism.

TARGETED WELFARE

The principal method used by the ALP to attack poverty was that of targeting assistance to those welfare recipients who were in greatest need, rather than utilising across-the-board increases in universally paid benefits. Targeting involved three aspects:

1 the elimination of universal payments via the introduction of an assets test on pensions, and the means-testing of family allowances
2 compliance initiatives such as regular reviews of unemployment beneficiaries and supporting parents, the use of the tax file number to identify applicants, and more stringent personal identification requirements that served to reduce the number of persons receiving payments (Weatherley, 1993)
3 the direction of greater resources to people in need. For example, the ALP Government met its long-standing commitment to a single old-age pension rate of 25 per cent of total average male weekly earnings — compared to the rate of 22.7 per cent it inherited. The government also increased the maximum level of rent assistance available by 150 per cent between 1983 and 1990, and extended it to new groups such as the unemployed (ALP, 1992: 167).

In addition, low-income families with children received substantial increases in their social security payments. Initiatives such as the Family Package of December 1987 served to reduce the percentage of children living in poverty by up to 40 per cent (Swan, 1995: 5–6).

The problem with this strategy of targeting benefits to particular needy or deserving groups was threefold. First, the targeting of social security benefits had little or no impact on inequalities within the paid workforce. The sole exception to this rule was the Family

Allowance Supplement which was paid to low-income workers with children. However, the supplement arguably has the potential to undermine the payment of adequate wages by legitimising the existence of a new 'working poor' (Jamrozik, 1991: 133).

Further, the increases in social security incomes were financed not by a redistribution of income from the rich to the poor that would improve the relative position of all low-income groups, but rather by a redirection of existing funds within the social security system. No action, for example, was taken to promote greater equity through the taxation system by imposing greater burdens on business and high-income earners. Rather, the overall intention of government policy was to restrain or reduce, rather than to increase, social expenditure (Gibson, 1990: 184–85).

In addition, the gains for beneficiaries were too often at the expense of the living standards and rights of other disadvantaged groups such as the homeless and the young unemployed (Gibson, 1990: 200).

INTEGRATING SOCIAL SECURITY AND THE LABOUR MARKET

Another major ALP initiative involved promoting closer integration of the social security, education and labour market systems to provide better opportunities for people to move from dependence on social security provisions into employment.

The government's initiatives in this area were inspired by Professor Bettina Cass's Social Security Review, which took place between 1986 and 1988. The review focused on three specific aspects of the social security system:

1 income support for families with children
2 social security programs and workforce participation, particularly in relation to unemployed people, the disabled and sole parents
3 the connections between social security programs and insurance-based income support measures, notably superannuation.

One of the major parts of the review was the inquiry into income support for the unemployed. This inquiry found that unemployment benefits (due to the increase in the rate and duration of unemployment in recent decades) had increasingly been perceived as a passive rather than active form of income support, resulting in a reduction of community support for the unemployment benefit program. Cass recommended the creation of an active role for income support for the unemployed, based on improved incentives to undertake training and retraining, and job search and closer integration between income support programs and labour market programs at the appropriate stages of unemployment (Cass, 1988: 4–7).

The government responded to the recommendations of the Social Security Review by introducing labour market programs designed to redress the disadvantages of the long-term unemployed (NewStart) and of sole parents (Jobs, Education and Training). It followed up these initiatives by introducing a Disability Support Package in October 1991 which was intended to help people with disabilities participate in the workforce.

In principle, these reforms were consistent with the traditional laborist emphasis on social protection through employment. They offered significant assistance to disadvantaged groups to learn new skills and improve their job prospects so as to potentially escape the chronic poverty associated with long-term dependence on social security payments.

For example, most commentators found that the Jobs, Education and Training scheme — a voluntary program that provides sole parents with individual assistance, information and support, access to labour market and educational programs, job placement and subsidised child-care — had been helpful in facilitating at least some access to the paid workforce (Shaver, 1993). Similarly, the NewStart program, which was originally introduced on a voluntary basis in 1988 and then transformed into a compulsory program in 1991, offered individual support and assistance to the long-term unemployed to improve their labour market prospects.

However, such programs (particularly NewStart) had two major deficits. Firstly, they placed considerable emphasis on improving the labour market skills of social security recipients, but did not involve any commitment by the government to directly intervene in the economy via public job creation and so increase the actual number of jobs available. Secondly, these programs were widely viewed as undercutting the traditional Australian notion of an entitlement to income support in favour of a contractual agreement conditional on labour market participation (Sheen and Trethewey, 1990: 32–35).

UNIVERSALISM OR SURVEILLANCE

Other ALP programs were arguably more successful in promoting egalitarian outcomes. The introduction of the Medicare health insurance scheme provided economic security for the two million people who were previously unable to afford health insurance. It also helped reduce hospital and medical costs for those on average weekly earnings (Watts, 1989: 119–20).

Similarly, the Better Cities Program served to improve infrastructure and support services such as housing, transport, education
and shopping centres for low-income families living in disadvantaged
outer suburbs (ALP, 1995: 13–17).

In addition, the ALP introduced the Child Support Scheme
which involved using the Taxation Office and the Department of
Social Security (DSS) to collect and distribute maintenance payments from non-custodial parents to contribute to the support of
their children. The Child Support Scheme was recognised as increasing both the proportion of non-custodial parents paying maintenance, and the amount of maintenance paid per child (Grattan and
Gruen, 1993: 190, 277).

Other positive initiatives included the introduction of free dental care for low-income earners, a maternity allowance and a parenting allowance, and service delivery reforms to make social
security payments more responsive and targeted to individual needs
(Baldwin, 1995).

NEOLIBERALISM AND ALP WELFARE POLICY

However, as already noted, the government failed to tackle broader
structural inequities. Hamstrung by a neoliberal economic agenda,
the government was limited to mitigating the social effects of economic restructuring. Tighter targeting of payments led arguably to
greater social exclusion of welfare recipients. In addition, too many
of the government's laudable initiatives were funded by reducing or
attacking existing welfare payments.

For example, unemployment benefits for 16 and 17 year olds
were substantially reduced which arguably contributed to the large
increase in the rate of youth homelessness (Burdekin and Carter,
1989: 160). In 1986, the Hawke Government proposed unsuccess-
fully that unemployed people (particularly young unemployed people) be required to work for the dole. There was also a large decline
in the number of the young unemployed actually receiving unemployment benefits (Grattan and Gruen, 1993: 193). In addition, the
Keating Government introduced measures in the 1994 White Paper
on Employment to tighten social security regulations and make beneficiaries more accountable.

The government also intensified surveillance and 'policing' of
welfare beneficiaries. Annual reports of the DSS contained numerous statistics about fraud control measures and their relative success
(Bryson, 1994: 297–98). However, research completed by Professor
Weatherley (1993) suggested that most welfare fraud in Australia
was committed by omission, rather than by deliberate commission.

For example, many people failed to notify the DSS of changed circumstances such as obtaining part-time employment or moving into a new relationship. Others are misled by the complexity of departmental rules and guidelines.

In summary, the ALP governments succeeded in the narrowest economic sense in raising the incomes of most poor Australians. However, the alleviation of poverty was accompanied by an increasing stigmatisation and marginalisation of social security recipients, and by an overall increase in income inequality. The latter occurred because the government chose to merely ameliorate the unfair economic and social consequences of free-market policies, rather than intervening directly in the market place through taxation, wage and public investment measures to promote a fairer distribution of wealth and income (Jamrozik, 1991: 257; Battin, 2000: 45–48).

THE ALP IN OPPOSITION: 1996–2002

Since the election defeat of 1996, many leading ALP figures have renewed the party's traditional commitment to socially just outcomes. Some of this rhetoric clearly has been directed pragmatically at firming up the support of traditional Labor voters who were alienated by the free-market agenda of the Hawke and Keating years. However, at least some of the rhetoric suggests a possible ideological shift back towards greater state intervention in the economy and to fairer income distribution by a future Labor government (Jungwirth, 1997; 1998).

Such social justice rhetoric is commendable, but the key question to be answered concerns the extent to which the ALP is willing to directly intervene in the market-place in order to promote a fairer distribution of income.

On this question, considerable doubt remains. To be sure, a number of ALP parliamentarians and activists have criticised the former government's reliance on the free market (Mendes, 1998d: 35). The 2000 ALP National Platform also suggested a greater commitment to government intervention. For example, the ALP argues that government has a critical role to play in 'achieving a more equitable distribution of wealth, income and status'. In addition, Labor promised to 'reach out, embrace, protect and support those in need' (ALP, 2000: 4).

However, corresponding ALP statements on taxation and economic policy suggest that any government intervention into the market-place will be insignificant. Whilst the ALP has promised to raise taxes on the wealthy through attacking tax avoidance, the party platform also emphasises that Labor will not increase taxation on lower- and middle-income Australians, and will not seek to raise the overall level of taxation revenue as a proportion of GDP (ALP, 2000: 55). It is hard to see how the ALP can promote a more equitable society whilst effectively ruling out the related options of raising greater revenue, or substantially increasing government spending.

The ALP has also offered a vigorous critique of Liberal Party policies on mutual obligation including particularly the cuts to social spending, and the huge rise in welfare breaches. However, the ALP appears to be opposed to the harshness of the implementation of mutual obligation, rather than to the principle. In fact, the ALP proudly claims to have invented the notion of reciprocal obligation, but argues that the Coalition Government has failed to meet its side of the bargain (Macintyre, 1999: 107). Specifically, the ALP has supported the work for the dole scheme as long as it involves real training. The ALP also endorsed the general recommendations of the McClure Report on welfare reform, and broadly shares the Liberal Party's concern to move income security recipients from welfare to work (ALP, 2000: 22, 26; Crean, 2001).

The ideological contradictions documented above suggest that the ALP is unlikely to substantially abandon its economic rationalist agenda. This reticence reflects in part the extent to which free-market ideas have become entrenched in ALP philosophy over the past two decades (Smith, 1994: 70–71). Any significant movement back towards traditional laborist ideas would require a radical break with dominant assumptions.

A CASE STUDY OF POLITICAL CONVERGENCE: WORKING NATION AND WORK FOR THE DOLE

In 1993, the Keating ALP Government appointed a high-level committee to address the future of work and the problem of long-term unemployment. The committee released a Green Paper in December 1993 followed by a White Paper in May 1994. The White Paper assumed that economic growth alone would not fix unemployment. Consequently, the government announced a 'Job Compact' for getting the long-term unemployed back into work (Keating, 1994).

The Job Compact guaranteed that job seekers on benefits for 18 months or more would receive temporary employment for 6–12 months as well as intensive training. Participants were promised that 'we will do all we can to help make you ready for a job' (Keating, 1994: 2). The preferred job location was in the private sector, and generous wage subsidies were offered. It was hoped that this job guarantee would assist the long-term unemployed to reconnect to the labour market, and to thereby compete more effectively for increased job opportunities. However, no direct job creation was envisaged (Finn, 1999; Edwards et al, 2001: 137–76).

As part of the *Working Nation* package, extensive case management activity agreements between the state and the unemployed were introduced. Case managers were expected to establish individually tailored employment and training assistance packages. *Working Nation* also extended the guidelines for the activity test that were introduced following the 1988 Social Security Review via the principle of reciprocal obligation. In return for the job guarantee, the long-term unemployed would be obliged to accept any reasonable training or job offer. Those who failed to comply faced greatly increased financial penalties (Finn, 1997: 33–34, 41–42; Fox, 2000: 14–15).

In contrast, the Howard Government introduced the work for the dole scheme for the young unemployed in February 1997. Initially the scheme was proposed as a trial program for long-term unemployed young people from selected regional and rural areas who would be required to work for their unemployment allowance. Later, the scheme was extended to those aged 25–34 years who had been unemployed for 12 months.

Prime Minister Howard depicted the proposal as a common-sense reaction to the long-standing problems of 'work shyness' and high unemployment. According to Howard, the scheme would teach the young unemployed work skills that would help them to attain employment, would discourage work dependency, and would reflect popular sentiment that the unemployed should do something in return for their unemployment payments.

Work for the dole is based on the notion of mutual or reciprocal obligation with the unemployed being viewed as owing something to the community supporting them. The scheme does not involve any structured labour market training or education programs, but rather aims to help the unemployed to re-adjust to the routines and demands of the labour market (Mendes, 1997c; ACOSS, 1999c).

We are not concerned here with the relative merits or effectiveness of these two schemes; rather, the focus is on the ideological convergence of the respective programs.

On the one hand, there were some significant differences. For example, *Working Nation* offered a guarantee of training or paid employment based on a substantially increased funding commitment by government. In contrast, work for the dole involves no obligation on the part of government to actually improve the participants' job prospects. Compared to *Working Nation*, work for the dole also assumes more explicitly that unemployment is attributable to personal or behavioural characteristics, rather than broader labour market conditions.

However, both programs are essentially dependent on private-sector growth as a solution to unemployment. And, most significantly, both programs erode the traditional rights-based payment of unemployment benefits as compensation from the community for the loss of the right to work. Instead, they introduce a conditional contract-based arrangement between the individual benefit recipient and the government (Macintyre, 1999: 108).

THE ALP AND THIRD WAY IDEAS

Over the past five years, the political concept known as the 'Third Way' has become highly influential, particularly in Britain but also in some other Western countries. Prominent advocates have included the British Prime Minister Tony Blair, the former US president Bill Clinton, and the German Prime Minister Gerhard Schroeder.

Yet, the Third Way remains a highly contested and ambiguous term (White, 2001: 3–4). Its supporters claim that it is a genuinely new centre-left political ideology which incorporates the best aspects of both social democracy and neoliberalism at a time of global social and economic change. However, its critics (particularly on the Left) argue that it is merely a pale imitation of Thatcherism designed to legitimise British Labour's surrender to global neoliberalism.

This chapter suggests that the Third Way (as reflected in still-developing British policies) does not constitute a mere repackaging of the Thatcherite agenda. There are significant differences, for example, between Third Way and neoliberal attitudes to inequality, poverty and welfare spending. Nevertheless, the Third Way does appear to accept, more than any other modern centre-left ideology, the predominant role of the market in addressing social problems.

The most prominent Australian Third Way advocate, ALP federal front-bencher Mark Latham, also favours private rather than public solutions to social and economic inequities. In addition, his critique of the existing welfare state and its inadequacies appears to be particularly close to that offered by Australian neoliberal politicians and commentators. Unlike British Third Way advocates, Latham makes little reference to structural causes of poverty and inequality. His intervention appears designed to reinforce the ALP's gradual abandonment of traditional interventionist and redistributionist ideas (Latham, 1998).

DEFINITIONS OF THE THIRD WAY

The British sociologist Anthony Giddens is generally regarded as the philosophical guru of the Third Way. Giddens refers to the Third Way as:

> a framework of thinking and policy-making that seeks to adapt social democracy to a world which has changed fundamentally over the past two or three decades. It is a third way in the sense that it is an attempt to transcend both old-style social democracy and neoliberalism. (Giddens 1998, 26)

According to Giddens, Third Way values include equality, protection of the vulnerable, freedom as autonomy, a strong civil society based on local community action in partnership with government, and no rights without responsibilities. For example, those who receive unemployment benefits should be obliged to actively search for work. Giddens argues for the entitlement-based protective welfare state to be replaced by a 'social investment state' in which recipients are provided with positive incentives to move from dependence to education, training and employment (Giddens, 1998).

Giddens specifically dismisses the notion that Third Way politics involves a rejection of the Left-Right divide, or a capitulation to neoliberal dogma. Rather, he argues that new ideas and policies are needed to implement the political values of the Left (Giddens, 2001: 5). For example, the Third Way emphasises the notion of 'social exclusion' in place of older terms such as poverty and disadvantage. This term emphasises the social as well as financial exclusion of people from mainstream economic and political systems and opportunities.

Other tenets of Third Way thinking include:

- a belief that class and structural inequalities no longer form the basis of political action. Instead local communities are likely to be the principal source of social and economic empowerment.
- that taxes should be reduced in line with international competition. High rates of income tax are no longer effective in reducing inequalities.
- that the existing welfare state has lost public legitimacy due to the existence of downwards envy, increased welfare dependency and inter-generational poverty, and the overload on government finances
- that welfare systems should exist to promote individual autonomy and participation, not to redistribute income to social groups or classes or impose abstract equality. Meritocratic social mobility is supported.

- that those welfare consumers who are unwilling to change their behaviour and attitudes regarding self-responsibility and work should be coerced to do so
- that the free market and successful entrepreneurs should be left relatively unhindered by government intervention to determine economic outcomes
- that governments should encourage the emergence of social entrepreneurs who use market principles to create wealth and growth at the local level. Significant power and resources should be transferred from the public sector to local community leaders and organisations. (Blair, 1998; Blair and Schroeder, 1999; Giddens, 2000)

Some Left critics of the Third Way contend that these ideas are far closer to neoliberalism than to any social democratic vision. They argue, for example, that the Third Way:

- may turn already vulnerable people into victims
- narrowly emphasises workforce participation at the expense of other forms of citizenship
- emphasises in an authoritarian and moralistic manner the responsibilities of the poor rather than all citizens
- redirects obligations from the collective community to the individual
- ignores the concentration of private power and its exercise in the interests of the powerful
- represents an abdication of government responsibility to promote greater equity. (See summary in Giddens, 2000: 22–25; Macintyre, 2001.)

In practice, however, the British application of Third Way thinking to the welfare state appears to be more complex than the above description might suggest. For example, the Blair Government emphasises that it is committed to a 'regeneration', rather than a dismantling of the welfare state. This is reflected in the slogan 'Work for those who can, security for those who cannot' (Blair, 1999). Paid work via the renamed Department of Work and Pensions will be the solution to growing inequality and poverty for those able to work, but welfare payments will still be available for the sick, the disabled, the retired and those engaged in full-time caring activities. In addition, the government promises to abolish child poverty within 20 years via increases to in-work benefits such as the Working Families Tax Credit (Millar, 2001: 31–32).

To be sure, British Prime Minister Blair also utilises the language of neoliberalism, referring to the importance of the work ethic, the negatives of welfare dependency, the responsibility of claimants to take up opportunities offered, and the struggle against benefit fraud (Blair, 1998). Nevertheless, British welfare reform appears to be fundamentally different to the neoliberal policies implemented by the former US Clinton administration. The US *Personal Responsibility and Work Opportunity Reconciliation Act* was highly punitive, involving time-limited payments, compulsory participation in workfare programs, and the right to deny benefits to unmarried teenage mothers and assign them to the care of government-appointed guardians. The scheme assumed that recipients lack work motivation, and its sole purpose appeared to be to push recipients off welfare rolls (O'Connor, 1999: 229–31).

In contrast, the British New Deal seems to use a carrot rather than stick approach. Lone parents are not obliged to work, and there is a stronger focus on job creation, wage subsidies, and the provision of education and training. The scheme recognises structural as well as individual barriers to joblessness, and assumes that business and government have a responsibility to actively promote employment opportunities for disadvantaged jobseekers (Curtain, 2000).

THE BRITISH AND AUSTRALIAN LABOR PARTIES AND THE THIRD WAY

The British and Australian labor parties have a long tradition of exchanging ideas, agendas and policies for government (Beilharz, 1994: 73). In particular, the electoral successes of the ALP from 1983 until 1996 provoked considerable interest in the United Kingdom. Prominent shadow ministers such as Tony Blair and Gordon Brown visited Australia, and developed significant relationships with leading ALP figures. Many in British Labour saw the Australian party as a model to emulate (Scott, 2000: 1–5)

Subsequently, the process has been reversed. Some leading figures in the ALP in Opposition now look to the British Third Way as a potential model for emulation (Scott, 2000: 255–57). For example, Shadow Finance Minister Lindsay Tanner praises many of the key tenets of Third Way thinking, including the emphasis on mutual obligation, community control of services, social entrepreneurship, and locational or place management. Tanner acknowledges the welfare state is facing a crisis of public legitimacy. He attributes this to a number of factors including intergenerational poverty and welfare dependence, and the emphasis on unpopular means-tested cash payments, rather than the provision of universal services such as Medicare, dental and child care assistance and public housing. He also accepts that government cannot promote equality of outcomes, whilst arguing that government should intervene in free markets in order to promote greater social inclusion. Overall, he rejects any simplistic association with the Third Way label (Tanner, 1999: 50–63).

Other Australian Labor figures are, however, more willing to carry the Third Way brand. They include, for example, the Western Australian Premier Geoff Gallop, who suggests a significant commonality between the Third Way and traditional social democratic ideas. Gallop argues in favour of state intervention to ensure adequate public services in areas like health and education, whilst recommending more participatory modes of service delivery (Gallop, 2001). Additional Third Wayers include the ALP-linked social policy researcher and Whitlam Institute Director, Professor Peter Botsman, and most notably the high-profile Federal front-bencher, Mark Latham.

MARK LATHAM AND THE THIRD WAY

The Federal Labor Member for Werriwa, Mark Latham, is the most prominent Australian advocate of Third Way views. After voluntarily spending a number of years on the back bench, Latham has now returned to the front bench as assistant shadow treasurer.

Latham has played a significant role in the ALP's welfare policy debate as the most vigorous opponent of old-style government intervention and redistribution (Watts, 2000a: 143, 148; Mendes, 2001b: 92, 98). He believes that a new Labor government should move even further down the path of free-market ideas by seeking to facilitate private and community-based, rather than statist, solutions to poverty and disadvantage. Nevertheless, whilst many of Latham's ideas closely resemble neoliberal agendas, he is not an unabashed admirer of the free market. He does, for example, recommend a continued role for government as a facilitator or enabler of socially inclusive programs. He also rejects the complete marketisation of welfare services (Latham, 2001c: 14–15).

A number of particular themes predominate in Latham's Third Way critique of the welfare state. Firstly, Latham damns the existing welfare state as obsolete. He argues that the centralised system designed to deliver welfare services in the 1950s and 1960s — a system of short-term earnings replacement as men moved from one job to another during an area of full employment and nuclear families — is no longer relevant to the globalised world of the twenty-first century. Instead, income security recipients need to be exposed to, and assisted to manage, the risks and uncertainties confronted by workers in the new economy. Latham advocates a new approach called the 'enabling state' based on active welfare to promote social capability, state facilitation rather than provision, risk taking, and case/place management (Latham, 1998: 200, 227, 253).

For example, whilst government should continue to provide central funding, Latham favours handing over control and provision of most welfare services from the state to local communities. He suggests the notion of place management whereby funding is targeted at social problems identified and prioritised by local experts. He also recommends the development of social entrepreneurs as a means of introducing dynamic new ideas and programs to poor neighbourhoods. Latham believes there is an urgent need for social and community relationships based on the notion of social capital to replace the isolated and individualistic transfer arrangements of the welfare state (Latham, 2001c: 22–24).

In addition, Latham argues that the welfare state has disabled its recipients, and led to their exclusion from social and economic norms. In particular, he condemns the increasing dependence of the poor on welfare payments. Using language analogous to that of the Howard Government, he argues that Australia's 'income dependency ratio — the proportion of the adult population relying on transfer payments for its principal source of income' has increased from 12 per cent in 1973 to just under 30 per cent in 1998 (Latham, 1998: 200).

Latham believes that poverty reflects not only material conditions, but also the impact of social isolation and destructive behaviour. He refers to a 'culture of dependency' which has been transferred to the children and grandchildren of welfare recipients, leading to the 'problem of inter-generational poverty' (Latham, 2001b: 15). He argues that unconditional transfer payments have 'given people a soft landing, rather than a bounce back into work. They function more like a safety net than a trampoline' (2001b: 16). He specifically rejects the argument that solutions to welfare dependency lie beyond the domain of the welfare state (1998: 254).

Latham endorses US philosopher Lawrence Mead's notion of mutual obligation or responsibility. He calls for the transformation of welfare from 'something-for-nothing into something-for-something'. There should be an end to unconditional entitlements. He argues instead that welfare payments should be conditional on people making an effort to learn new skills, improve their health, edu-

cate their children and, whenever possible, accept new work opportunities (Latham, 1998: 204).

He suggests that case managers be employed to assist 'welfare
dependent people'. Their job would be to link people into suitable
employment training, education and support programs. They
would also be granted the power to ensure that recipients met their
side of the welfare contract. As a last resort, case managers could
recommend sanctions including reduced welfare payments
(Latham, 1998: 207).

Finally, Latham persistently critiques the role played by professional welfare groups and sectional interest groups in the existing
welfare state. In particular, he has vigorously attacked ACOSS for
allegedly focusing on the 'immediate material conditions of welfare
recipients', rather than assisting 'welfare-dependent communities to
rebuild the habits of self-help and achievement'. Latham accuses
ACOSS of speaking only for itself, rather than on behalf of poor people (Latham, 1999).

The concerns and agendas raised by Latham pose significant
challenges to existing welfare state policies. As noted in Chapter 4,
there is little doubt that many poor and disadvantaged people are
disempowered by current services. In addition, many welfare services do not actively engage with the actual social milieu and cultural networks of income security recipients.

It would be beneficial in some circumstances for individual
case managers to provide more specialised support and assistance
to individual welfare recipients. It would also be useful for income
security assistance to be offered in a more flexible and less paternalistic manner. In addition, local communities can offer particular expertise and knowledge in dealing with specific manifestations
of larger social problems (Frankel, 2001: 37–38). And the examples of social entrepreneurialism cited by Latham suggest that
there is significant potential for new and innovative services in the
welfare sector.

Having said that, Latham's framework also has considerable
limitations. Many of his key arguments are based on exaggerated,
and overly generalised assumptions. Firstly, as noted in Chapter 4,
the welfare state is *not* dead and it continues to promote greater
equity.

Secondly, the first and prime responsibility of the welfare state
is to protect the poor and disadvantaged. Promoting greater social
or economic participation is arguably at best a secondary role. In
contrast, it is the responsibility of government and the private
sector to promote positive macroeconomic and employment

opportunities and outcomes, and to reduce the existing imbalance between supply and demand in the labour market (Mendes, 2000b: 28).

Thirdly, Latham's condemnation of intergenerational welfare dependency is arguably about blaming the victim, rather than addressing the real causes of poverty (Watts, 2000a: 148–52). In addition, his specific recommendations pertaining to case management of all welfare recipients are likely to lead to further intrusive measures of social control. The unemployed and more recently sole parents are already exposed to considerable policing and surveillance under the existing mutual obligation framework. Proposals for further intrusions into their private lives would arguably involve a discriminatory and coercive restriction of their civic rights (Masterman-Smith, 2000).

Fourthly, whilst social entrepreneurship may have the potential to deliver more innovative services at the local level, it does not offer any alternative solution to state provision of income security payments (Frankel, 2001: 39). Social entrepreneurship remains at best a developing idea limited by inherent tensions between the principles of individual entrepreneurship and those of collectivist community development (Ziguras, 2001).

Finally, as we shall see in Chapter 7, Latham's outright denigration of welfare professionals and welfare bodies reflects a simplistic and ill-informed view of the welfare sector. For a start, some of the key activists in welfare bodies are current or former welfare recipients. In addition, ACOSS arguably retains an important role in defending the income security safety net from those who would prefer a harsher system based solely on private and family provision.

CONCLUSION

The Labor Party has historically been a laborist party committed to government intervention in the free market to promote a fairer distribution of income, and social protection for the poor/disadvantaged. However, the Hawke/Keating years saw an abandonment of traditional laborist concerns around equity and fairness in favour of free-market agendas. Social welfare policies were relegated to the mere alleviation of poverty, rather than being concerned with attacking structural inequities.

Since the election defeat of 1996, the federal ALP has veered in its rhetoric from affirming traditional interventionist and redistributionist policies on the one hand to endorsing the Third Way solutions favoured by the British Labour Party on the other. However, it appears far more likely that the ALP will move in the latter direction.

Whilst there are some significant differences between the ALP and British Labour, the Third Way model can be seen as representing at least a partial recycling and/or extension of the earlier Australian Labor experience (Frankel, 1997; Scott, 2000: 1–5). Given this policy linkage, it is probable that future ALP policies will contain a combination of older Hawke/Keating ideas, and newer lessons from Britain and elsewhere. There may perhaps be a greater emphasis than previously on community involvement in welfare service delivery, and switching the unemployed from welfare to work. But overall, the ALP's policy statements suggest an entrenched support for free-market ideas including low taxation and limited social expenditure.

Questions for consideration

1 Did the welfare policies of the Hawke/Keating governments involve a fundamental break with Labor Party traditions and principles?
2 Does Labor retain a genuine commitment to promoting greater social and economic equity?
3 Does the Third Way represent a viable response by social democrats to economic globalisation?

Exercise

Identify which ideological tendency or tendencies is present in these quotes from prominent Labor Party figures:

1 A comprehensive social security scheme was an indispensable concomitant of, a stabiliser in, full employment policy. It would help sustain purchasing power on which full employment depended, while full employment would keep social security costs to a minimum. (Labor Government Treasurer Ben Chifley, 1943)
2 A welfare state is a state in which organised power is deliberately used (through politics and administration) in an effort to modify the play of market forces. (Federal Labor Opposition Leader Gough Whitlam, 1967)
3 Social justice is the ALP's reason for existence. It is a common goal that unites all Party members. Through its objectives, policies and programs, the ALP works to create a fairer society for all ... Our attachment to social justice springs from many sources including democratic socialism ... It is broader than the social

wage ... it seeks to redistribute power, privilege and opportunity, to democratise economic and social life, to protect basic rights and freedoms, and to change the structural causes of inequality. (ALP, 1991 Policy Platform)

4   Labor believes the welfare system must do two things. It must alleviate poverty so that no family is left destitute, and it must give families the skills and the opportunities they need to achieve a measure of independence, to get ahead. (Federal Shadow Minister for Family and Community Services Wayne Swan, 1999)

part three

INTEREST GROUPS
AND THE
WELFARE STATE

The following four chapters explore the impact of local interest and lobby groups on the welfare policy debate. The term 'interest' or 'lobby group' is generally used to refer to 'a formal organisation of people who share one or more interests or objectives or concerns, and who try to influence the course of public policy to protect or to promote these objectives' (Jaensch, 1991: 169).

International literature suggests that interest groups play a key role in debates about the future of the welfare state. There is some evidence, for example, that pro-welfare interest groups have succeeded in blocking attempts at radical retrenchment (Pierson, 1994; Mishra, 1999: 59–71).

In contrast, the Australian literature on interest groups and the welfare state has been far less analytical. Some attention has been drawn to the role played by ACOSS in social policy debates (Warhurst, 1997; Brown, 1999). However, relatively little consideration has been given to the social welfare views of other important groups representing various socio-economic sectors and interests. It is, however, arguable that these groups — including those committed to a substantial retrenchment of the welfare state — enjoy as much influence, if not greater influence, than ACOSS in the current welfare policy debate (May, 2001: 261).

The following four chapters extend the existing analysis to a broader range of interest groups. Chapter 7 examines the activities of ACOSS, which is the foremost defender of the Australian welfare state. Chapter 8 explores the views and influence of a number of interest groups including the business sector, the union movement, the social work profession, the media, and local government. Chapter 9 explores the particular social policy philosophy and role of the Australian churches. Lastly, Chapter 10 considers the political influence of unemployed action groups.

7

DEFENDING THE WELFARE STATE: THE AUSTRALIAN COUNCIL OF SOCIAL SERVICE

This chapter examines the activities of the peak non-government welfare lobby group, the Australian Council of Social Service. Attention is drawn to the key role played by ACOSS in defending the Australian welfare state. This chapter begins by outlining the basic composition and objectives of ACOSS. It then examines the principal lobbying strategies utilised by ACOSS; and discusses the extent of its influence with both recent Labor and Coalition governments. The last sections examine, firstly, factors which may inhibit the effectiveness of ACOSS's interventions; and a case study of its participation in the GST debate, which serves to illuminate both the strengths and limitations of ACOSS's lobbying strategies.

THE ROLE AND OBJECTIVES OF THE WELFARE LOBBY

Established in 1956, ACOSS is the peak lobby group of the community welfare sector. It aims to represent the voice of low-income people in policy debates, and to promote alternatives to the dominant neoliberal agenda. ACOSS appears to have been successful in defending the fundamental structures of the welfare state from attack, and in protecting its constituency from potentially even greater hardship and distress. However, it has arguably had only minimal success in convincing governments to introduce measures that would lead to greater social or economic equity.

Councils of Social Service were established in most Australian states in the 1940s and 1950s. Their establishment reflected the rapid growth of the government welfare sector under the ALP Government from 1941 to 1949, and the corresponding concern of the leading non-government welfare agencies to maintain their influence on government policy (Mendes, 1996: 61).

Formed in humble circumstances, ACOSS gradually gained recognition as the political representative of the non-government welfare sector. ACOSS also became an increasingly effective lobby group in terms of its ability to influence and alter government policy agendas. Notable policy reforms influenced by ACOSS lobbying included:

- the 1963 increase in payments to civilian widows
- the 1969 health care reforms introduced by the Gorton Government and the later introduction of Medibank by the Whitlam Government
- the establishment of the Henderson Poverty Inquiry by the McMahon Government and the subsequent broadening of that inquiry by the ALP
- the introduction of the Supporting Mother's Pension by the Whitlam Government
- the expansion of interpreter and other migrant support services in the early to mid-1970s
- the easing of harsh invalid pension criteria introduced by the Fraser Government. (Mendes, 1996: 547–49)

Today, ACOSS claims to represent the interests of low-income and disadvantaged people in social and economic policy debates. Key policy priorities include:

- economic development and tax
- social security and low incomes
- employment, education and training
- community services
- Aboriginal rights and reconciliation
- housing and urban development
- health
- law and justice
- rural and regional communities.

ACOSS's major aims are:

- to promote a fairer and more equitable society
- to eliminate poverty
- to improve the access of low income and disadvantaged Australians to government services and facilities

- to attain a recognised role for the non-government welfare sector in national policy making.

Overall, ACOSS espouses a social democratic or social justice ideology which emphasises tackling the structural causes of poverty and inequality (Lyons, 1995: 682; Marsh, 1995: 64–65).

ACOSS has a highly diverse membership, and claims to represent 11 000 community welfare organisations. The council's principal affiliates include:

- the eight state and territory Councils of Social Service
- major religious and secular welfare agencies such as the Salvation Army, the St Vincent de Paul Society, Centacare, Lifeline, Mission Australia, Relationships Australia, the Smith Family, and Anglicare Australia
- key professional associations such as those of social workers and psychologists, and peak bodies which specialise in particular policy areas or population groups including the National Association of Community Legal Centres, and National Shelter
- the major low-income consumer groups such as the Association of Civilian Widows, the National Council for Single Mothers and their Children, and the National Association of People Living with HIV/AIDS. (ACOSS, 2001a: 6)

ACOSS's claim as a professional advocacy body to represent the interests of low-income and disadvantaged Australians has often been questioned by governments, and even by the poor themselves (May, 2001: 254). One of the reasons is the potential conflict of interest within the ACOSS membership itself between welfare service providers and service users. For example, some traditional charities remain committed to highly conservative agendas on social issues such as abortion and illicit drugs. ACOSS affiliates may also disagree on the extent to which welfare services are best provided by public or private agencies. As we will discuss in Chapter 9, this is an important philosophical divide which may gain added momentum given the increasing involvement of church-based agencies in employment services. Nevertheless, ACOSS remains united in its support for a publicly funded welfare safety net supported by a progressive taxation system.

Another reason is that ACOSS has rarely been able to satisfactorily involve consumer groups in its policy development and decision-making. This has been particularly the case with the unemployed, although this is not to deny the structural difficulties involved in ensuring such representation (Mendes, 1996: 539–40). We discuss the relationship between ACOSS and the unemployed in greater detail in Chapter 10.

An associated critique from the political Left attacks ACOSS for keeping its arguments within the framework of the dominant economic rationalist discourse. ACOSS is alleged to have reinforced the tendency of both ALP and Liberal governments to target resources to particular needy groups at the expense of other disadvantaged groups, rather than undertaking a broader redistribution of income from rich to poor (Cox, 1993: 273). Traditional Marxists go further, arguing that ACOSS's support for the allegedly benevolent welfare state has misled and disarmed the working class, especially low-income earners and social security beneficiaries. Such authors call on ACOSS to overthrow the capitalist welfare state, rather than attempting to wield it as a weapon on behalf of the poor (Lennie and Skenridge, 1978; Mowbray, 1980).

These criticisms have some legitimacy in that ACOSS has often narrowed its critique to the government's specific priorities, rather than rejecting the overall economic rationalist model. Nevertheless, it is also likely that stronger criticism of the government's overall agenda would lead to ACOSS's complete isolation from the political mainstream (Mendes, 1996: 282).

It would appear that this Leftist critique of ACOSS is explicitly linked to the broader debate of whether the interests of the poor are best represented by government-funded lobby groups linked to the traditional welfare state, or alternatively by radical activist/protest groups committed both to financial and political independence from government agendas. According to May (2001: 271), an effective anti-poverty movement requires both these forms of advocacy.

LOBBYING STRATEGIES AND TARGETS

ACOSS operates as an 'insider' lobbying group concerned to retain an ongoing consultative status with government. This means ACOSS typically engages in certain types of accepted lobbying activities such as preparing well-researched submissions, and giving evidence to official committees which government officials judge to be representative and responsible (Matthews, 1989: 212). ACOSS also primarily uses co-operation and persuasion strategies, rather than contest strategies, to promote change. Key lobbying targets are:

- government, both politicians and leading public servants
- other key opinion leaders, including the media, business and unions
- general public opinion.

Lobbying strategies used include:

- submissions to and meetings with leading public servants and government ministers. ACOSS generally meets with the prime minister and other prominent ministers at Budget time, and to discuss other major policy initiatives such as the Welfare Reform Package. ACOSS has had over 60 formal meetings with ministers, Opposition leaders and other federal politicians, and departmental officers during the last year.
- presentations to parliamentary inquiries and hearings such as the inquiry into the tax treatment of charitable organisations. ACOSS may also meet with or attempt to influence internal party policy committees and groups. For example, one ACOSS seminar examined the organisational structure of the Liberal Party including the various internal groupings such as the Young Liberals, the Menzies Resource Centre and the Lyons Forum.
- public campaigns such as the 1992 Day of Action on Unemployment, during which delegations of churches, welfare organisations, unions, community workers and unemployed people visited all Federal parliamentarians. ACOSS also ran a vigorous public campaign in the early 1980s against the Fraser Government's crackdown on invalid pension eligibility criteria. Campaign activities included a public rally and seminar, the attainment of support from state ministers, the collection of information regarding the unfair treatment of applicants, and the distribution of a petition.
- extensive contact with the media, since media coverage can be crucial in influencing government policy outcomes. During 2000/2001, for example, ACOSS issued 39 press releases, held 12 press conferences, and monitored over 1200 references to ACOSS concerns on national and local press, radio and television outlets.
- addresses to public forums such as the National Press Club. For example, the former ACOSS president, Robert Fitzgerald, addressed the Press Club in April 1996 and called on the Howard Government to honor its promise to maintain the welfare safety net.
- alliances with other lobby groups such as churches, trade unions, business and environmental groups. For example, at the time of the 1987 election, ACOSS arranged a letter concerning child poverty by the heads of all the major churches which greatly influenced the subsequent government's family assistance package. In addition, as we will discuss below, ACOSS formed an alliance with

the Australian Chamber of Commerce and Industry to promote tax reform. (May, 1996: 265–67; Mendes, 1996: 285–95)

More recently, ACOSS has participated in the Australian Collaboration project alongside a number of conservation, ethnic, Aboriginal, church and other community groups. The project aims at promoting a socially, culturally and environmentally sustainable Australia, and has produced a major report titled *A Just and Sustainable Australia* (Yencken and Porter, 2001). It has also met with a number of state and territory governments, and union and business leaders to promote its objectives.

ACOSS'S POLITICAL INFLUENCE

ACOSS is a non-party political organisation committed to dialogue with both major political parties, and also the minor parties in the Senate. It has traditionally enjoyed closer relations with the ALP than with the Liberal Party due to the greater symmetry of their ideological positions. However, ACOSS's relationship with both Labor and Liberal-National Coalition governments has always involved a mixture of co-operation and criticism. It does not seek a formal alliance with any particular government or political party which may lead to a diminution of its own political choices. Rather, it aims to influence all parties to develop policies which benefit people affected by poverty and inequality.

During the Hawke/Keating years from 1983 to 1996, ACOSS became one of the most important lobby groups in the country. It attained substantial access to government including regular meetings with the prime minister, the treasurer and other leading ministers. It had representation on various government forums and advisory bodies including the influential Economic Planning Advisory Council, and leading government figures regularly spoke at ACOSS's congresses. It was recognised by government as the legitimate representative of the welfare sector (Mendes, 1996: 296–306; Warhurst, 1997: 111).

In short, ACOSS became an accepted member of what Smith (1993) calls the government's 'policy network', whereby information is formally exchanged between the state and approved interest groups. Its access to government meant opportunities to influence and alter government policy agendas. It achieved significant successes in its lobbying on social security policy, and at times in other areas, such as taxation, superannuation and labour market programs (Gruen and Grattan, 1993: 64).

In addition, ACOSS attained a prominent media profile which enhanced its capacity to influence government policy outcomes. It also formed a co-operative relationship with other key lobby groups such as the ACTU on issues of mutual concern such as taxation and social security reforms (Mendes, 1996: 312–22, 523–38).

ACOSS's influence with government arguably reflected its adherence to a number of key strategies identified as crucial for lobbying success. These include the provision of well-researched case studies, professional expertise, speaking with a united and representative voice, topicality and timing in its interventions, moderate and considered recommendations, and an emphasis on broader national concerns rather than narrow self-interest (Lyons, 1995: 691–92; Abbott, 1996: xi-xvi).

Nevertheless, ACOSS's influence was almost certainly less than that of groups like the ACTU or the BCA because welfare groups cannot initiate economic sanctions to further their aims (May, 2001: 253). Nor was the relationship with the Labor Government free of tension. Both the Hawke and Keating governments tended to be intolerant of criticism from presumed allies such as ACOSS. Often, the prime minister or ministers would respond to criticism from ACOSS by vigorously questioning its credibility and legitimacy. Thus, its relationship with the Labor Government, whilst generally co-operative, also included significant periods of confrontation (Mendes, 1996: 333–37).

ACOSS's association with the current Coalition Government has been far less harmonious. To put it briefly, its views and those of the Liberal Party are ideologically incompatible. The contemporary Liberal Party favours a neoliberal agenda — smaller government, lower taxation and greater private provision of welfare. In contrast, ACOSS advocates a traditional social democratic approach — higher taxation, a larger public sector, and substantial government intervention to reduce poverty and unemployment.

Since the election of the Howard Government in March 1996, ACOSS's major priority has been to preserve the welfare safety net at a time of cutbacks to government programs and spending. On a number of occasions, it has called upon the Liberal Government to keep its promise to maintain existing social security expenditure levels. While ACOSS appears to enjoy considerable access to the Liberal Government — including regular meetings with the prime minister and treasurer — most ACOSS proposals and criticisms of government policy have been rejected by the government. Overall, its influence seems far less than under the preceding ALP Government.

Despite its increasing marginalisation and lack of common

ground with the government, ACOSS is determined to remain an insider lobby group involved in responsible negotiations with the government. As we shall see, its approach to the GST debate was predicated on the assumption that it could more effectively influence the Coalition Government as a lobby group with recognised 'insider status', rather than as a harsh critic from outside the policy mainstream. ACOSS also identified the need to develop new alliances with business groups which (unlike the ACTU) were on good terms with the government.

INFLUENCES ON EFFECTIVENESS

A number of internal and external factors are likely to limit the influence of ACOSS's interventions. One factor is that ACOSS has limited funds compared to the business lobby and neoliberal interest groups. As we noted in Chapter 2, the BCA and the National Farmers' Federation alone spend a combined total of more than $7 million per year on lobbying activities. In contrast, ACOSS's total income in 2001 was $1 064 406 (ACOSS, 2001a: 24).

Another limitation is that ACOSS is continually forced to confront the political dominance of economic rationalist ideas. Both major political parties are wholly committed to free-market ideas such as smaller government, lower taxes, freedom of choice, and individual responsibility (Frankel, 2001: 150, 153).

In addition, ACOSS is not a producer group, and cannot initiate sanctions such as strike action to further its aims. Consequently, ACOSS appears to be successful only when its agenda does not clash fundamentally with that of the government. For example, its 1993 campaign for a jobs development levy failed even though it had considerable public support. Similarly, although ACOSS appeared to have won the public and media debate on tax reform in calling for an efficient and equitable package that did not involve a change in the tax mix from income to consumption, its campaign ultimately failed since it clashed with the Howard Government's election-driven agenda which was to introduce a GST accompanied by large personal income tax cuts.

Further, ACOSS's public advocacy on behalf of its constituency is limited by the general political apathy and powerlessness of the poor. For instance, many income security beneficiaries feel stigmatised by their situation and do not wish to be involved in public activities or protests.

Finally, ACOSS continues to be dependent on government grants for 40 per cent of its total funding. This financial reliance on government may compromise its independence, and prevent it from speaking out against government policies. For example, when John Hewson was leader of the Liberal Party, he threatened if elected to government to cut ACOSS's funding (Mendes, 1996: 434–37).

Nevertheless despite these limitations, ACOSS continues to speak out loudly and effectively on behalf of its low-income constituency. Whatever the pressures to compromise, ACOSS continues to maintain a significant independent public voice and influence in terms of offering viable alternatives to the dominant neoliberal policy agenda (Frankel, 2001: 150).

A CASE STUDY OF ACOSS AND TAX REFORM: THE GST

From mid-1996 until the Federal election of August 1998, ACOSS played a central role in Australia's tax reform debate. Prospects for serious tax reform had seemed dead and buried after the 1993 Hewson election debacle, and Prime Minister Howard's May 1996 statement ruling out any consideration of a GST. However, ACOSS's informal alliance with the powerful business sector to promote a more equitable and economically efficient tax system served to re-ignite the tax debate.

ACOSS's contribution to the debate was recognised as influential and informed by numerous media and public commentators, and both major political parties sought its support for their respective tax packages. Some observers went so far as to suggest that ACOSS held a power of veto over any taxation reform proposals (Mendes, 1998e: 50).

Yet Australia now has a new taxation system which is sharply at odds with ACOSS's key policy concerns and recommendations. In addition, ACOSS has largely been frozen out of the tax debate by the Howard Government since the 1998 federal election. This section seeks to critically examine the strategies pursued by ACOSS in the tax reform debate, and to explain why ultimately they weren't successful.

ACOSS AND THE TAX DEBATE

In accordance with its social democratic views, ACOSS has consistently favoured a more progressive and equitable tax system that would increase the amount of revenue available for support programs for low-income earners. In particular, it has argued for higher taxes on high-income earners, such as taxes on capital gains, fringe benefits and wealth, the abolition of tax concessions for superannuation payments, and an end to loopholes and distortions in business tax.

ACOSS has historically opposed proposals for consumption taxes on the grounds that they are regressive — taking a proportionately larger sum out of a small income than out of a large one. For example, ACOSS played a key role in defeating the Hawke Government's 1985 proposed consumption tax by arguing that the poor could not be adequately compensated for the associated rise in consumer prices. Similarly, ACOSS campaigned against the Liberal Party's proposed consumption tax in 1991–93 (Mendes, 1996: 348–57).

However, from mid-1996, ACOSS suggested in its public statements that it was no longer opposed in principle to a GST. A number of complex factors appear to have prompted this change of heart. The most significant factor was ACOSS's increasing concern at the fall in government tax revenue, and its implications for government spending on community services. According to ACOSS, Australia's overall level of tax revenue was the third lowest in the OECD. Revenue as a percentage of GDP had declined from 27 per cent to 25 per cent over the last decade — a loss of $10 billion. Another concern was that regressive indirect or consumption taxes had already increased substantially over the past decade (ACOSS, 1996a).

Contrary to numerous media reports, ACOSS did not favour a new consumption tax or GST in isolation. However, it did support consideration of an extended wholesale sales tax or national consumption tax as part of a broader tax reform package which maintained or improved the progressive nature of the system, and broadened and strengthened the tax base (ACOSS, 1998a).

ACOSS's reform proposals received enormous media coverage and considerable praise from respected academic economists and tax experts. In addition, reports and editorials in pro-business newspapers such as the *Australian* and the *Financial Review* regularly suggested that ACOSS was an informed and key player in the debate with the power to strongly influence its ultimate outcome.

ACOSS AND THE BUSINESS LOBBY

To the surprise of many, ACOSS established an informal alliance with the powerful business sector to promote tax reform. Groups such as the BCA and the Australian Chamber of Commerce and Industry (ACCI) have always been highly effective lobby groups, but have arguably become even more influential in recent years due to the election of an ideologically sympathetic Coalition Government, and associated economic trends (Argy, 1998: 230–33).

However, traditionally ACOSS and the business sector have not enjoyed close relations. As we will explore in greater detail in Chapter 8, this is because the business community generally favours a free-market agenda at odds with ACOSS's advocacy of higher government spending (Mendes, 1996: 398–99, 435–36). Nevertheless, and despite the diverse economic and political interests which they represent, ACOSS and the key business groups managed to find considerable common ground in the tax reform area. In October 1996, for example, ACOSS and the ACCI revived the dormant tax debate by co-convening the National Tax Reform Summit.

The summit gained nation-wide media coverage, and suggested the possibility of welfare and business groups jointly agreeing on a tax package which would meet both equity and efficiency concerns. Subsequently, ACOSS and ACCI formed a Tax Reform Consultative Committee to review proposed reforms, and attempt to attain a consensus (Mendes, 1998e: 50).

Both ACOSS and the business groups appeared in the short term to gain from their joint campaign. ACOSS, for example, attained the support of a key interest group for its concerns that any tax reform package address equity as well as efficiency issues, and ensure provision of an adequate revenue base to provide necessary government services. The business community also broadly supported ACOSS's opposition to a tax-mix switch from income to consumption, and acknowledged the need to address income tax loopholes and shelters (ACOSS, 1996b).

Similarly, the business community, which regarded ACOSS as sufficiently powerful to influence the success or otherwise of a tax reform package (Westfield, 1999: 71–72), attained its co-operation for an extended consumption tax, and measures to lower unnecessary compliance costs which reduce business productivity.

However, in the long term, the alliance collapsed due to the business sector's perfidy. When it came to the political crunch, the business sector abandoned their coalition with ACOSS, re-asserted their narrower interests and priorities, and lined up firmly behind the government's tax package (Frankel, 2001: 226–27).

THE COALITION GOVERNMENT'S TAX REFORM PACKAGE AND ACOSS

In August 1997, the Howard Government established a Taxation Task Force to prepare options for reform of the taxation system. Five principles were to be taken into account:

- there should be no increase in the overall tax burden
- any new taxation system should involve major reductions in personal income tax with special regard to the taxation treatment of families

- consideration should be given to a broad-based indirect tax to replace some or all of the existing indirect taxes
- there should be appropriate compensation for those deserving of special consideration
- reform of Commonwealth/state financial relations must be addressed. (Costello, 1998a)

Notably, the package conflicted with a number of ACOSS's key concerns including opposition to a tax-mix switch, and scepticism about the efficacy of any compensation package. In addition, there was no reference to maintaining existing public revenue levels, to tackling loopholes and distortions, or to restoring the overall progressivity of the tax system (Davidson, 1997).

With hindsight, it seems clear that at this point, ACOSS should have re-assessed its position of in-principle support for tax reform. The government's stated reform principles suggested that any tax package would move in a direction fundamentally at odds with ACOSS's core concerns. At the very least, ACOSS should have moved away from its insider vantage point, and adopted a position of outright opposition to the unacceptable aspects of the government proposals.

Instead, ACOSS chose to continue its negotiations with the government in an attempt to attain policy concessions. It appears that ACOSS attained some minor wins from this dialogue, including squashing early government proposals to reduce overall tax revenue, and to directly use the GST to fund big personal income tax cuts.

Essentially, ACOSS assumed that the Liberal Party would win the next election, and that ACOSS should retain an ongoing dialogue with the government in order to avoid being isolated from the debate. However, it is possible that a stronger ACOSS critique at this time may have influenced the government into reconsidering their reform principles, given their continuing fears about the possible political consequences of ACOSS's opposition.

The government's tax package was finally released in August 1998, and confirmed ACOSS's worst fears. The major components of the package were a 10 per cent GST to replace ten existing indirect taxes, massive personal income tax cuts, compensation for low-income earners, and measures to tighten tax arrangements for trusts.

The government ignored many of ACOSS's key recommendations including its call for the exemption of food from any GST, its opposition to any increase in the overall indirect tax burden, and its proposed broadening of income tax to remove unfair loopholes and shelters such as negative gearing, income-splitting, work-related deductions and superannuation tax breaks (Costello, 1998b).

In response, ACOSS criticised the tax plan as 'unbalanced and unfair', demanding sweeping changes including the exemption of food, and the revamping of the allegedly regressive tax cuts so that they favoured low-income earners rather than the wealthy (ACOSS, 1998b).

ACOSS's criticisms led to a vigorous public brawl with the government. ACOSS President Michael Raper and Treasurer Peter Costello went head-to-head on just about every television public affairs program. The government attempted to minimise the impact of ACOSS's criticisms by suggesting that it was just another interest group which was not even representative of the whole welfare sector, and that its stated concerns about the allegedly regressive nature of the package were based on inadequate information (Mendes, 1998e: 51).

THE POST-1998 ELECTION DEBATE

Following the Liberal Party's election success, ACOSS continued to seek changes to the proposed tax legislation. In a 115–page submission to the Senate Select Committee on a New Tax System, ACOSS argued for the exclusion of food from the GST, a reduction in the income tax cuts especially for high-income earners, and a serious attempt to close off loopholes and shelters in the personal income tax system (ACOSS, 1999a).

ACOSS lobbied senators such as those from the Democrats and Brian Harradine, who together held the balance of power to amend the package, and it appears from media reports to have exerted considerable influence on their bargaining position. ACOSS subsequently welcomed the exclusion of food from the package, but argued that the package was still unfair due to the regressive tax cuts, and the failure to close loopholes (ACOSS, 1999b).

However, with the exception of its influence on the Senate debate, ACOSS was clearly marginalised in the post-election period. Once re-elected, the Coalition Government no longer felt any need to curry favour with the body.

ACOSS AND THE ALP

In addition to ongoing negotiations with the business sector and the Coalition Government, ACOSS also engaged in regular discussions with the Opposition ALP. Throughout the period of the tax debate, the ALP was highly critical of ACOSS's willingness to consider a GST, arguing that it had lent legitimacy to Howard's regressive tax agenda. Senior ALP figures threatened on a number of occasions that ACOSS could face retribution from a future ALP Government should it continue to co-operate with the Liberals on tax reform (Brown, 1999: 90).

In August 1998, the ALP released its own tax package based on an unequivocal opposition to a GST. The ALP argued that it could instead fund personal income taxes for lower- and middle-income earners by tackling tax loopholes such as family trusts and other income-splitting devices. Labor supported a progressive tax system, and opposed any shift in the tax mix from income to consumption. Overall, the ALP's position appeared to be far closer to ACOSS's agenda than that of the Liberal Party. However, ACOSS was strongly critical of the Labor Party's proposed tax package, arguing that it was 'fair enough, but not good enough' (ACOSS, 1998c).

ACOSS's relationship with the traditionally friendly ALP appears to have been significantly damaged by the tax debate. It may be that this conflict was unavoidable, since the ALP was always going to view any endorsement by ACOSS of a GST (however qualified and complex) as a threat to its own political strategies and fortunes (Brown, 1999: 97).

In addition, ACOSS was for a number of reasons never going to simply bow to ALP pressure to shut up. Firstly, ACOSS is expected by its broad and ideologically fluid constituency to maintain a dialogue with both major political parties. Further, its relationship with past Labor governments has also involved a mixture of co-operation and criticism (Mendes, 1996: 322–37). Finally, ACOSS retained some justified scepticism as to the ALP's intentions on tax, since it had been the previous Labor Government that had permitted the revenue base to decline by such a significant proportion.

Nevertheless, it does appear with hindsight that ACOSS should have considered retreating from any dialogue with the government once the unacceptable tax reform principles were released in August 1997. That ACOSS chose not to do so despite those flawed principles leading inevitably to a regressive tax package suggests that ACOSS did not properly consider an alternative or 'Plan B' option involving an alliance with the ALP. Whether or not such an alliance in opposition to the government's tax plans would have led ultimately to better policy and political outcomes for ACOSS can, of course, only be considered hypothetically.

CONCLUSION

The GST debate encapsulates both the strengths and weaknesses of ACOSS's lobbying activities. On the one hand, it is a highly competent and professional research and advocacy body which has managed to acquire significant respect and recognition from a range of sources including government, the media and other key interest groups.

On the other hand, ACOSS has little real social or economic power in terms of an ability to mobilise its constituency. Its greatest strength is its perceived moral authority, and ability to prick the social conscience of other groups. But this strength is often overridden by the vested interests of more powerful groups such as government, unions and business (May, 2001: 253).

Despite limited funding, ACOSS arguably continues to be an effective and independent advocate for the interests of its constituency, and for an alternative approach to social policy agendas. However, it is unlikely to break the current neoliberal consensus unless it can find ways and means of more effectively introducing its affiliates — including welfare service providers, professionals and consumers — into the policy debate. The discussions which follow in Chapters 8 to 10 suggest at least some potential for movement in this direction.

Questions for consideration

1 Is ACOSS the most appropriate representative of poor and disadvantaged people in our society?
2 Why do government and the media appear to view ACOSS as an important and influential lobby group?
3 Given that ACOSS is a welfare lobby group concerned primarily with welfare payments, why has it intervened in broader macroeconomic debates around taxation?

Exercise

Read the following case scenario. If you were the director of ACOSS, what actions might you take in response to this policy initiative?

> The Prime Minister Mr Tough-Love today announced the abolition of all social security benefits including the aged pension.
>
> Mr Tough-Love said that most poor people are able to receive help from family or friends. Those who are genuinely destitute should contact their local charity.
>
> Mr Tough-Love simultaneously announced huge tax cuts to Australia's 50 biggest companies as an incentive to employ people previously on social security benefits. He also abolished the minimum wage.
>
> Mr Tough-Love said that his aim was to make Australia a work, rather than welfare, society.

8
OTHER INTEREST GROUPS

Besides the political parties and ACOSS, there is a range of other interest groups representing sections of the Australian polity which contribute to the debate over the welfare state. This chapter discusses the roles played by these groups. Firstly, it examines the various business groups, and the major employees' group, the ACTU. It also studies the major professional social work organisation, and looks in detail at the Australian Association of Social Workers (AASW). It then examines the role of media in the welfare debate, and lastly, of local government bodies. (The roles of the churches and the unemployed are the subjects of Chapters 9 and 10.)

THE BUSINESS SECTOR, SOCIAL RESPONSIBILITY AND THE WELFARE STATE

Business organisations are consistently amongst the most powerful lobby groups in society. They are well organised and adept at linking their own interests to national issues like jobs and efficiency. Their influence reflects their key structural role in the economy, the resources available to them, and their capacity to mobilise public opinion. In addition, they have a major impact on the funding of political parties (overwhelmingly favouring the conservative side of politics), and on the funding and output of some of the most influential neoliberal think-tanks as well as the media (Singleton, 1997; Argy, 1998: 231–33).

The business sector has been able to retain significant influence on the development and implementation of government policy, regardless of which political party is in power. For example, the former ALP Education and Employment minister, John Dawkins, admitted that the BCA had dominated the ALP Government's economic policy agenda (quoted in Stilwell, 2000: 148). The subsequent election of the Howard Government in 1996 has led to even greater access for business groups (Warhurst, 1997: 122–23).

Whilst the business sector includes diverse interests from the smallest corner store to the largest multinationals, representative peak groups have consistently adopted a hostile approach to welfare spending. In general, business argues that economic goals and wealth creation should take precedence over social goals and expenditure. Consequently, business taxes should be reduced regardless of the negative impact on government revenue, and the associated ability to fund social expenditure (Langmore and Quiggin, 1994: 224; Argy, 2001: 74–75).

During the 1983–1996 period of ALP governments, for example, business groups frequently called for cuts to unemployment benefits and job training assistance, and for overall cuts to government social expenditure (BCA, 1991: 36–42). More recently, business groups such as the Australian Chamber of Manufacturers and the ACCI have called for substantial cuts to welfare spending. In particular, they have called for changes to social security to encourage participation in the workforce such as limiting the period of unemployment benefits, freezing unemployment benefit levels, extending work for the dole, and removing benefits for job refusal. For example, the Victorian Chamber of Commerce and Industry called for $3 billion to be cut from welfare spending in the 1999 budget.

BUSINESS AND HOWARD'S SOCIAL COALITION

In 1999, Prime Minister Howard called for a social coalition between business, families, individuals, welfare and charitable organisations, and government to tackle social problems. This concept was based on the notion of mutual obligation whereby those who have been successful have an obligation to contribute back to the welfare of their community. Specifically, Howard urged the business sector to increase its contribution to the provision and funding of welfare services. Howard criticised business for contributing less than 5 per cent of total funds available to the non-government sector, and urged development of a greater philanthropic tradition in Australia (Mendes, 2000c: 39).

The subsequent Reference Group on Welfare Reform report urged business to do more to employ long-term jobless people, and to meet community expectations regarding their social responsibility. The report also suggested the establishment of a national framework of triple bottom-line (social, environmental and economic) auditing for the corporate sector (RGWR, 2000: 35–37).

In order to encourage a higher level of business philanthropy, Howard introduced a $51 million package of tax concessions for business contributions. The government also allocated $13.4 million over four years for a Business and Community Partnerships initiative designed to strengthen the links between the corporate and community sectors. The partnership comprises an 11–member consultative board designed to develop and promote a culture of corporate and individual social responsibility in Australia. In addition, the government announced the establishment of the Prime Minister's Awards for Excellence in Community Business Partnerships.

A study commissioned by the consultative board investigated 115 large companies on their attitude and commitment to community involvement. The study found that three quarters of the companies now supported an expanded role in the community as a social responsibility. Most linked community involvement to their long-term commercial interests and reputation, but a minority viewed community involvement solely as a means of 'putting back into the community' (Centre for Corporate Public Affairs, 2000).

The Body Shop offers a highly positive example of commitment to the notion of corporate social responsibility. The Body Shop adheres to what has been called the 'stakeholder approach' as opposed to a narrow commitment to shareholder concerns. This refers to the concept that companies are responsible to a range of groups influenced by their practices including local communities, the natural environment and future generations (Murphy and Thomas, 2000: 142–43).

The Body Shop is well known for its involvement in corporate volunteering — that is encouraging and supporting staff involvement in community programs including those with indigenous groups and disadvantaged youth. Particularly valuable is their Community Management Project in the Victorian region of Mornington Peninsula which provides a free management consultancy service for small community agencies, neighbourhood services and local resident groups. The Body Shop also specifically encourages communities in the development of skills in advocacy and policy debate (Murphy and Thomas, 2000).

However, a number of large companies are less enthusiastic. The general view seems to be that their primary obligation is to generate investment and economic growth, and provide profits to their shareholders. Their willingness to acknowledge any broader social obligation is limited, and they do not wish to share the burden of funding social welfare. According to a number of business leaders, the responsibility of providing assistance to the poor and disadvantaged belongs solely to government (Buckingham, 1998; Paterson, quoted in Henderson, 2000).

In addition, some companies such as the big banks issue social responsibility statements relating to individual community activities and services in which they are involved, but fail to integrate social responsibility values and principles into their business practices. Examples of this hypercritical behaviour include retrenchments, the closure of branches in regional and rural communities, and the refusal to accept a legally imposed social obligation to service poorer customers (Bretherton, 2002).

Another limitation is that many big-business groups prioritise community partnerships that offer publicity and marketing opportunities. This is particularly the case when they are concerned to restore a public image which has been damaged by involvement in dishonest, unsafe or environmentally damaging activities. Consequently, many are not willing to engage with smaller local community groups which lack high public profiles (Mission Australia, 2002: 17; Murphy et al, 2002: 4).

The prime minister's initiatives have also provoked a number of broader questions and concerns. In particular, some commentators have questioned whether the government intends to use increased business donations as an excuse to reduce government spending and so undermine the welfare safety net. Some have also criticised the government for not considering the alternative option of asking business to pay greater taxes so that government can continue to afford a generous welfare safety net.

Overall, there seems to be an inherent contradiction in the notion of corporate social responsibility. On the one hand, business organisations are increasingly claiming to contribute via community partnerships to the social cohesion of the community. On the other hand, most business groups have consistently opposed socially responsible policies by government which address structural inequities. Many also continue to engage in actions such as downsizing which increase, rather than decrease, unemployment and social hardship (Edgar, 2001: 96).

AUSTRALIAN COUNCIL OF TRADE UNIONS

The Australian union movement has traditionally adopted a laborist approach to social policy issues. The union movement concerned itself primarily with the wages and working conditions of wage and salary earners, rather than focusing on a broader redistribution of income from rich to poor (Castles, 1985). This laborist philosophy paid little attention to the needs of those who do not participate in the workforce, except for the sick and the aged. During the 1930s Depression for example, the union movement, whilst expressing sympathy for the unemployed, with some exceptions generally made little attempt to organise the unemployed or to lobby on their behalf for adequate unemployment relief (Louis, 1968: 156–92).

However, in the mid- to late 1960s, the 'rediscovery' of poverty by welfare groups and academic researchers encouraged the union movement to begin considering broader social policy issues. For example, an ACTU Congress promoted the establishment of a national health service, and called for increases in all the existing forms of social service payments.

In 1969 Bob Hawke was elected president of the ACTU. Hawke immediately declared his intention to develop policies beyond the traditional areas of wages and working conditions. Under Hawke's presidency, the union movement involved itself in a number of broader social and policy issues not directly related to employment conditions, such as the green bans of the Builders Laborers' Federation, anti-uranium strikes, work bans on the Newport power station, support for Medibank, and opposition to oil drilling on Aboriginal land (Cupper and Hearn, 1980).

THE SOCIAL WAGE

During the Fraser Government years from 1975 to 1983, the union movement promulgated the notion of the 'social wage' — that standards of living are affected by far more than just private incomes received by individuals through wages and salaries. The movement argued that government spending on services such as education, health, social security and welfare, and housing and community amenities, was just as important.

The social wage campaign reflected the growth of unemployment and its detrimental impact on union strength. Large numbers of union members were not only forced to survive on social security benefits, but also ceased to pay their union dues and/or terminated their involvement with the movement. In response, the union movement developed a political strategy that was designed not only to protect the immediate economic interests of unemployed and employed via increasing the social wage, but also to buttress the overall strength of the union movement by promoting policies that would hopefully reduce unemployment and so reverse the decline in union membership (Mendes, 1998c: 111).

The prime force behind the social wage campaign was the left-wing Amalgamated Metal Workers' and Shipwrights' Union. The union published a series of pamphlets criticising government attacks on the social wage. The pamphlets were particularly critical of the widespread growth in poverty and unemployment under the Fraser Government and the erosion of social security benefits (Singleton, 1990: 61–69).

The ACTU also displayed increased interest in social welfare policies. Consecutive ACTU congresses published lengthy documents on the social security system, calling for increases in unemployment benefits and job creation schemes, and condemning attempts to blame the unemployed for their predicament.

THE ALP/ACTU ACCORD

The ultimate creation of the trade union social wage campaign was the ALP/ACTU Accord of 1983. The Accord endorsed a 'fairer taxation system and social wage involving increased provision by the government of health, education, housing and social welfare services' (ACTU and ALP, 1983: 3). The Accord also promised to:

> address anomalies in welfare coverage; to foster social equity by striving to improve the relative position of the most disadvantaged; to take urgent action to restore the position of the recipients of unemployment benefits; and to develop automatic indexation provisions (and restoration of the relative value of pensions) to the basic rate of 25 per cent of average male earnings. (ACTU and ALP, 1983: 12)

The ACTU's endorsement of the Accord reflected a commitment to broader social democratic objectives beyond mere wages and conditions, including particularly a commitment to a secure welfare safety net. Defenders of the Accord pointed to significant social wage gains including the introduction of the Family Allowance Supplement for low-income working families, indexed family allowance payments, the introduction of Medicare, the establishment of helpful labour market schemes such as NewStart and Jobs, Education and Training, extended child-care funding, and rental assistance for social security beneficiaries (Evatt Foundation, 1995: 169–75).

However, whilst the ACTU devoted a considerable time to formulating its social welfare objectives, the actual implementation was arguably lacking. As we noted in Chapter 6, the social security reforms promised in the Accord were largely subordinated by the Hawke and Keating ALP governments to the achievement of macro-economic objectives such as appropriate wage outcomes, and a reduction in public spending as a proportion of GDP. Consequently, the union movement's commitment to specific social security objectives, whilst genuine, were not of high priority. Narrow laborism based solely on wages policy arguably triumphed over the broader social democratic prospects raised by the Accord.

In particular, critics of the Accord argued that it favoured the interests of the employed and union members at the expense of welfare recipients. For example, the use of tax cuts as alternatives for wage increases may have benefited those in employment, but tended to limit the expenditure available for social security initiatives. In general, the union movement did not challenge or protest government spending cuts that hurt and disadvantaged low-income earners (Ewer et al, 1991: 26; Langmore, 2000: 25).

Since the election of the Howard Government in 1996, the union movement has, with some minor exceptions, generally refrained from comment on social welfare issues. For example, no union submission was made to the government's Welfare Reform review. The relative silence of Australian unions arguably reflects the declining influence world-wide of traditional mass trade unions (Rodger, 2000: 1). Nevertheless, at least some European unions continue to play a prominent role in defending welfare state provisions (Mishra, 1998: 61, 68–69; Yeates, 2001: 142–43).

RELATIONS BETWEEN THE UNION MOVEMENT AND THE WELFARE LOBBY

Prior to the Fraser Government years, there was little contact between ACOSS and the union movement. Stronger ties were formed during this period due to a common concern at the growth in unemployment. However, the relationship tended to be ad hoc.

During the Hawke/Keating years, ACOSS developed a stronger, more formal working relationship with the union movement. Yet this relationship remained too fitful and inconsistent to be designated a formal alliance. On some issues such as opposition to a consumption tax, advocacy of a 'jobs levy', and support for social security reforms such as the family allowance supplement, ACOSS and the ACTU acted in close alliance. However, on other issues such as tax cuts and superannuation, ACOSS and the ACTU sat on opposite sides (Mendes, 1998c: 117–20).

Since the election of the Howard Coalition Government in March 1996, ACOSS and the ACTU have tended to minimise their differences whilst forging a common opposition to government policies. Both organisations are concerned to protect the rights of low-income earners, and to prevent the development of a larger group of 'working poor' in Australia (Belchamber, 2000).

For example, in 1996 ACOSS joined the ACTU in opposing the Coalition's proposed industrial relations reforms on the basis that they would hurt low-income workers. ACOSS also intervened for the first ever time in a major national wage case to support the ACTU's call for a significant wage rise for low-paid workers. In its submission to the Australian Industrial Relations Commission, ACOSS argued that wages and welfare policies were closely connected, and that the interests of income security recipients and low-wage earning households are 'one and the same' (ACOSS, 1997: 5).

Over the last decade, there have been numerous calls for a closer alliance between the welfare sector and the union movement. From the viewpoint of ACOSS, closer co-operation with the ACTU offers the potential of support for social welfare objectives from an influential and powerful lobby group. Equally from the viewpoint of the unions, closer co-operation with ACOSS and other social movements offers a broadening of the union movement's own dwindling base of support. This is particularly important in the current political climate where the ACTU is able to exert little influence on the policies of the Howard Government (Jamrozik, 2001: 141).

The underlying assumption of much of this argument is that a 'natural alliance' exists between the representatives of the working class including the working poor (the trade unions) and the representatives of the poor and disadvantaged, whether employed or social security recipients (the welfare sector). This alliance would be based on a common commitment to a social democratic agenda.

Yet, such an alliance can be problematic, for the interests of the workers (including well-paid workers) have not always proven to be the same as the interests of the poor. In addition, the narrow laborism of the union movement, based on wage protection rather than broader social democratic concepts, has tended to militate against such an alliance (Mendes, 1998c: 106–107).

For the union movement to move beyond laborism and take responsibility for the whole working class, including social security recipients, instead of just its membership, would require a radical break with its history and ideological framework. Equally, the welfare sector's caution about forming firm alliances with a union movement which it regards as representing a relatively privileged proportion of the population (those in employment) is unlikely to change.

It is perhaps more likely that the two groups will continue to work together on specific matters of mutual concern, and more broadly to promote ideas for greater social and economic equity.

However, both organisations will retain a specific and sometimes disparate commitment to the particular agendas of their separate constituencies (Mendes, 1998c: 121–25; Stilwell, 2000: 216).

PROFESSIONAL SOCIAL WORK ASSOCIATIONS AND SOCIAL ACTION

The profession of social work has long been closely linked with the ideas and values of the modern welfare state (Ife, 1997: 6–7). Professional social work associations have consistently espoused at least a rhetorical commitment to promoting more equitable social policy outcomes.

Internationally, Lyons (1999: 11–12) argues that professional social work has a core and unifying commitment to 'defending and promoting the human and civil rights of usually the least powerful individuals and groups in society, in the pursuit of social justice'. This commitment is formally reflected in both the Code of Ethics and policy statements of the International Federation of Social Workers and its national affiliates.

Yet too often the actions have failed to live up to the rhetoric. This will become particularly evident in our case study of the AASW.

CASE STUDY: THE VICTORIAN BRANCH OF THE AASW

This study explores the social action history of the Victorian state branch of the AASW. Through a number of issues, attention is drawn both to the highlights and lowlights of the branch's social policy interventions.

The AASW has six core objectives:

- to promote the profession of social work
- to provide an organisation through which social workers can develop a professional identity
- to establish, monitor and improve practice standards
- to contribute to the development of social work knowledge and research
- to advocate on behalf of clients
- to actively support social structures and policies pursuant to the promotion of social justice.

Since its formation, the AASW has given most priority to the establishment of social work as a serious and recognised profession, and the creation of the structures of professionalism such as education and accreditation, a Code of Ethics, and verifiable practice standards. Supporting social justice has had less emphasis.

The Victorian branch has been chosen for a number of reasons. Firstly, the branch has long been the largest state branch in terms of membership. In addition, the limited historical evidence that is available would suggest that the Victorian branch has been the most politically active branch. Furthermore, although the AASW is a national organisation, much of its history of social action has taken place at a state rather than national level, particularly in the earlier years of the organisation. Nevertheless, some of this study will necessarily refer to and overlap with discussions of actions by the national AASW.

The Victorian Association of Social Workers was formed in 1935. Following the formation of the national AASW in 1946, the Victorian AASW also began to develop and grow. Branch activities included the formation of sub-committees for public relations, social legislation and migration (Lawrence, 1965). During 1958, the Victorian branch established its first Social Action and Public Relations Committee concerned with both short- and long-term action on social issues. The branch subsequently became more outspoken under the presidency of Concetta Benn. Benn urged social workers to move beyond the confines of casework, and speak out on broader social and community issues and problems. Members of the AASW began to appear on radio and television to discuss their profession.

Nevertheless, these activities arguably only constituted the slim beginnings of a serious commitment to social action. Noticeably, there was no attempt to publicly challenge repressive social policies such as the removal of Aboriginal children, or the coerced adoptions of children born to single mothers. Overall, the association was arguably most notable for its political timidity, which probably reflected a number of factors.

One factor was the continued emphasis on individualistic casework in Australian social work education and practice, at the expense of alternative methods such as social and community development. An associated factor was the lack of specialised knowledge about broader social policy debates and theories. Some social workers were also inhibited by their employment in statutory agencies (Lawrence, 1965: 183–84; Weeks, 2000: 121).

Another important influence was almost certainly the general political conservatism of the period, including the lack of social policy initiatives from the long-standing Menzies Government. An additional more specific political influence may have been the *Bulletin* magazine's 1961 attack on alleged communism in the Melbourne University Social Studies Department. This attack, which was associated with the general McCarthyism of the Cold War, appears to have damaged the academic careers of two prominent researchers, Geoff Sharp and Lois Bryson (Mendes, 2001d).

The branch was particularly nervous of any perceived alignment with Labor or Left political groups. For example, in 1965 the branch rejected an approach from the Victorian ALP to provide an expert advisor to the party's social welfare committee on the grounds that the national constitution prevented affiliation with any organisation limited by politics, religion or sex. The branch even rejected a compromise suggestion that the same offer be made on a non-partisan basis to the Liberal Party. Instead, the branch agreed to encourage social workers who were members of the ALP to join the ALP Social Services Committee (Benn, 1967: 29).

In the late 1960s, the AASW began to move in a more activist direction. This was reflected most prominently in the joint AASW/Victorian Council of Social Service (VCOSS) 1967–68 campaign on health insurance. This campaign was led by Marie Coleman, a Melbourne social worker who later became the director of VCOSS and subsequently of the Whitlam Government's Social Welfare Commission.

The joint AASW/VCOSS report urged all social workers to press the Federal Government for a public enquiry into the national health insurance scheme. The report argued that the existing hospital and medical benefits scheme failed to meet the needs of the most vulnerable groups — the chronically ill and families on low incomes. Instead, the scheme tended to subsidise upper- and middle-income groups. The report urged that consideration be given to introducing a government-controlled compulsory health insurance scheme that would be available to all, with contributions varying according to income.

The report received considerable media coverage in all Victorian newspapers, radio and television programs, and some interstate papers including the *Australian*. Subsequently, a combined AASW/ACOSS delegation met with the Federal minister for Health. The report arguably played an important role in the reforms introduced by the Gorton Government in 1969 on hospital and medical insurance for patients with chronic conditions (AASW and VCOSS, 1968; Coleman, 1968).

Nevertheless, social action continued to face barriers at both a state and national level. At the end of 1975, the AASW membership voted to split the association (which still held formal trade union registration under the *Conciliation and Arbitration Act*) into two separate bodies:

- a trade union to be known as the Australian Social Welfare Union (ASWU) which would represent all social welfare workers rather than just qualified social workers, and participate in political and social policy debates
- the rump professional association, which would concentrate on professional education and accreditation issues. (Davis, 1987: 52–55)

The split with the ASWU inevitably left the AASW weakened in terms of numbers and resources. Nevertheless, the Victorian branch continued to pursue some social action objectives. However, membership apathy continued to present a barrier to effective action. By 1984, the AASW Social Action Network had ceased to exist, and there was a significant decline in branch activity. The following decade saw little organised branch commitment to social action or reform.

Under the presidency of Robyne Schwarz (1991–93), there was a mini-revival of social action commitment. Unfortunately, this revival was short-lived. For the next three years, branch comment on social policy issues was the notable exception rather than the rule. This non-activity probably reached its embarrassing trough at the time of the controversial 1996 Victorian child protection strike, during which the branch maintained a conspicuous silence. When reproached, a branch representative laid the blame at the old bogey of membership apathy (AASW Victorian Branch Newsletter, 1976–1996).

At the beginning of 1997, the Victorian branch appointed a full-time social policy officer to lift the public and media profile of the AASW. During this period, the branch attained regular coverage in the print and broadcast media. Issues covered included child welfare and child protection, social work ethics, and cuts to social work services. A second component of social action involved the strengthening of links with other key welfare bodies such as VCOSS, the Children's Welfare Association of Victoria, and the Victorian Department of Human Services.

A third component was the holding of quarterly public forums on issues such as child protection and the media, problem gambling, the stolen generation and youth suicide. A fourth component involved the revamping of the State Newsletter as the *Victorian Social Work* bulletin and the concentration of individual editions on specific social policy topics such as racism, youth suicide, drug reform and political activism (Mendes, 2003).

However, at the end of 1997, the branch decided to re-classify the social policy position as an executive officer job, and to significantly downgrade the emphasis on social action. Since that time, the branch has been relatively silent on social policy issues, with the exception of some statements regarding the stolen generation of Aboriginal children (AASW Victorian Branch Newsletter, 1997–2002).

Ironically, the apparent demise of social action within the Victorian branch has coincided with what appears to be the revival of a serious social policy commitment at the national level. For example, the national AASW has established a social policy committee and a half-time position for a policy officer. Submissions have been made to a number of important government inquiries, including those on welfare reform and substance abuse. In addition, close links have been established with ACOSS.

This study demonstrates that the Victorian Branch of the AASW has historically had a strong commitment (at least in principle) to social action, but that in practice the association has often failed to meet its stated objectives. There appear to be a number of key factors that have contributed to this gap between rhetoric and action.

Firstly, professional social work education does not appear to effectively prepare graduates to implement the objectives of social action within their everyday practice. The most obvious explanation for this deficit is that the subjects of social policy and social change are generally taught separately from the subjects of social work theory and practice. In addition, the AASW does not currently require social policy to be taught by qualified social workers (Ife, 1997: 170–72).

Herein lie two problems. Firstly AASW policies leave open the possibility of social policy subjects being taught in a highly dry and theoretical manner by armchair theorists with little practice-based application. Whilst most social policy lecturers obviously do not fit this generalisation, many graduates have described social policy subjects as boring and irrelevant.

In addition, the distinction between social work practice subjects and generic social policy appears to leave social work students with the impression that social policy is simply about theoretical knowledge, without any need for practical application. Few students, for example, complete their fieldwork practicums in social policy agencies, although this decision probably also reflects the popular view that social work employment is to be found in direct practice, rather than in broader policy work.

The AASW has some potential to turn around these negatives. For example, it could require all social policy courses to be taught by qualified social workers, or at the very least by academics with direct practical experience in social policy activities, who are able to offer practical as well as theoretical content. It could also substantially upgrade the references to social policy activism in its own Continuing Professional Education Policy (AASW, 1997).

Another potential barrier to effective social action has existed within the internal structure of the AASW. For example, many association leaders at both a state and national level have been employed by public sector agencies, which restricts their ability to speak out publicly against government policies. An associated problem has been that few AASW leaders have enjoyed prominent public and media profiles outside the social work profession. Conversely, the AASW has always found it difficult to attract high-profile social workers into its leadership (Mendes, 1998b: 12–13).

These structural issues suggest that the AASW needs to be very careful in its choice of public spokespersons. Some comparative organisations such as ACOSS use their elected president as their media figurehead, whilst other organisations have been known to use a paid director as their public voice. The key is to select and adequately resource a person who can speak freely and effectively to an audience other than the social work profession, and who can also mobilise the AASW membership, including individual workplaces, in campaigns (Arkley and Jones, 1991: 219–20). Overall, the AASW needs to reconstruct itself as an activist rather than a reactive organisation.

An associated problem is that many of the statements issued by the AASW do not appear to express a firm opinion or viewpoint. It has been suggested elsewhere that the AASW desperately needs to adopt a coherent political philosophy and ideology that explicitly identifies the types of social structures and policies it supports, and the strategies it advocates to achieve these changes. Unless the AASW is clearly identified with a core belief or value position, it is unlikely that the media will be interested in hearing what it has to say (Mendes, 1998b: 12–14).

A further problem is that the AASW still seems unsure who it is claiming to represent. In earlier times, the AASW had only a small membership, and was understandably tentative about claiming to speak on behalf of the whole social work profession (Scott, 1981: 118). However, the AASW now has over 6000 members, and can reasonably claim to speak authoritatively on behalf of social workers in the same way the Australian Medical Association claims to represent doctors.

However, the AASW should not and cannot claim, as it has done on occasions, to represent the views or interests of social work clients unless these persons are directly represented on the AASW board. In fact, groups such as the unemployed, the homeless, the disabled and the aged are properly and effectively represented by other consumer and self-help groups. What the AASW can do is to present the informed and value-based views of a professional group regarding the impact of government policies on welfare services and outcomes.

SOCIAL POLICY AND THE MEDIA

There is considerable evidence to suggest that the media plays an important role in setting the public policy agenda. Given the narrow ownership of the mass media, there also appears not surprisingly to be a significant bias in favour of neoliberal ideas (Argy, 1998: 224–25). Much of the Australian media is owned by two companies: Rupert Murdoch's News Limited, and Kerry Packer's Consolidated Press. Newspapers owned by these companies generally defend the socio-economic status quo. They support pro-business agendas, oppose militant trade unions, reject government intervention and prefer the Liberal Party to the Labor Party (Bessant and Watts, 1999: 353–59).

Commercial television news and current affairs shows are particularly powerful. They influence the policy process in two ways. First, the more attention given by the media to an issue, the more likely it is to appear on the government's agenda. Second, those issues which receive significant coverage by the media are also perceived by the public to be important issues for government. Media interest reflects a set of values which determine what is newsworthy including the presence of human drama, visual attractiveness, entertainment, the involvement of important people, negative or bad news, and the role played by public personalities.

Conversely, many social problems are neglected by the media because they are not easily dramatised, or amenable to simple solutions (Beresford, 2000: 136–38). For example, the media has been poor at exploring such issues as poverty, racism and homelessness. Both Windschuttle (1988) and Beresford et al (1999) argue that overall the media reinforces conservative explanations of, and solutions to, social problems. Similarly, Putnis (2001) suggests that the media has contributed to an increasing tolerance of social inequality and poverty.

Talkback radio shows have also increased in importance. High-rating commentators such as Alan Jones, John Laws and Neil Mitchell offer a right-wing view which targets populist issues such as paedophilia, drugs, immigration, crime and sentencing, asylum seekers, and Aboriginal affairs. They generally limit open-ended pol-icy debate, and make no attempt to achieve balance. Their aim appears to be to reinforce rather than challenge public prejudices, and to tell people what they want to hear (Adams and Burton, 1997).

The above discussion suggests that the media may play an impor-tant role in social policy debates by shaping the direction of public attitudes and values. Often highly complex issues are presented in simplistic black-and-white terms. Below we discuss the media's role in the debate in Victoria over child abuse; some other significant recent examples of media influence include:

- The long campaign to promote public hostility towards the unemployed, and to portray them as welfare cheats and dole bludgers. A prime example of this campaign was the vicious 1996 attack by Channel Nine's 'A Current Affair' on the Paxtons, three naive, unemployed young people from Melbourne's disad-vantaged western suburbs. Overall, media coverage seems designed to shore up public support for conservative solutions to unemployment, such as reduced welfare expenditure and the introduction of the work for the dole scheme (Beder, 2000: 158–67; Twentyman, 2000: 83–88).
- The campaigns by the Victorian tabloid newspaper, the *Herald Sun*, to destroy proposed drug law reforms pertaining firstly to the decriminalisation of marijuana, and later to the introduction of supervised injecting facilities. According to David Penington, the chairman of the Victorian Drug Policy Expert Committee:

  A survey of opinion carried out by an independent firm showed that opinion for or against the trial of supervised injecting facilities was strongly correlated with educational level and family income level. No doubt this perception had much to do with the *Herald Sun* stance as it appeals very much to the lesser educated and lower income levels in society compared with the readership of *The Age*. (Penington, 2000: 7)

- The associated 1997 campaign by talkback radio hosts and the Sydney tabloid newspaper the *Daily Telegraph* to destroy Federal Government support for the ACT's proposed heroin trial. According to Lawrence et al (2000: 254) 'the Prime Minister pulled the plug on the ACT experiment ... because the debate ignited by the proposed trial, driven mainly by the Sydney-based *Daily Telegraph*, shifted unfairly from the medical benefits to a much wider issue of supposedly rewarding addicts'.
- The 2002 campaign by the *Herald Sun* to end the application of harm minimisation principles to the practice of 'chroming' (inhaling fumes from spray paint) by young people in state care.

The campaign appears to have played a critical role in the Victorian Government's decision to shut down a program based on the monitoring of chroming on residential premises (Mendes, 2002b).

CASE STUDY: THE PORTRAYAL OF CHILD ABUSE IN THE VICTORIAN PRESS

This study compares the coverage of high-profile cases of child abuse and debates within the two daily Melbourne newspapers, *The Age* and the *Herald Sun*. Evidence is presented to demonstrate that the *Herald Sun* has consistently pursued a broader socially conservative agenda based on defending traditional nuclear families from allegedly subversive or deviant groups. In contrast, *The Age* has generally eschewed simplistic coverage of individual cases in favour of broader structural reform agendas.

In order to illustrate the difference between what I have called the social justice and social conservative approaches to the reporting of child abuse, I will now draw on examples from the local coverage of high-profile cases of child abuse and surrounding debates within the two daily Melbourne newspapers during the 1996–97 period.

During this period, the *Herald Sun* devoted considerable attention to individual child abuse cases involving either the deaths of children known to protective services, such as Amanda Clark, Katy Bolger and Dillion Palfrey, or alternatively the removal of children (allegedly without sufficient grounds) from their families by protective workers. All these reports had the following characteristics in common:

- sensationalist headlines accompanied by poignant photos of children, those who either had died or been removed from their families. Examples include: 'Death of an Angel', 'Death of Innocents', 'House of Squalor', 'Snatched', 'Military-Style Swoop' and 'The Fatal Mistakes'.
- advocacy of simplistic and immediate solutions to complex problems of child protection
- attacks on individual child protection workers who were portrayed either as 'bungling and incompetent wimps', or alternatively as bullies
- a consistent re-affirmation of family values by means of contrasting grieving members of the extended family (and never questioning their past contribution to or alternatively lack of involvement in the child's life) with the state professionals who it was claimed deserve to be blamed for the child's death

- a failure to even consider the complexities of practice, such as the oft-documented legislative contradiction between parental rights and civil liberties versus children's rights, or broader structural issues such as the limited availability of resources to support carers with intellectual or psychiatric disabilities in the community.

In contrast, *The Age* has generally rejected the sensationalising of individual cases and deaths in favour of serious and broader analysis of the problem. In February 1997, for example, *The Age* reported extensively on the out-of-control behaviour of many adolescents in state care, including prostitution, violent crimes, drug-taking and other substance abuse. These reports arguably played a key role in the Victorian Government's subsequent decision to allocate $5.3 million for 'high-risk adolescents' in the 1997 State Budget.

Similarly, *The Age* gave considerable coverage to the alleged involvement of state wards with organised paedophile networks. In combination with the disclosures of the Wood Royal Commission into the NSW Police Service, these reports arguably played some role in the Federal Government's decision to establish a National Council for the Prevention of Child Abuse.

In addition, *The Age* has tended to be sober and considered in its reporting of individual cases. For example, it cited the support of civil libertarians and child welfare lobbyists for the Department of Human Services' highly publicised removal of a newborn baby from its intellectually disabled mother. Similarly in reporting on the Victorian Child Death Review Committee's annual report, *The Age* emphasised the identification of structural deficits such as poor training and inadequate resources, rather than the details of individual cases (Mendes, 2000d).

LOCAL GOVERNMENT

Historically, local governments have not had a significant impact on Australian social policy debates. However, recent developments suggest that their influence is starting to grow. In Victoria particularly, local governments have been at the centre of recent policy debates around issues such as illicit drugs and prostitution.

This change reflects two particular factors. Firstly, the restructuring of local government by the former Kennett Coalition State Government greatly enhanced the potential resources and power of the newly amalgamated local councils. A number of the 78 new local governments have begun community development and social advocacy projects in a range of policy areas including economic development, environmental protection and human services. For example, the Wyndham Council played a prominent role in supporting the community campaign against a toxic dump in Werribee. Similarly, the Moonee Valley Council provided assistance to the Niddrie Quarry Action Group's struggle against a toxic tip in Moonee Valley (Strangio, 2001: 186).

In addition, the newly formed local government body — the Victorian Local Governance Association — has considerably supported and assisted these collective advocacy campaigns (Hill, 2000). Consequently, Victorian local governments are now far more able than in the past to play an important role in broader policy debates.

Given the impact of economic globalisation (described in Chapter 3), it is likely that local governments and communities will become an increasingly important source of counter ideas and initiatives to neoliberal agendas (Ife, 2002: 145–46).

CONCLUSION

This chapter has explored the views and influence of a number of interest groups including the business sector, the trade union movement, professional social work associations, the media, and local government. Some of these groups including business bodies and key sections of the media have played a significant role in promoting neoliberal agendas. Other groups such as the ACTU, the AASW, other parts of the media, and some local governments, have been active in promoting socially equitable policies.

The examples cited would suggest that the ideas and agendas presented by some non-welfare interest groups around welfare policy are as important if not more important in determining outcomes than those proposed by ACOSS and other welfare lobby groups.

Questions for consideration

1 What are some of the direct and indirect ways in which the business sector influences the level of welfare spending?
2 Does the union movement's approach to social policy still matter given its declining political influence?
3 Why has the social work profession failed to exert a significant influence on social welfare debates?
4 How and in what direction does the media influence public attitudes to social policy ideas and controversies?
5 What is the connection between economic globalisation and the increasing influence of local governments in social policy debates?

9

THE CHURCHES AND SOCIAL JUSTICE

Over the past decade, churches and other Christian welfare agencies have played a prominent role in social welfare debates. Utilising a broad set of moral and ethical values, many church groups have been vigorous and effective critics of free-market economic rationalist agendas (Langmore and Quiggin, 1994: 226; Beresford, 2000: 118).

The involvement of the churches in these debates reflects their significant historical role in the provision of Australian welfare. Since the late nineteenth century, charitable organisations such as the Salvation Army, the St Vincent de Paul Society and the various City Missions have been prominent in caring for the poor (Dickey, 1980: 89–90, 106–110, 200–201).

This role has arguably become even more important in recent years with the growth of some Christian welfare agencies into large providers of government-funded programs including the Jobs Network. For example, the Salvation Army, the Brotherhood of St Laurence, the Wesley Mission and the Anglican Retirement Villages rank amongst the 20 largest community organisations in Australia. Some of these agencies have also diversified into business ventures that help to fund their welfare activities (Industry Commission, 1994; Lyons, 2001: 34, 36).

Despite their central role in welfare services, many critics of the churches dispute the legitimacy of their policy interventions. One argument is that religion is a private affair, and that churches have no proper role in politics. An associated argument broached by some internal church critics defends the right of the church to intervene on alleged matters of the faith such as abortion and euthanasia.

However, they reject the legitimacy of broader social justice activities, claiming they are inspired by Marxist ideology rather than by Christian teachings.

In response, church leaders point to the coherent set of Christian social teachings on which their interventions are based; and the central role played by churches in the provision of non-government welfare services. They also reject the notion of religion as a private affair, and emphasise the importance of churches as public bodies contributing to debates in a democratic society.

This chapter examines the policy influence of the churches as both welfare lobbyists and welfare providers. It begins with an introduction to the Christian social teachings on which church social justice activism has been based. Attention is also drawn to the long history of church activism on issues of social justice, and to the current activities of Christian welfare lobby groups. The next section describes a case study of church social justice activism: the 1992–93 campaign against the proposed GST. This chapter then discusses attacks on church social justice interventions by political parties and neoliberal lobby groups and considers alternative arguments. It then examines some of the potential tensions and dilemmas posed by church involvement in the privatised Jobs Network. The final section examines internal divisions within the churches, and draws some conclusions about the legitimacy of church social justice interventions.

It should be noted that no detailed reference is made in this chapter regarding the response of non-Christian religions to social welfare debates. This is because, to date, groups such as Jews and Muslims have not participated collectively in any formal or institutional campaigns for social justice.

Nevertheless, Jewish religious teachings include a core commitment to concepts of Tzedakah (private charity aligned with social justice), and Tikkun Olam (heal, repair and transform the world). These teachings predispose many Jews towards sympathy for oppressed and disadvantaged groups (Vorspan and Saperstein, 1992: 165–89). The Federation of Australian Jewish Community Services has been a long-time affiliate of ACOSS, and some Jewish individuals including the late Walter Lippmann have been prominent in the welfare discourse.

Equally, the Australian Muslim community has started to develop a substantial social welfare infrastructure. Representatives of this community have begun to speak out on social welfare issues, and related concerns about racism and discrimination (Humphrey, 2001).

CHRISTIAN SOCIAL TEACHING

In opposing economic rationalism, the churches call upon a set of social teachings which emphasise the responsibility of government and the community to redress structural poverty and inequality. The core principles of these teachings include:

- that each person possesses a fundamental dignity that comes from God, not from any human quality or accomplishment, nor from race, gender, age or economic status
- the concept of the 'common good', which holds that individual rights should be adjudged within the context of promoting the common good. Thus, Christian social teaching can be interpreted as requiring the state to actively intervene in the free market in order to promote a fair distribution of wealth.
- the principle of 'solidarity', which holds that individuals are responsible for the welfare of one another. This is closely linked to the idea of the common good.
- the 'universal purpose of goods', which affirms the right to hold private property, but also teaches that this right is not absolute: 'It is subordinated to the right to common use, to the fact that goods are meant for everyone'
- the 'preferential option for the poor', according to which Christians are required to give priority to the poor and oppressed, and to support them in their struggles for justice
- the 'value of work', which upholds the dignity of workers. Labour is granted priority over capital. Workers should have a right to belong to trade unions. (ACSJS, 1990: 10–14; Catholic Bishops, 1992: 17–29)

A Uniting Church document summarises these principles in more laymen's terms:

- Christians stand for a just and equitable society with minimal gap between rich and poor
- Christians should advocate for those who are voiceless, poor or marginalised
- Christians have a prophetic responsibility to transform those conditions and structures that create social injustice in the first place. (Uniting Church, 1996)

THE HISTORY OF CHURCH SOCIAL JUSTICE ACTIVISM

Australian churches have been actively involved in social policy debates since at least World War II. Influenced by the war and the

Great Depression, the Catholic bishops decided in 1940 to publish an annual statement on social justice matters. The statements, which reflected the papal teachings of *Rerum Novarum* and *Quad-rangesimo Anno*, were intended to promote a fairer and more equitable society. Continuing until 1962, they covered such issues as a just family wage for workers, nationalisation of industry and post-war reconstruction, social security, full employment, socialisation, and industrial relations. Each statement was circulated to around 100 000 church members (Hogan, 1990; Duncan, 2001: 33–39).

A number of churches were also involved in welfare lobby activities via membership of the state and Australian Councils of Social Service. They included the national welfare bodies of the Catholic, Anglican and Methodist Churches, and the Salvation Army. Church representatives such as David Scott of the Brotherhood of St Laurence, EH Burgmann, the 'Red Bishop' of Goulburn (Hogan, 1987: 220–21) and Bishop Sambell of the Melbourne Diocesan Centre were amongst the most vigorous advocates for political action on behalf of the poor and disadvantaged. In 1972, Marcus Loane, the Anglican Archbishop of Sydney, the Anglican Primate and 24 Anglican diocesan bishops strongly supported ACOSS's call for a national inquiry into social welfare in Australia (Mendes, 1997b: 146).

The Catholic Church also renewed its social justice statements under the auspices of the Catholic Commission for Justice and Peace. From 1973 to 1987, the commission issued forthright and often highly controversial statements on such issues as poverty, unemployment, wealth and responsibility, international justice and development, and young people. The body was an integral member of the wider welfare lobby, and worked closely with other church-based welfare groups such as the Brotherhood of St Laurence and the Salvation Army (Woolfe, 1988; Hogan, 1993: 93–112).

During the 1987 federal election campaign, the leaders of all the major Christian denominations joined together to sign a letter calling upon the Hawke ALP Government to take decisive action against child poverty. The letter reportedly played a key role in convincing the government to introduce the often-praised family assistance package (Lyons, 1988: 89).

A number of newer Christian welfare lobby groups emerged during this period. One was the Fair Share Network which was formed by a number of Christian denominations in 1983 to promote church awareness and action on issues of poverty and growing inequality. Fair Share had an educational focus, producing occasional booklets and a regular newsletter, *Poverty Watch* which appeared for a period in the now defunct *National Outlook* journal. It also held occasional public rallies, and organised a letter of concern about poverty to the prime minister prior to the 1984 federal election. Fair Share finished in December 1995 (Burke, 1995: 282–83).

Another Christian lobby group is the Australian Catholic Social Justice Council, which is an agency of the Australian Catholic Bishops' Conference. Formed in 1987, the council aims to promote Catholic social teaching, and an awareness of the reality and causes of poverty, hunger, oppression and injustice. The council publishes a regular newsletter titled *Justice Trends*, and occasional papers on such issues as unemployment, housing, and social justice (Burke, 1995: 241–43).

An associated lobby group is Catholic Welfare Australia (CWA), formerly known as the Australian Catholic Social Welfare Commission. Formed by the Australian Catholic Bishops' Conference, the CWA has 'a mandate of advocacy, co-ordination, support, research and advice in the field of social welfare'. The CWA seeks to influence public policy debates via active contact with parliamentarians and the media. It publishes a regular newsletter, *Common Wealth*, which considers such issues as taxation, privatisation, citizenship, unemployment, minimum wages and the labour market, housing and Wik (Burke, 1995: 246–47).

A third Catholic lobby group is the Bishops' Committee for Justice, Development and Peace. Formed in place of the controversial Catholic Commission for Justice and Peace, the committee conducted a national inquiry into wealth distribution from 1988 to 1992. The subsequent publication, *Common Wealth for the Common Good*, attracted considerable media and public attention. The study questioned the current distribution of wealth and income in Australia, and recommended a government wealth inquiry with the objective of establishing a fairer society (Catholic Bishops, 1992; Burke, 1995: 243–45).

Uniya, established by the Jesuit Order, is another example. It aims to 'promote justice through competent research, effective action and participation in the life of the Australian community, especially among marginalised people'. Uniya has attempted to influence the national political debate through the holding of public forums on issues such as the White Paper on Employment; unions, churches and social justice; and the Industries Commission's Inquiry into Charitable Organisations (Mendes, 1997b: 148).

Probably the best known Christian welfare lobby group is the

Brotherhood of St Laurence. The Brotherhood was formed in 1930 by Father Tucker, an Anglican Priest, to address the problems of unemployment, homelessness and the inner-city slums during the Depression. In more recent decades, it has played a key role in welfare lobby campaigns around child poverty, social security payments and a fairer taxation system.

The Brotherhood emphasises structural change and a fairer distribution of income in order to promote a socially just society. A number of the its directors and research officers including the future governor-general Peter Hollingworth, Michael Challen, and Alison McClelland have been particularly prominent in national social policy debates (Keen, 1996).

Other Christian welfare agencies such as the Salvation Army, the St Vincent de Paul Society, and Uniting Care Australia have also been increasingly outspoken in calling for action to address the growth of poverty and inequality. All these agencies utilise research based on the demonstrated needs of their service users to influence social policy debates. Some of their recent publications include:

- Catholic Welfare Australia and the Australian Catholic Social Justice Council (2001) used Catholic social teaching to identify five important social issues facing Australians during the 2001 Federal Election
- Salvation Army (2001) condemned the punitive nature of current welfare breaching policies
- St Vincent de Paul Society (2001) called for action to address the widening gap between rich and poor
- Uniting Care Australia (2001) urged the development of a fairer and more equitable social security system
- Brotherhood of St Laurence (2001) called on the incoming Commonwealth Government to work for a fairer future for all Australians
- National Coalition Against Poverty (2001) asked the incoming government to commit to a fairer Australia
- Catholic Social Services Victoria (2001) recommended a review of social policies to give social equity a much higher priority
- Anglicare (2002) urged government to take action to reduce the high rate of child poverty.

In addition, many Christian groups have been active in the National Coalition against Poverty convened by the Victorian Synod of the Uniting Church. However, to date, the Howard Government has ignored its call for the elimination of poverty.

CASE STUDY: THE CHURCHES AND THE CONSUMPTION TAX DEBATE OF 1993

In the lead-up to the 1993 federal election, a number of church bodies attacked the Federal Liberal Party's proposed GST, and the associated *Fightback* Package. The argument with the Liberal Party reflected philosophical differences over the legitimacy of government intervention. *Fightback* particularly emphasised the need to reduce the size and cost of government, to place greater reliance on the free market, and to end unnecessary dependence on government welfare. The churches took issue with all of these concepts.

The most prominent criticism came from the Australian Catholic Social Welfare Commission. In May 1991, the commission released a paper questioning the impact of a GST on low-income earners and families. A follow-up paper released in October 1992 argued that any taxation on food was regressive and unjust, and would contravene Catholic social teaching.

Criticism of the consumption tax was also voiced by the Uniting Church National Assembly. The Uniting Church argued that the tax package and the Liberal Party's proposed tax cuts would benefit the wealthy at the expense of the disadvantaged. In addition, that church criticised the proposed cuts to social security benefits.

The Liberal Party responded to these criticisms by questioning the motives and propriety of its critics. For example, front-bencher Senator Fred Chaney described the Catholic Social Welfare Commission as a 'bunch of shysters'. Yet, the churches refused to relent. Ultimately, the Liberal Party was forced to capitulate to the churches and ACOSS. The Liberal Party leader Dr John Hewson agreed to exempt food from the GST. Hewson referred specifically to the 'intensity of criticism of *Fightback* as being unfair by a range of church leaders and other community leaders' (Mendes, 1997b: 148–49).

POLITICAL ATTACKS ON THE CHURCH

The Christian campaigns on the various incarnations of the GST, and on other social policy issues, have provoked vigorous criticism from political leaders and commentators. There is nothing new about these attacks. Politicians of both Left and Right have long attempted to discredit the legitimacy of church political interventions on social justice issues. They have suggested instead that the churches should stick to providing private spiritual guidance and assistance. On welfare, they have welcomed the involvement of the

churches in the provision of band-aid welfare services, whilst rejecting any criticism of the government policies which create social
problems and inequities in the first place.

A number of historical examples demonstrate this tradition. A
statement in 1972 by the Anglican archbishop of Sydney, expressing concern about growing poverty and unemployment in
Australia, was greeted by Liberal Party Prime Minister William
McMahon with the following comments: 'It is obvious to me that
the Archbishop does not have a great knowledge of the problems
associated with inflation or for that matter unemployment'. A 1979
statement by the Catholic Commission for Justice and Peace criticising the high level of unemployment was attacked in similar terms
by Liberal Party Prime Minister Malcolm Fraser. And a statement in
1990 by the Anglican Archbishop of Brisbane Peter Hollingworth
criticising the ALP Government's record on child poverty prompted the following aside from Prime Minister Hawke: that as prime
minister, he would continue to refrain from 'entering into some dissertation on the mysteries of the Holy Trinity' if the archbishop
would 'show a similar reluctance before entering into a dissertation
on the mysteries of the unholy trinity of economic policy — monetary policy, fiscal policy and wages policy'.

The church campaign against the GST provoked allegations
from Liberal politicians that the Australian Catholic Social Welfare
Commission was motivated by leftist political views rather than
those of Christianity. The deputy leader of the Liberal Party,
Senator Fred Chaney, argued that 'criticism of Opposition policy
had come from small left-wing social policy units within the churches and did not represent the views of the churches as a whole'.
Similar allegations of political bias were levelled against the churches by Liberal-National Party politicians during the 1996 federal
election campaign.

The former Victorian Liberal Premier Jeff Kennett continued this
tradition of slamming the church messenger, instead of addressing the
substance of the message. Kennett consistently denied the legitimacy
of church involvement in political matters, condemning the alleged
'use of the pulpit for political purposes'. According to Kennett,
churches should stick to their primary purpose which is spiritual uplift-
ing, and stay out of the political arena (Mendes, 1997b: 151–52).

THE NEW RIGHT AND THE CHURCHES

Church political interventions have also provoked criticism from
the New Right — the group of free marketeers based in the
media, academia and corporate-funded think-tanks — who favour

a significant retrenchment of the welfare state. As we noted in Chapter 2, neoliberals strongly oppose the arguments propounded by the churches for increased government intervention and welfare spending. They also contest the legitimacy of church involvement in social policy debates. Utilising public choice theory, neoliberals argue that church involvement in political advocacy reflects a self-interested concern to protect its own institutions, rather than a genuine desire to advance the interests of the poor and disadvantaged (Johns, 2000: 13).

Some elements within the New Right, however, also favour socially conservative agendas promoted by sections of the church, such as preservation of family values and opposition to single parenthood, homosexuality, abortion and euthanasia. Their argument (highly artificial and contentious) appears to be that the church has a right to intervene on these matters because they are central to private faith and morality, rather than involving broader public policy issues (Mendes, 1997b: 152).

Neoliberal critiques also have some history. The joint statement by the Catholic, Anglican and Uniting Churches of 1983, titled *Changing Australia*, which advocated a fairer distribution of national wealth and income, provoked a furious response from the free-market think-tank, the CIS. The CIS organised seminars in Sydney and Melbourne attacking the statement, and also published a book titled *Chaining Australia: Church Bureaucracies and Political Economy* (Brennan and Williams, 1984).

More recently, the CIS has established a 'Religion and the free society' program in an attempt to combat left-wing influences within Australian churches. This program mirrors similar pro-business programs established by neoliberal think-tanks in the United States to combat Christian social justice teachings (Duncan, 2000: 18).

The CIS program offers moral arguments for the free market, and criticises the views of Church justice groups including 'their hostility to the market, a tendency to demonise major corporations, endless demands for government regulation, as well as a profound ignorance of economics'. In August 1999, Catholic Archbishop George Pell presented the first Acton Lecture for the CIS on the topic of 'Religion and Liberty'. The CIS has also published two books by the program's former director, Samuel Gregg (1999a; 1999b).

CORRESPONDING ARGUMENTS IN FAVOUR OF CHURCH SOCIAL JUSTICE ACTIVISM

The churches have advanced a number of arguments in favour of their social policy interventions:

- They contest the notion that churches should restrict their interventions to the private realm. They insist that there is no legal or theological restriction to religious bodies participating in public debates on which they have some interest or expertise. Churches represent a considerable cross-section of the community and are as entitled as any other community group to express their opinion.
- They do not accept that Christianity is limited to personal, private salvation. They believe that churches must act on and attempt to implement the social teachings of Christianity if they are to remain relevant to contemporary society. Social justice activists reject as hypercritical the notion that they should restrict their interventions to matters of personal morality such as abortion and homosexuality. They believe that Christian teachings are equally applicable to issues such as poverty and unemployment.
- Churches reject the narrow concept of democracy free of the influence of interest groups, as advanced by public choice theorists. For a start, churches do not restrict their social justice interventions to lobbying for changes in government policies. They also provide direct services to those in need.

Churches are the principal providers of non-government welfare services which contribute more than half of all welfare services in Australia (Lyons, 2001: 34–35). Consequently, the churches believe they are as well placed as any group to assess and critique the impact of government policies on poor and disadvantaged Australians (Mendes, 1997b: 153–54).

CHURCHES AND THE JOBS NETWORK

The introduction of compulsory competitive tendering by state and Federal governments in recent years has posed a challenge to the church's dual role of service provider and advocate. As we noted in Chapter 2, one of the principal aims of the tendering process is to exclude welfare providers and lobby groups from policy-making processes. The new privatised Jobs Network exemplifies this dilemma.

The Jobs Network was introduced by the Coalition Government in May 1998. It consists of about 300 private, community and government organisations which have successfully competed for the right to provide government-funded employment placement services. Many of the contracted agencies are Christian-based, including most noticeably the Salvation Army's Employment Plus which holds contracts worth millions of dollars.

The prominence of Christian-based providers in the Jobs Network has provoked two related controversies. Firstly, concern has been expressed that Christian agencies may discriminate against jobseekers who are not practising Christians. This concern prompted the intervention of the Human Rights and Equal Opportunity Commission which drafted guidelines pertaining to freedom of religion and belief (HREOC, 2000). Christian agencies have generally responded by emphasising their commitment to dispassionately serving all disadvantaged people without discrimination. However, suspicion remains that some agencies may display judgemental attitudes either towards particular jobseekers, or alternatively towards particular forms of employment.

A second concern is that the social justice values of many Christian agencies may be undermined by their obligation under contractual arrangements to 'breach' jobseekers who are failing to meet the requirements of mutual obligation. Herein lies a potential tension between performing business contracts on behalf of government, and remaining an effective advocate for the poor and unemployed (Preece, 2002: 43).

Many Christian agencies claim to manage this tension by administering the system in a particularly fair and compassionate manner. In addition, the largest agencies such as the Salvation Army and Mission Australia were amongst the sponsors of a recent independent review of social security breaches and penalties (Pearce et al, 2002). However, the suspicion remains that some agencies will find themselves compromised by their dual roles. For example, Christian agencies administering contracted work for the dole schemes may find their criticisms of the notion of mutual obligation increasingly muted.

INTERNAL CRITICISM OF CHURCH SOCIAL JUSTICE ACTIVISM

One of the most persistent arguments made against church social justice activism is that its adherents may not accurately represent church opinion. This possibility is acknowledged by Father David Cappo, the former national director of the Australian Catholic Social Welfare Commission. According to Cappo:

Social activist lobbying ... can be identified most noticeably in the social welfare and social justice structures of the mainstream churches, some parishes and other church organizations. Yet, even these structures are subject to a mixture of support, suspicion and/or rejection by those within. (Cappo, 1994: 3)

Cappo's admission reflects the reality that much of the strongest criticism of Christian social justice activism comes from economic and social conservatives within the church. For example, two Uniting Church ministers — Warren Clarnette and John Williams — have consistently argued that Christian social teachings are more akin to the economic rationalist agenda than to that of social justice (Williams, 1988; Clarnette, 1993).

Conservative Christian individuals and organisations such as the National Civic Council and the Galatians Group have regularly contested the right of the social justice bodies to speak on behalf of the church. The termination by the Catholic Bishops of the Catholic Commission for Justice and Peace in 1987 was due as much to its loss of support from within the church as to criticism from outside (Hogan, 1987: 267).

In my opinion, the divisions within the church on social justice activism reflect different theologies of church and the meaning of 'mission'. As Simons has noted, Christian social teaching contains a number of problematic elements including:

> a confusing openness to contradictory interpretations; an apparent lack of consistency between the principles of the Church's social teachings and the principles which appear to guide its internal governance; the absence of a modern theory of society; and its tendency to resort acritically to religious language and theological concepts. (Simons, 1995: 116)

Both the Catholic social justice activist Chris Sidoti and the former Liberal politician Fred Chaney can agree, for example, that there is no strict or rigid Christian position on contemporary issues such as poverty and inequality. This is why Sidoti can advocate redistribution of wealth as a Christian solution to poverty, whilst Chaney is opposed. Internationally, there is an enormous divergence within Catholic social teaching between Michael Novak who endorses neoliberal economics, and liberation theologists such as Paulo Freire and Donald Dorr who mount a socialist critique of the marketplace.

This ambivalence was expressed, for example, in the 1995 public struggle for control of the Catholic charity, St Vincent de Paul. The incumbent president (Brian Murnane) and his supporters argued that Christians had a duty to advocate political and structural changes that would reduce poverty and inequality, rather than just providing charitable hand-outs. Murnane's critics, including the National Civic Council, argued, in contrast, that St Vincent de Paul should restrict its activities to charitable care for the poor and homeless rather than undertaking political actions that would divide its membership. The secessionists won out, Murnane's broader agenda being rejected by a majority of St Vincent de Paul members (Mendes, 1997b: 155–56).

Similarly during the 1998 federal election campaign, a number of church groups publicly opposed a GST. However, some of the impact of this campaign was muted by the Melbourne Archbishop George Pell who commented that 'there was no one Catholic position on something as complex as taxation' (Warhurst et al, 2000: 172).

More recently, a pronouncement by a section of the Anglican Church on the distribution of work and wealth was marked by serious ideological divisions. On the one hand, the General Synod Task Force employed Dr Samuel Gregg from the CIS to undertake research for the document. The final report, which appears to have been strongly influenced by Gregg's initial draft, argues in favour of wealth creation, private property, incentive-based taxation, and merit-based rewards. However, a minority report published in the final document criticises the main report for ignoring the implications of Christian social teachings regarding social and economic equity (Anglican Church, 2001).

None of this division means that Christian social justice activists should not attempt to apply Christian social teachings to contemporary social justice issues. Whilst there is no policy blueprint, Christian teachings do offer a guide to social change based on values and principles of peace, justice and compassion. For example, they suggest distinctive perspectives on contentious issues such as welfare reform (Massaro, 1998: 151–67; 2000: 197–201). In addition, the prominent Christian welfare lobby groups referred to earlier are officially endorsed by the church hierarchies, and almost certainly represent a significant proportion of church members.

Nevertheless, the ambivalence of much Christian teaching suggests that individual Christians influenced by different interpretations of the theological mission will continue to identify different solutions to problems such as poverty and inequality (Chaney, 1999: 210–11; Preece, 2002: 43). This is something that Christian social justice activists need to keep in mind when they claim a Christian mandate for their particular policy agendas.

CONCLUSION

Churches have long made a significant contribution to the Australian welfare system both as service providers and social justice lobbyists. This contribution has been magnified in recent years with the emergence of some Christian agencies as major providers of government-tendered employment and training services. This has also led to an increasing community perception that the churches face a potential conflict of interest between their business and advocacy activities.

Historically, the independence of the churches has been fundamental to their effectiveness as advocates of social justice. This has included both ideological independence in terms of commitment to core theological teachings rather than contemporary political dogma, and structural independence in terms of avoiding co-option by government agendas. The danger for some Christian agencies is that their involvement in government-funded business operations will progressively undermine their independence, including particularly their commitment to exploring alternative policy agendas and directions based on Christian teachings (Cleary, 2001).

Questions for consideration

1 Discuss the relationship between Christian social teaching and contemporary social welfare policies. Is there a specifically Christian view on issues such as poverty and wealth distribution?
2 Why do churches continue to have a significant influence on social policy debates?
3 Do Christian welfare agencies and lobby groups have a vested interest in the outcome of social policy debates?

10

THE POLITICAL POWERLESSNESS OF THE UNEMPLOYED

According to official statistics, there were 694 000 unemployed Australians in January 2002 making an unemployment rate of 6.3 per cent. This figure included 385 000 people who had been on unemployment payments for over 12 months. The unemployed easily comprise the largest group of workforce age Australians receiving income security payments — 31 per cent in 1998 (Newman, 1999: 4–5). Some commentators argue that the real unemployment figure is far higher. For example, the above figure excludes at least another 514 000 people who wanted work but had given up seeking work, and at least another 188 000 people who worked less than 16 hours per week but would like to secure full-time employment. This suggests that the true unemployment figure is about 1.4 million people (ACOSS, 2001c: 1).

The contemporary unemployed are a highly diverse group. Unemployment rates are particularly high for young people aged 15–19 years, older males aged 55–64 years, people with disabilities, Aboriginal and Torres Strait Islanders, female-headed sole-parent families, and migrants with low English-language proficiency (ACOSS, 2002: 22–23). Unemployment also varies with location. Some rural and regional centres have suffered disproportionately from the decline in manufacturing industry.

In addition, the proportion of the labour force employed part-time has increased from 10 per cent in 1970 to 25 per cent in 1997, with the vast majority being either young people or married women. Most of these part-time jobs are low-paid and casual positions, with no security and no entitlements such as sick or annual leave

(Gregory and Sheehan, 1998: 109–110; Jamrozik, 2001: 131–47).

Proposed solutions to unemployment vary according to political and ideological perspectives. Neoliberals tend to favour 'fight inflation first' policies, and greater labour market flexibility including wage cuts and tighter access to welfare payments. In contrast, social democrats prefer economic growth, redistribution of work opportunities, and publicly funded job creation. Overall, recent Australian governments from both sides of politics have tended to approximate the neoliberal model with the major emphasis on preparing the individual unemployed for work, rather than providing full employment (Watts, 2000b; Bell, 2001).

Yet surprisingly, the high unemployment of the last two decades appears to have provoked little political activism on the part of the unemployed. This chapter attempts to explain the factors contributing to the recent political acquiescence of the unemployed.

Attention is drawn firstly to the changes in the nature and distribution of work in an attempt to explain the relative decline in protest activities. Secondly, emphasis is placed on the research of British sociologist Paul Bagguley, who argues that the absence of effective political protest can be attributed to the centralised control of income maintenance, and to the lack of requisite organisational and cultural resources for mobilisation.

In addition, we consider the traditional laborism of the Australian labor movement which has tended to marginalise those who are not in the workforce; the failure of welfare lobby groups to politically mobilise the unemployed; and the subtle social control mechanisms used by recent Australian Governments to discourage political action.

HISTORICAL BACKGROUND

Both the political Left and Right have traditionally assumed that high unemployment would provoke mass support for radical and revolutionary movements. As noted by Jill Roe, since the 1790s, the Right has feared the radical 'mob', and regarded the unemployed as a threat to public order. Similarly, the Left saw mass unemployment as proof of the long-awaited breakdown of capitalism, a portent of 'the coming struggle for power' (Roe, 1985: 46).

Three particular factors were seen as likely to contribute to political activism amongst the unemployed. The first was that the unemployed were left (prior to the introduction of a uniform national system of unemployment benefits) with little if any money to pay for their basic needs and those of their family. The second was that compared to the paid workforce, the unemployed generally had plenty of free time to spare to participate in political activities. The third factor was the likely development of a sense of group solidarity among the unemployed — particularly amongst single, unmarried males based in one geographical area (Croucher, 1987: 20–21).

Some of these assumptions about political protest were confirmed during the Great Depression of the 1930s when collective movements of the unemployed were active in wrenching political concessions from the state. Perhaps the most effective protest group was the British National Unemployed Workers' Movement which operated from 1920 to 1940. Under the leadership of the Communist Party, the movement used a variety of methods including national hunger marches and local demonstrations to force more adequate forms of unemployment relief. Similarly in the United States, a large unemployed workers' movement formed under the auspices of the Workers' Alliance of America to demand more generous unemployment relief (Hannington, 1936; Piven and Cloward, 1982: 48–92).

In Australia, the Unemployed Workers' Movement — strongly influenced by the Communist Party — organised demonstrations to demand adequate unemployment relief, defend free speech, and prevent the eviction of tenants. By 1934, the Australian movement claimed around 68 000 members in the eastern states. Some authors argue that the protest movements succeeded in forcing significant concessions from both hostile and apathetic governments. However, others disagree, maintaining that the unemployed workers of the Depression were dispirited and disorganised, making few attempts to disrupt the existing system (Mendes, 1999a: 45; Fox, 2000: 8–9).

Certainly, unemployed movements faced severe obstacles, such as:

- the indifference of much of the trade union movement. As we noted in Chapter 8, the union movement generally made little attempt to organise the unemployed or to lobby on their behalf for adequate unemployment relief. According to historian LJ Louis, unemployed workers quickly became isolated from the mainstream union movement (1968: 157–59).
- the psychological impact of unemployment which left many individual workers isolated and demoralised
- the inability of the politically powerless unemployed to initiate economic sanctions such as strikes to win their demands
- political violence and political repression including regular police surveillance and harassment (Mendes, 1999a: 45).

CONTEMPORARY UNEMPLOYED ACTIVISM

Most developed countries including Australia have experienced high levels of unemployment since the mid-1970s. This appears to reflect the influence of neoliberal orthodoxy on government macroeconomic policy, and particularly the abandonment of any commitment to full employment in favour of balanced budgets and low inflation (Grieve Smith, 1997). Yet, political protest by the unemployed has been sporadic and marginal.

There has been some significant local exceptions. In the mid-1970s, a viable and militant Victorian Unemployed Workers' Union (UWU) emerged and existed in varying manifestations until approximately 1990. The broad aims of the UWU (1991) were 'to unite the unemployed and to defend and to extend their rights, and to organise and politicise the unemployed as to the nature of unemployment and the capitalist system'. More specific objectives were:

- to secure either full-time employment or a full wage for the unemployed
- to oppose temporary job creation and training schemes
- to end intimidation and harassment of the unemployed by field officers
- to secure independent benefit status for unemployed women involved in de facto relationships
- to attain free public transport for all the unemployed
- to attain better conditions for unemployed workers at Commonwealth Employment Service (CES) and DSS offices. (UWU, 1982–89)

Activities taken to pursue these objectives included the publication of regular bulletins and newsletters; production of a weekly program on community radio station 3CR; publication of leaflets and booklets defending the rights of the unemployed; establishment of a Job Watch Project to expose exploitative employment and training schemes; and the establishment of a Women Against Social Security Injustice group to protest the jailing of beneficiaries for alleged welfare fraud.

In addition, the UWU undertook various forms of direct action including leafleting and street theatre inside CES and DSS offices; and public demonstrations such as annual Unemployed Days, Right to Work campaigns, and occupations of the elitist Melbourne Club and the Victorian ALP headquarters. Some activities were also taken in conjunction with the Coalition Against Poverty and Unemployment, a broad coalition of poor, unemployed, welfare organisations, trade unions and community groups (Mendes, 1999: 45–46; Fox, 2000: 35–43).

Similar unemployed worker groups were formed in Victorian provincial cities such as Shepparton and Ballarat, and in other major cities such as Hobart, Launceston, Newcastle, Wollongong, Canberra, Adelaide, Brisbane, Darwin, Perth and Sydney. Overall, somewhere between 30 and 100 unemployed workers groups appear to have existed in the late 1970s.

Some groups secured considerable support from local trade unions. One of the most prominent was the Wollongong Out of Workers' Union which sponsored a popular 'march for jobs' to Sydney. In addition, a National Union of Unemployed People was formed in the mid-1980s (Tomlinson, 1982: 107–108, 134–36; Lowenstein, 1997: 130–39).

To what extent were these unemployed workers' groups successful in their endeavours? The question does not yield an easy answer. On the one hand, government concessions appear to have been minimal. At least in Victoria, the UWU succeeded in forcing the Victorian Government to provide free travel on public transport for people going to seek work, and to provide public toilets in CES and DSS offices. Squatters also sometimes won the right to reside in unused housing. However, most of the key objectives of unemployed groups were not achieved (Mendes, 1999a: 46).

In addition, most of the groups appear to have attracted only a small membership. For example, Alec Pemberton estimated in 1980 that no unemployed group had been able to attract even 1 per cent of the unemployed in its area to membership (1980: 75). Similarly, Rodney Smith found that only 3 per cent of the young Sydney unemployed regularly attended unemployed organisations (1995: 156).

Some of the factors that may have contributed to this minimal support included the militant left-wing ideology of most groups, their involvement in highly confrontational direct action activities sometimes bordering on the dangerous or illegal, and the decline in trade union support following the election of the Hawke Labor Government in 1983.

On the other hand, activist groups almost certainly contributed to publicising and politicising the plight of the unemployed amongst trade unions, bureaucrats, politicians and the general public. In the absence of any systematic research, however, it is difficult to judge whether their activities exerted any influence on policy debates or government policy-making. It would appear that the overwhelming majority of unemployed Australians did not participate in protest activities (Mendes, 1999a: 46).

Today, four unemployed groups exist in Melbourne. They are

the Victorian Unemployed Workers' Coalition, the Oakleigh Unemployed Action Group, the Victorian Social Justice Council, and the Brunswick Unemployed Workers' Group. These groups have campaigned against recent government policies such as the work for the dole scheme, the Common Youth Allowance, and the 'dole diary'. They appear to be less politically militant than earlier groups, and to be more concerned with developing a sense of social solidarity amongst and support services for the unemployed within local communities.

A newer group called the Dole Army recently gained notoriety through perpetrating a hoax on two Melbourne TV current affairs shows. The group, which is linked to radical anti-globalisation protest groups, pretended to be living in suburban drains and hunting in bins for food. In addition, the Unemployed People's Embassy continues in Sydney, whilst a number of unemployed groups exist in country and regional areas such as the Illawarra (Mendes, 1999a: 46).

Most prominent at a national level is the Brisbane-based Australian National Organisation for the Unemployed (ANOU) headed by Kevin Brennan and Ron Baker. The ANOU describes its mission as 'unemployed people speaking for themselves and fighting for their rights'. It aims to mobilise the unemployed as a collective group to participate in social welfare debates. In particular, it hopes to emulate the success of the Irish National Organisation of the Unemployed in gaining formal government recognition as a key stakeholder in unemployment policy (Botsman, 2001).

The ANOU is currently unfunded, and staffed by unpaid volunteers. However, some logistical assistance has been provided by ACOSS, the Queensland Trades Hall Council and the Brisbane Institute think-tank. The ANOU has created an excellent website, and begun to develop a media profile. However, neither state or Federal governments appear as yet to have included the ANOU in any of their consultation or decision-making processes (Brennan, 2000a; 2000b). Noticeably, none of the contemporary Australian groups appear to have employed public protests.

Internationally, there appears to be a similar story of sporadic militancy and protest. In Britain, for example, there were large 'right to work' marches in the 1970s and 1980s. There were also unemployment centres created by the trade unions to provide support services to the unemployed. Similarly, the 1980s featured large protests by the unemployed and homeless in the United States (Imig, 1996). However, there has been no influential mass movement of the unemployed similar to that of the 1930s.

More recently, large movements of the unemployed have formed in France, Germany and other European countries to demand more adequate payment levels. Many of these movements appear to receive significant support from local trade unions, and have engaged in some formal negotiations with government. For example, a 1997–98 campaign by the French unemployed movement, including occupations of Assedic offices — the French equivalent of Centrelink — led to increases in social security payments. Similarly, a 1998 national campaign by the German unemployed featured large protest marches against proposed cuts to welfare payments (Gager, 1998: 49; Klein, 1998).

In addition, a major campaign by the unemployed in Argentina featured large road blockades organised primarily at the local level. Demonstrators demanded state-funded jobs administered by local unemployed workers' associations, food parcels and job creation. Similar movements have also emerged in other Latin American countries such as Bolivia, Colombia, Brazil and Paraquay, and in South Korea (Petras, 2002; Ranald, 2002: 200–201).

WHY THE ACQUIESCENCE?

The first explanation for the lack of widespread political activism is that the contemporary labour market is radically different to that of the 1930s. In particular, the earlier was based around the concept of gendered full-time employment where the husband served as the breadwinner, and the wife acted as the housewife and the mother (Giddens, 1998: 16). In contrast, the contemporary labour market is based more and more on the casualisation of labour where mixed gender groups compete for a mixture of insecure and often short-term, full-time, part-time and casual employment.

The changing dynamics of the workforce have arguably influenced the ideology and politics of the unemployed in two particular ways. First, there appears to be less unity and cohesion between the increasingly heterogeneous groups of workers both inside and outside of the workforce. Consequently, there is less likelihood of mass political action (Solas, 2000: 29).

Second, the high level of youth unemployment has combined with a generational change in attitudes to the work ethic so that many young people now expect to be unemployed, and do not view this as a particularly stressful or traumatic outcome. In fact, as noted by Lackner (1998), some young people choose not to engage in paid work. Consequently, many unemployed people do not consider unemployment per se to be an issue worthy of political protest.

However, an arguably more effective and comprehensive explanation is presented by the British sociologist Paul Bagguley (1991). He argues that the recent political acquiescence of the unemployed, compared to the mass protest movements of the 1930s, can be explained by a number of key variables.

The first is the changing form of the state's income maintenance system, which favours centralised (typically middle-class) pressure groups. In the 1930s, the existence of democratically organised local decision-making over the forms and levels of unemployment relief provided a clear and accessible target for collective protest. In contrast, today's income maintenance systems are centralised and bureaucratic, essentially shielding them from the impact of collective action by the unemployed. For example, it is hard to imagine a protest at one regional Centrelink office exerting any impact on the level of income security payments.

In addition, effective protest requires particular kinds of cultural resources based on high levels of working-class solidarity, and a belief in the efficacy of participation in collective action (Bagguley, 1991: 3–4, 203). However, the close-knit working-class communities that spawned local protest activities in the 1930s are long gone. Many of the unemployed today have little experience of employment, and hence little experience of the role played by the wider labour movement in supporting struggles of the poor and disadvantaged (Burgmann, 2000: 8).

As already noted, the contemporary unemployed are characterised more by their diversity than by a shared or homogeneous set of values and experiences. For example, a group of long-term unemployed at one Centrelink office could potentially include:

- persons from 50 different ethnic backgrounds including many with minimal English language skills
- age groups from 17 to 65 years
- those with widely ranging employment histories, from those who have never worked to those who were retrenched from one job after 40 years
- residents of comfortably middle-class areas alongside long-term residents of Housing Commission estates
- married men with large dependent families, and single women with no children.

According to May (2001: 264), such diverse groups are unlikely to collectively identify with each other in terms of their poor or unemployed status. Rather, they are more likely to form groups based on commonalities of gender, ethnicity, age, disability or Aboriginality.

Other factors include:

- the absence of a political group or party similar to the Communist Party that is able to take a central organisational role in politicising the unemployed (Bagguley, 1991: 103, 140)
- the associated individualisation of unemployment whereby most of the unemployed hope to escape their situation by individually finding work, rather than improve the situation of the unemployed by collective action (Ashton, 1986: 160; Bauman, 1998: 93)
- the continued reluctance of most trade unions, which are potentially the key allies of protest movements, to provide organisational resources and/or political support to unemployed people. As we noted in Chapter 8, the ACTU has largely been a passive observer of recent social welfare policy debates.
- overt political repression and control. Freeland notes, for example, the action taken by the Federal Government to end attempts by Community Youth Support Schemes in New South Wales to organise a collective voice for the unemployed (Freeland, 1992: 170). Similarly, there was action taken by the Northcote City Council in Melbourne to physically demolish the headquarters of the Victorian UWU.
- subtle state control of the unemployed through the provision of unemployment benefits, and the imposition of compulsory training schemes such as work for the dole. Populist attacks on the unemployed such as the Paxton family saga referred to in Chapter 8, and the 'dob in a dole bludger' hotline further emphasise to the unemployed that their behaviour is under surveillance. Most of the unemployed are not willing to place their inadequate (but 'sufficiency-level') unemployment payments at risk in order to take political action (Fox, 2000: 29; May, 2001: 263).
- the particular unpopularity of the unemployed in Australia. Numerous surveys have found the unemployed to be the least popular group among welfare recipients. Most Australians think that the unemployed are at least partly to blame for their own predicament. Only a minority of Australians favour greater public spending on the unemployed (Smith, 1993: 44–46; Eardley and Matheson, 1999).

In addition there is the failure of ACOSS and the welfare lobby to seriously support or assist the establishment of a national unemployed group similar to groups for other income security recipients (Mendes, 1996: 278–79, 540). Disability groups and single mothers are effectively represented within the ACOSS structure, but not the unemployed. Whilst this may be no easy task due to the transient nature of unemployment, unemployed groups have reasonably questioned ACOSS's right to speak on behalf of the unemployed.

To be fair, ACOSS has recently begun to actively assist local unemployed workers' groups in a number of rural and urban areas, and has declared that the 'voices of unemployed people should be heard by the community, business, unions and government' (Kusuma, 1998). Some state Councils of Social Service have also resourced unemployed workers networks (McCormack, 2001). ACOSS could further empower the unemployed by ensuring that they have a representative on the ACOSS board, and are guaranteed regular input into ACOSS deliberations on unemployment.

None of this criticism is meant to detract from ACOSS's forceful advocacy on behalf of the unemployed, including its recent campaign to end the massive increase in social security breaches (ACOSS, 2001b). However, this does not diminish ACOSS's responsibility to facilitate collective action by the unemployed themselves.

CONCLUSION

The factors noted by Bagguley (1991: 203) are likely to preclude the emergence of mass unemployed protest movements akin to those of the 1930s. Unemployed political activism seems to have declined rather than increased in the last decade. Newly introduced mutual obligation measures have provoked only minor protest.

Nevertheless, as long-term unemployment continues to rise, and becomes for many a way of life rather than a stigmatised and short-term condition, it is possible that unemployed groups will become louder and more effective in their collective protest. Demands are likely to focus on increased employment and training opportunities, on some direct representation of the unemployed in policy- and decision-making, and on a guaranteed minimum income for those unable to work. Closer links may also be formed with related consumer groups such as the Council of Single Mothers and their Children which have been effective contributors to social policy debates. As we note in Chapter 11, an effective unemployed voice could make a significant contribution to campaigns against welfare retrenchment.

At least locally, much will arguably depend on the willingness of the welfare lobby and trade unions to provide the resources necessary to organise protest activities, and to engage the diverse groups currently excluded from the workforce.

Questions for consideration

1 Compare the responses of workers in the 1930s and today to long-term unemployment.
2 Consider some of the means by which trade unions and/or ACOSS could seek to mobilise the unemployed. What potential role might employees of Centrelink, including social workers, play in such a strategy?
3 What might be the political response of the Federal Coalition Government to a militant unemployed workers movement?

Exercise

Australian governments currently consult with a range of consumer groups, but explicitly exclude representatives of the unemployed from policy and decision-making processes. What political changes would be required to facilitate the collective political representation of welfare consumers?

11

THE FUTURE OF THE AUSTRALIAN WELFARE STATE

This book has examined the role of key socio-economic players and their respective ideologies in the political struggles around the Australian welfare state. Here, we attempt to draw a concluding assessment of the local and international political factors and forces which are contributing towards or against welfare retrenchment — the reduction or abolition of state-funded welfare services and programs. In analysing the political transition of welfare states, we do not assume that retrenchment occurs in uniform fashion across all welfare states. Rather as noted in Chapter 3, we believe that changes to welfare states reflect different processes of adaptation among welfare states.

The first section below explores the factors contributing to welfare retrenchment, including the absence of political alternatives to neoliberalism and the increasing financial pressures on welfare states. Consideration is also given to specific political influences such as neoliberal lobby groups, the dominance of neoliberal ideas within the major political parties, and the impact of global social policy actors. The next section considers some of the factors limiting welfare retrenchment, including the strength of public opinion, the impact of lobby groups, and the growth of international campaigns against corporate globalisation.

FACTORS CONTRIBUTING TO WELFARE RETRENCHMENT

Probably the strongest factor contributing to retrenchment is the absence of a viable alternative model or strategy for managing the economy and distributing social benefits. As noted by Mishra (1999), the collapse of communism and the decline of social democracy has removed any political challenge to the domination of free-market ideas. Capitalist systems no longer fear potential revolutionary threats from labour movements or the disadvantaged. Consequently, governments have far less political incentive to address questions of social injustice.

In addition, global economic pressures, including particularly the enhanced power of financial markets, appear to have increased the policy constraints on national governments. Although, as we have argued, governments are not powerless and continue to have a range of political choices, many social democratic and laborist governments seem to lack the political will to adequately fund the welfare state. Few governments, particularly in Anglo-Saxon countries, seem willing to challenge the dominant neoliberal discourse. Little attempt is being made to challenge the associated massive increase in social and economic inequality and exclusion.

A further factor is the considerable resources available to free-market lobby groups, and their strong influence on key opinion-makers in the public service, media and political parties. For example, local commentator Fred Argy (1998: 230) has documented the strengthening alliance between business, finance and the policy elites (senior politicians, ministers, minders and bureaucrats) in favour of economic rationalist ideas.

The concentrated ownership of the mass media has clearly assisted the dominant neoliberal agenda. Many leading journalists are vigorous advocates of welfare retrenchment. They include Alan Wood, economics editor of the *Australian*, Andrew Bolt and Paul Gray from the *Herald Sun*, Paddy McGuiness from the *Sydney Morning Herald*, Christopher Pearson from *The Age*, and Piers Akerman from the *Daily Telegraph*. In addition, the leading Australian newspapers give considerable space to the representatives of the neoliberal think-tanks, and their prescriptions for radical change in the welfare system. Journalists committed to alternative positions such as Mike Steketee and Phillip Adams of the *Australian*, and Pamela Bone and Ken Davidson of *The Age*, appear to be far less influential.

The ruling Federal Liberal Party seems to be dominated by neoliberal ideas at both the parliamentary and organisational level. The party's think-tank, the Menzies Resource Centre, is vigorously critical of the welfare state and welfare spending. The parliamentary Liberal Party and the Centre enjoy co-operative relationships with the leading neoliberal think-tanks such as the CIS. There is almost a total exclusion of social liberal perspectives favouring a role for the state in both intervening in the free market and protecting the poor.

Nevertheless, the naturally cautious Prime Minister Howard remains highly sensitive to public opinion. Earlier backdowns on minimum wages and the proposed extension of mutual obligation principles to the disabled suggest that he is likely to withdraw radical reforms when confronted with poll-based evidence of their unpopularity (Mendes, 2000a: 109–110; Wilson and Turnbull, 2001: 397).

The ALP seems unwilling to challenge the dominant neoliberal discourse. On key debates such as work for the dole and welfare reform, the ALP has supported (albeit reluctantly) Liberal Party policies for fear of losing public support. Only one Opposition front-bencher, Dr Carmen Lawrence, has been willing to oppose the consensus in favour of mutual obligation (Lawrence, 2000). In contrast, another influential front-bencher, Mark Latham, wishes to extend the ALP's support for mutual obligation. At best, the ALP can be described as favouring what Boris Frankel calls 'economic rationalism with a human face' (Frankel, 2001: 32).

Internationally, organisations such as the IMF and the OECD remain key influences in favour of neoliberal agendas of expenditure reduction, and deregulation of the labour market. Their views were clearly reflected in the Maastricht Treaty requirement to limit government borrowing in the period leading up to European Monetary Union which explicitly mitigated against social protectionist policies. In contrast, there are no corresponding global organisations which represent non-corporate interests and argue for different policy agendas.

Locally, both Liberal-National and ALP Australian governments remain keen to be seen as conforming to the prescriptions of the IMF, OECD, and international credit rating agencies for fiscal responsibility. Once accepted, these prescriptions in turn greatly limit the capacity of governments to interfere with the free market in order to reduce social and economic inequities.

Policy-makers are also influenced by the political and economic policies of some of Australia's major regional trading partners in East Asia, and their far lower levels of social expenditure (Frankel, 2001: 76).

FACTORS AGAINST WELFARE STATE CONTRACTION

One important restraint on the contraction of the welfare state is that national and international pressure groups continue to have some success in policy debates. For example, trade unions (particularly in Belgium, France, Italy and Germany) continue to play an important role in blocking substantial welfare retrenchment (Mishra, 1999: 59–61; Hinrichs, 2001: 172–73).

In addition, many individual welfare programs enjoy the support of large constituencies. Welfare consumers and service providers are influential defenders of the welfare state. In the United States, for example, the Association of Retired People has a membership of 28 million people. Not surprisingly, lobby groups for the aged have been highly effective in defending social security pensions. Governments engaged in welfare retrenchment may experience considerable electoral backlash (Pierson, 1996: 146; Mishra, 1999: 65–67).

However, as Pierson (1994) notes, governments can take action to reduce the impact of such groups by withdrawing funding from public interest organisations, and reducing the strength of unions. The cohesive industrial working class which provided significant support for the welfare state appears to be seriously weakened. Taylor-Gooby (2001a: 177) suggests that there are now far fewer ideological and political barriers to welfare retrenchment.

There is also evidence that some countries are doing far better than others in terms of reducing inequality, and promoting the inclusion of the poor in mainstream social and economic structures. As we noted in Chapter 4, the Netherlands have enjoyed considerable success in pursuing both social and economic goals. Other European countries have also managed to achieve employment rates similar to those of the much-praised United States without commensurate increases in poverty and inequality. These outcomes suggest that neoliberal policies do not provide the only path to national competitiveness in the global economy, and that Australia could benefit from following European social policies rather than those of the under-performing Britain and United States.

A further factor is public opinion. Consistent surveys in OECD countries reveal public support for government intervention funded by existing or even higher levels of taxation to create employment and retain social programs and benefits (Hirst and Thompson, 1999: 173–74; Mishra, 1999: 57–59). Such support has led to the election of social democratic governments in some European countries including Germany and Britain, and in New Zealand and most Australian states, although there has been a number of recent electoral reverses particularly in Europe. Nevertheless, the problem remains that electoral politics and party competition hardly matter anymore. Parties of both the Left and Right appear to be following a similar neoliberal political agenda. Those differences that exist appear to be cross-national, rather than party political (Mishra, 1999: 54–56).

The failure of many social democratic parties (particularly in the Anglo-Saxon world) to implement social democratic policies increasingly seems to transform public altruism into cynicism. For example, British attitudes to the poor and public spending appear to have significantly hardened since the election of the Blair Labour Government (Wilby, 2001). Confronted by evidence that social democratic policies to reduce poverty or inequality either no longer work or are not allowed to work, the middle classes increasingly appear to focus on maximising their personal rewards and aspirations (Emy, 2001: 9).

It will be interesting to see, therefore, how the British public responds to the tax rises announced in that county's April 2002 budget. The rises are linked to a promise to rebuild public services and particularly the under-funded National Health Service. The crucial question is whether voters will welcome or reject the underlying rationale that such a high standard of public services cannot be funded by low neoliberal tax rates.

There is also evidence of a distinction between universalistic health and education services which remain popular, and income support programs targeted specifically to the poor which are less so. For example, the broad Dutch welfare system appears to retain considerable public support based on perceived self-interest, whereas this factor may be less significant for residual welfare systems (van Oorschot, 2001: 48–49). In addition, there appears to be greater support for programs directed at the aged, rather than those which focus on groups perceived as less deserving. These variables provide a potential opportunity for neoliberal politicians seeking to reduce welfare spending by playing off one disadvantaged group against another (van Kersbergen, 2000: 29).

Similarly in Australia, there is evidence that the use of 'wedge politics' by the Howard Government has reduced public sympathy for the poor. In particular, the government has used a range of political tactics in order to induce a hardening of community attitudes towards particular disadvantaged groups such as the young unemployed, single mothers and new migrants (Wilson and Turnbull, 2001). Although surveys continue to suggest some support for higher taxes and higher social spending, and while most Australians support more spending on aged and disability pensions (Baldry and Vinson, 1998; Saunders, 1998: 28–30), when it comes to income security payments for unpopular groups, attitudes appear to be much harsher.

A recent *Age* survey, for example, found that only 22 per cent of respondents supported greater spending on single-parent benefits, whilst 29 per cent favoured the reduction of benefits. Similarly only 17 per cent supported greater spending on unemployment benefits, whilst 31 per cent supported less spending. In addition, 88 per cent of Australians support work for the dole (Mackay, 2001). Other surveys have similarly found that Australians strongly favour the application of mutual obligation to the unemployed. However, there is greater compassion for those with parenting responsibilities and disabilities (Eardley et al, 2000).

Another potential factor is the development of a counter-weight to the neoliberal think-tanks. Currently, social democratic think-tanks such as the Evatt Foundation and the Fabian Society continue to promote political alternatives, but appear to lack the political lobbying skills and resources of the neoliberals. In addition, their recommendations often tend to be cautious and supportive of the status quo, and of little interest to policy-makers or the mass media.

However, recently, the Canberra-based Australia Institute has enjoyed some success in promoting progressive alternatives to the neoliberal agenda. Two of its recent publications on mutual obligation and aged-care funding have gained considerable exposure in the mainstream media, and provoked significant public debate (Kinnear, 2000; 2001). The success of these publications suggests that a social democratic think-tank committed to relevant and accessible research has the potential to influence welfare policy debates. It is possible, for example, to see such a think-tank organising prominent visitors from the Scandinavian countries who can extol the virtues of extending, rather than cutting, welfare programs.

An additional factor is the increasing demand for international agencies such as the IMF and the World Bank to become more representative, democratic and accountable. At the very least, these agencies are beginning to acknowledge the importance of a 'social dimension' in Third World development. Nevertheless, such changes in rhetoric do not appear as yet to have been translated into policy.

A final and probably crucial factor is attempts to confront 'globalisation from above' with 'globalisation from below'. For example, the 1999 meeting of the WTO in Seattle was confronted with massive protests of 50–80 000 people organised by a coalition of unionists, conservationists, clerics and consumer groups. Protesters demanded that the WTO incorporate labour and environmental standards into its rulings. Mishra (1999: 129) recommends the establishment of international institutions similar to the IMF which have the power to promote and implement binding social rights at a global level.

In addition, there is increasing evidence of local community resistance to corporate global agendas. As Ife notes (2002: 144–47), global capital may be able to intimidate national governments, but arguably has far less capacity to threaten local activists. Local communities have the potential to introduce new economic, social, cultural and political initiatives based on principles of social justice. They are also increasingly utilising the Internet to link their campaigns and experiences with similar local movements elsewhere.

CONCLUSION

The above discussion suggests that there are significant ideological and political factors and forces contributing to welfare retrenchment. They include most notably:

- global economic pressures
- policy prescriptions of global social policy actors such as the IMF and OECD
- neoliberal think-tanks, such as the CIS, IPA and Tasman Institute
- business organisations such as the ACCI and the Australian Chamber of Manufacturers
- the National Farmers' Federation
- the Australian Liberal Party
- mainstream print and broadcast media.

In addition there are various forces contributing to welfare state retrenchment with a 'human face', including:

- the Australian Labor Party
- advocates of the Third Way
- Patrick McClure (Mission Australia) and Reference Group on Welfare Reform.

In contrast, other factors and forces may mitigate against welfare state contraction including:

- public opinion (albeit highly variant)
- the Australian Council of Social Service
- the Australian Council of Trade Unions
- church welfare agencies
- the Australian Greens party and small radical Left groups
- some dissident Labor parliamentarians and activists
- the Australian Association of Social Workers

- the Victorian Local Governance Association and many local governments
- the Australian National Organisation for the Unemployed
- the Australia Institute think-tank
- local and global resistance by local communities.

This opposition would almost certainly be more influential if an effective means could be found for facilitating the collective political representation of the poor and unemployed.

At this time, the political momentum is clearly towards further welfare retrenchment. The debate between the Liberal Party and the Labor Party is not so much about ending welfare state entitlements, given that both parties favour a shift from welfare to work. Rather, the debate is about how quickly this transformation should occur, whether it should extend to all working-age recipients of income security payments including single parents and the disabled, and what level of support should be provided to income security recipients as they move into the labour market.

Nevertheless, public opinion remains an unpredictable variant. The current neoliberal consensus suggests that policies based on principles of mutual obligation will produce more effective and fairer outcomes for all, including the poor. However, evidence of policy failure, including greater social costs, may sway public opinion in another direction. The onus will then be on social democrats to show that they can develop new ideas and initiatives for regenerating the welfare state.

Questions for consideration

1 Why does Australian public opinion appear to be more sympatheric to the needs of those on aged and disability penions, rather than those of sole parents and the unemployed?
2 Why are social democratic parties including the ALP so reluctant to defend the welfare state?
3 Are there any significant political barriers to further retrenchment of the Australian welfare state?

Exercise

Write down the stated views of your family and peers on welfare spending and welfare recipients. Consider the similarites and differences between the views of the two groups, and consider the factors and experiences that may have influenced their development. Then consider what actions you might take if necessary to influence a change in their opinions.

GLOSSARY

associationalism the involvement of self-governing, voluntary, publicly funded and publicly accountable associations in the delivery of welfare services

civil society social networks embedded in family, neighbourhood and the community which are distinct from both government and the market; closely associated with Third Way (qv) ideas

classical liberalism a preference for free-market, rather than state or collectivist, solutions; more recently called neoliberalism (qv)

community development building and strengthening community structures and processes

decommodification the extent to which social rights such as minimum standards of health, education, housing and income are guaranteed independently of the market

economic rationalism a preference for the free market over government intervention; the Australian variant of neoliberalism (qv)

feminism views gender as the key structuring principle of social practices and institutions. Feminists believe the patriarchal structure of the welfare state reinforces women's subordination and dependence on men through the tying of payments to families, of which men are normally considered the head.

globalisation the integration of trade and financial markets at a global level; tends to produce greater influence of supranational economic forces, and decreased national control

guaranteed minimum income a scheme designed to ensure that everyone in the community receives an income on or above the poverty line

interest groups groups of people who share one or more interests or objectives, and who try to influence policy debates to protect or to promote those objectives

laborism a concern with improving the relative conditions of the working class. Laborists seek to attain fair or higher wages through direct state intervention in the market to determine wage levels, rather than seeking a broader non-market distribution of income via progressive taxation and other transfers.

Marxism the belief that class-based inequalities are entrenched in the economic, political and social structure of capitalist society. The Marxist view of welfare contains contradictory tendencies. Marxists believe the welfare state acts to repress and control the working class, but they also acknowledge that welfare programs improve the lives of the poor and disadvantaged.

mutual obligation the belief that welfare recipients have contractual duties and obligations to society as well as needs and rights; closely associated with the neoliberal (qv) agenda including particularly the Howard Government's work for the dole scheme

neo-conservativism see 'neoliberalism'

neoliberalism sometimes known as 'economic rationalism' (in Australia) or the 'New Right' or 'neoconservatism' (in North America: qqv). Neoliberals emphasise individual rights and initiatives, the rationality of the free market, and the necessity for the size and influence of the state and government to be limited as much as possible.

New Right a group of free-marketeers committed to reducing government spending, lowering taxation, and deregulating the economy and labour market from government control

post-modernism influenced by the emergence of social movements and identity-politics based on race, gender, sexuality, disability and age, post-modernists reject the traditional universalist focus of social policy on income redistribution. Instead, they favour a fractured definition of inequality.

public choice theory the belief that all individuals seek to maximise their personal welfare at the public expense. The only constraint on this pursuit of self-interest is the free market. Adherents favour private rather than public provision of goods whenever possible.

residualism the belief that social welfare institutions should come into play only when the normal structures of supply — the family and the market — break down; usually results in selectivist or targeted forms of social welfare restricted to the poor and disadvantaged

social capital stable interactive relationships based on mutual trust and co-operation which help to promote desirable social outcomes

social citizenship refers to the right of every member of a society to be able to participate fully in that society. Social rights, enshrined in welfare state policies, are necessary to enable disadvantaged people to also exercise their political rights (such as the right to vote) and legal rights (such as the right to free speech).

social coalition the notion that business and community groups as well as government have an important role to play in tackling social problems; associated with neoliberal (qv) ideas around the limits of government spending.

social conservatism a commitment to traditional institutions and values such as the monarchy and the nuclear family

social democracy a belief that inequalities in the distribution of power and resources within capitalist society lead to the disadvantage of some groups of people. Social democrats advocate greater government intervention in the economy and a wide-ranging welfare state to alleviate market-based inequality and ensure minimum standards of support for all citizens.

social entrepreneurship the use of market principles and social partnerships between communities, business, and government to promote social and economic growth at the local level

social justice refers to the fair distribution of life chances, wealth, income, rights and responsibilities

social liberalism a belief in the necessity of state intervention to protect the social and economic rights of the underprivileged

social responsibility the belief that the corporate sector has broader obligations to the social, environmental and economic welfare of the community beyond the mere making of profits

targeted welfare the residual (qv) limiting of welfare payments to those in greatest need

Thatcherism neoliberal (qv) ideas associated with former British prime minister Margaret Thatcher, particularly the belief that there is no such thing as a society, only individuals and their families

think-tanks public policy institutes engaged in scholarly research independent of government or political parties

Third Way a highly contested term popularised by the British Labor Prime Minister Tony Blair. Advocates see it as an attempt to blend the positives of social democracy and neoliberalism. Its foremost values appear to be equality, freedom as autonomy, a strong civil society based on local community action in partnership with government, and no rights without responsibilities.

universalism defines welfare as a normal, front-line function of modern industrial society. Social welfare is a right for all, regardless of income or position. Allocation takes the form of positive discrimination programs rather than means tests.

wedge politics a calculated political tactic based on the exploitation of divisive social issues to gain political support, weaken opponents, and maintain control over the policy agenda

welfare retrenchment reduction or abolition of state-funded welfare services and programs

welfare state group of social policies intended to maintain the basic well-being of citizens, especially in relation to education, health, personal social services, housing and incomes

REFERENCES

Abbott, Keith (1996) *Pressure Groups and the Australian Federal Parliament.* AGPS, Canberra.

Adams, Phillip and Burton, Lee (1997) *Talkback: Emperors of Air.* Allen and Unwin, Sydney.

Alber, Jens and Standing, Guy (2000) 'Social dumping, catch-up or convergence? Europe in a comparative global context'. *Journal of European Social Policy* 10(2): 99–119.

Alcock, Pete (2001) 'The comparative content'. In Pete Alcock and Gary Craig (eds) *International Social Policy.* Palgrave, Basingstoke, pp 1–25.

Alcock, Pete and Craig, Gary (2001) 'The United Kingdom: Rolling back the welfare state?' In Pete Alcock and Gary Craig (eds) *International Social Policy.* Palgrave, Basingstoke, pp 124–42.

Alford, John, O'Neill, Deirdre, McGuire, Linda, Considine, Mark, Muetzelfeldt, Michael and Ernst, John (1994) 'The contract state'. In John Alford and Deirdre O'Neill (eds) *The Contract State.* Deakin University Press, Melbourne, pp 1–20.

Allan, Rodney (1997) 'Money for nothing: The ethics of social welfare'. *Policy, Organisation and Society* 14: 1–22.

Alston, Margaret and McKinnon, Jenny (2001) 'Introduction'. In Margaret Alston and Jenny Mckinnon (eds) *Social Work: Fields of Practice.* Oxford University Press, Melbourne, pp xv–xxxiv.

Anglican Church of Australia (2001) *The Distribution of Work and Wealth in Australia.* Anglican Church, Sydney.

Anglicare (2002) *State of the Family 2002.* Anglicare, Melbourne.

Antcliff, Susan (1988) 'Behind the rhetoric: A closer look at the New Right'. *Australian Quarterly* Autumn: 63–69.

Appleyard, RT (1965) 'Pockets of poverty in Australia'. *Social Service*, 17(1): 1–10.

Argy, Fred (1998) *Australia at the Crossroads.* Allen and Unwin, Sydney.

—— (2001) 'Liberalism and economic policy'. In John Nieuwenhuysen, Peter Lloyd and Margaret Mead (eds) *Reshaping Australia's Economy.* Cambridge University Press, Melbourne, pp 67–85.

Arjona, Roman, Ladaique, Maxime and Pearson, Mark (2001) *Growth, Inequality and Social Protection*. OECD, Paris.

Arkley, Sally and Jones, David (1991) 'The social work profession and professional public relations'. In Bob Franklin and Nigel Parton (eds) *Social Work, the Media and Public Relations*. Routledge, London, pp 218–26.

Ashton, David (1986) *Unemployment Under Capitalism*. Wheatsheaf Books, London.

Australian Association of Social Workers (AASW, 1969–2002) *Victorian Branch Newsletter/Victorian Social Work*. AASW, Melbourne.

—— (1997) *Continuing Professional Education Policy*. AASW, Canberra.

Australian Association of Social Workers and Victorian Council of Social Service (1968) 'The National Health Act'. *Australian Journal of Social Work* 21(1): 29–34.

Australian Catholic Social Justice Council (1990) *Social Justice in Everyday Life*. Collins Dove, Melbourne.

Australian Council of Social Service (ACOSS, 1996a) *Documents for the National Tax Summit*. ACOSS, Sydney.

—— (1996b) 'The ACOSS-ACCI Tax Summit'. *Impact* November: 8–9.

—— (1997) *Living Wage*. ACOSS, Sydney.

—— (1998a) *Agenda for Tax Reform*. ACOSS, Sydney.

—— (1998b) *The Government's Tax Package: ACOSS Analysis*. ACOSS, Sydney.

—— (1998c) *Labor's Tax Package: ACOSS Analysis*. ACOSS, Sydney.

—— (1999a) *Making the Tax Package Fairer*. ACOSS, Sydney.

—— (1999b) *Revised Tax Package: ACOSS Analysis*. ACOSS, Sydney.

—— (1999c) *Work for the Dole — Briefing Paper*. ACOSS. Sydney.

—— (2001a) *Annual Report 2000–2001*. ACOSS, Sydney.

—— (2001b) *Breaching the Safety Net: The Harsh Impact of Social Security Penalties*. ACOSS, Sydney.

—— (2001c) *Generating Jobs*. ACOSS, Sydney.

—— (2002) *The Obligation is Mutual*. ACOSS, Sydney.

Australian Council of Trade Unions and Australian Labor Party (ACTU and ALP, 1983) *Statement of Accord*. ACTU and ALP, Melbourne.

Australian Labor Party (ALP, 1992) *Poles Apart*. ALP, Canberra.

—— (1995) *Shaping the Nation: Achievements of the Labor Government*. ALP, Canberra.

—— (2000) *ALP Platform*. ALP, Canberra.

Bagguley, Paul (1991) *From Protest to Acquiescence: Political Movements of the Unemployed*. Macmillan, London.

Balanya, Belen, Doherty, Ann, Hoedeman, Olivier, Ma'anit, Adam and Wesselius, Erik (2000) *Europe Inc.: Regional and Global Restructuring and the Rise of Corporate Power*. Pluto Press, London.

Baldry, Eileen and Vinson, Tony (1998) 'The current obsession with reducing taxes'. *Just Policy* 13: 3–9.

Baldwin, Peter (1995) *Beyond the Safety Net: The Future of Social Security*. AGPS, Canberra.

Battin, Tim (2000) 'Labourism and the Australian Labor Party'. In Paul Boreham, Geoffrey Stokes and Richard Hall (eds) *The Politics of Australian Society*. Longman, Sydney, pp 38–50.

Bauman, Zygmunt (1998) *Work, Consumerism and the New Poor*. Open University Press, Buckingham.

Beder, Sharon (1997) *Global Spin.* Scribe Publications, Melbourne.
—— (2000) *Selling the Work Ethic.* Scribe Publications, Melbourne.
Beilharz, Peter (1994) *Transforming Labor.* Cambridge University Press, Melbourne.
Beilharz, Peter, Considine, Mark and Watts, Rob (1992) *Arguing about the Welfare State.* Allen and Unwin, Sydney.
Belchamber, Grant (2000) 'Exploring the real relationship of work, wages and welfare'. In ACOSS *Work, Wages and Welfare.* ACOSS, Sydney, pp 5–11.
Bell, Stephen (2000) 'The unemployment crisis and economic policy'. In Stephen Bell (eds) *The Unemployment Crisis in Australia.* Cambridge University Press, Melbourne, pp 1–20.
Benn, Connie (1967) 'Social work in the industrial society'. In *Broader Horizons: 10th National Australian Association of Social Workers Conference Proceedings.* AASW, Brisbane, pp 23–39.
Bennett, James and Di Lorenzo, Thomas (1985) *Destroying Democracy.* Cato Institute, Washington DC.
Beresford, Peter (2002) 'User involvement in research and evaluation: Liberation or regulation?' *Social Policy and Society* 1(2): 95–105.
Beresford, Peter, Green, David, Lister, Ruth and Woodard, Kirsty (1999) *Poverty First Hand.* Child Poverty Action Group, London.
Beresford, Quentin (2000) *Governments, Markets and Globalisation.* Allen and Unwin, Sydney.
Bessant, Judith and Watts, Rob (1999) *Sociology Australia.* Allen and Unwin, Sydney.
Blair, Tony (1998) *Welfare Reform Green Paper.* Department of Social Security, London (www.dss.gov.uk/hq/wreform).
—— (1999) 'Beveridge revisited: A welfare state for the 21st century'. In Robert Walker (ed) *Ending Child Poverty.* Polity Press, Bristol, pp 7–18.
Blair, Tony and Schroeder, Gerhard (1999) *The Third Way/Die Neue Mitte.* Labour Party and SPD (www.labour.org.uk/lp/new/PMSPEECHES).
Block, Fred, Cloward, Richard, Ehrenreich, Barbara and Piven, Frances Fox (1987) *The Mean Season: The Attack on the Welfare State.* Pantheon Books, New York.
Boreham, Paul, Dow, Geoff and Leet, Martin (1999) *Room to Manoeuvre: Political Aspects of Full Employment.* Melbourne University Press, Melbourne.
Borland, Jeff, Gregory, Bob and Sheehan, Peter (2001) 'Inequality and economic change'. In Jeff Borland, Bob Gregory and Peter Sheehan (eds) *Work Rich, Work Poor.* Victoria University, Melbourne, pp 1–20.
Botsman, Peter (2001) 'Putting the Mutual into Mutual Obligations'. In Peter Botsman and Mark Latham (eds) *The Enabling State: People Before Bureaucracy.* Pluto Press, Sydney, pp 173–83.
Brecher, Jeremy and Costello, Tim (1994) *Global Village or Global Pillage.* South End Press, Boston.
Brennan, Deborah (1998a) 'Government and civil society'. In Paul Smyth and Bettina Cass (eds) *Contesting the Australian Way.* Cambridge University Press, Melbourne, pp 124–36.
—— (1998b) 'In defence of the welfare state'. In David Lovell, Ian McAllister, William Maley and Chandran Kukathas (eds) *The Australian Political System,* second edn. Longman, Melbourne, pp 652–53.

Brennan, Geoffrey and Williams, John (1984) *Chaining Australia: Church Bureaucracies and Political Economy*. Centre for Independent Studies, Sydney.

Brennan, Kevin (2000a) 'Unemployed people speak out'. *ACOSS Impact* September: 5.

—— (2000b) 'Gaining a seat at the table: Unemployed groups form national organisation'. *ACOSS Impact* December: 1.

Bretherton, Tanya (2002) 'Do Australian businesses suffer from a scrooge complex?' *Australian Quarterly* 74(1): 33–36.

Brett, Judith (1994) 'Ideology'. In Judith Brett, Murray Goot and James Gillespie (eds) *Developments in Australian Politics*. MacMillan, Melbourne, pp 1–22.

Brotherhood of St Laurence (2001) *Towards a Fairer Future*. Brotherhood of St Lawrence, Melbourne.

Brown, Jerome (1999) 'The tax debate, pressure groups and the 1998 Federal Election'. *Policy, Organisation and Society* 18: 75–101.

Brown, Kevin, Kenny, Susan, Turner, Bryan and Prince, John (2000) *Rhetorics of Welfare*. Macmillan, London.

Brown, Ray (1963) 'Poverty in Australia'. *Australian Quarterly* June: 75–79.

Browning, Bob (1990) *The Network: A Guide to Anti-Business Pressure Groups*. Canonbury Press, Melbourne.

Bryson, Lois (1994) 'The welfare state and economic adjustment'. In Stephen Bell and Brian Head (eds) *State, Economy and Public Policy in Australia*. Oxford University Press, Melbourne, pp 291–314.

—— (2000) 'Family, state, market and citizenship'. In Wendy Weeks and Marjorie Quinn (2000) *Issues Facing Australian Families*, third edn. Pearson Education, Sydney, pp 43–54.

—— (2001) 'Australia: The transformation of the wage-earners' welfare state'. In Pete Alcock and Gary Craig (eds) *International Social Policy*. Palgrave, Basingstoke, pp 64–84.

Buckingham, David (1998) 'Service delivery and the future of the welfare state'. Address to IPAA National Conference, Hobart (www.bca.com.au).

Bull, Sandra (1996) 'Hotline to report job-offer refusals'. *Mercury* 10 April.

Burdekin, Brian and Carter, Jan (1989) *Our Homeless Children: Report of the National Inquiry into Homeless Children*. Human Rights and Equal Opportunity Commission, Canberra.

Burden, Tom (1998) *Social Policy and Welfare*. Pluto Press, London.

Burgmann, Verity (2000) 'Protesting unemployment, past and present'. *Australian Options* 21: 6–9.

Burke, Christine (1995) Credible Christian participation in public discourse towards a just society. PhD thesis, Monash University, Melbourne.

Business Council of Australia (BCA, 1991) *Government in Australia in the 1990s*. BCA, Melbourne.

Butlin, NG, Barnard, A and Pincus, J (1982) *Government and Capitalism*. Allen and Unwin, Sydney.

Callinicos, Alex (2001) *Against the Third Way*. Polity Press, Cambridge.

Calwell, Arthur (1963) *Labor's Role in Modern Society*. Lansdowne Press, Melbourne.

Cappo, David (1993) 'Fear of engagement: A crisis in contemporary Christian churches'. Paper to Uniting Church Forum on Faith and Society, Melbourne.

Carey, Alex (1987) 'Managing public opinion: The corporate offensive'. In Stephen Frenkel (ed) *Union Strategy and Industrial Change*. UNSW, Sydney, pp 12–54.

Carey, David (1999) *Coping with Population Ageing in Australia*. OECD, Paris.

Carney, Terry and Hanks, Peter (1986) *Australian Social Security Law, Policy and Administration*. Oxford University Press, Melbourne.

Cass, Bettina (1988) *Income Support for the Unemployed in Australia: Towards a More Active System*. Social security review issues paper no. 4, AGPS, Canberra.

—— (1989) 'Defending and reforming the Australian welfare state.' In Lionel Orchard and Robert Dare (eds) *Markets, Morals and Public Policy*. Federation Press, Sydney, pp 134–56.

—— (1998) 'The social policy context'. In Paul Smyth and Bettina Cass (eds) *Contesting the Australian Way*. Cambridge University Press, Melbourne, pp 38–54.

Cass, Bettina and Whiteford, Peter (1989) 'Social security policies.' In Brian Head and Allan Patience (eds) *From Fraser to Hawke: Australian Public Policy in the 1980s*. Longman Cheshire, Melbourne, pp 273–303.

Castles, Francis (1985) *The Working Class and Welfare*. Allen and Unwin, Sydney.

—— (1991) *On Sickness Days and Social Policy*. Discussion paper no 25, Australian National University Graduate Public Programme, Canberra.

—— (1996) 'Australian social policy: Where we are now?' *Just Policy* 6: 12–15.

—— (1998) *Comparative Public Policy*. Edward Elgar, Cheltenham, UK.

Castles, Francis and Mitchell, Deborah (1992) 'Identifying welfare state regimes: The links between politics, instruments and outcomes'. *Governance* 5(1): 1–26.

Catholic Bishops of Australia (1992) *Common Wealth for the Common Good*. Collins Dove, Melbourne.

Catholic Social Services Victoria (2001) *Surviving, Not Living: Disadvantage in Melbourne*. Catholic Social Services, Melbourne.

Catholic Welfare Australia and Australian Catholic Social Justice Council (2001) *Searching for the Common Good — Federal Election 2001*. Catholic Welfare Australia, Curtin.

Centre for Corporate Public Affairs (2000) *Corporate Community Involvement*. Department of Family and Community Services, Canberra.

Chaney, Fred (1999) In *Discerning the Australian Social Conscience*. Jesuit Society, Melbourne, pp 207–17 and 227–29.

Chossudovsky, Michel (1999) *The Globalisation of Poverty*. Zed Books, London.

Clarke, John (2001) 'US welfare: Variations on the liberal regime'. In Allan Cochrane, John Clarke and Sharon Gewirtz (eds) *Comparing Welfare States*. Sage, London, pp 113–52.

Clarnette, Warren (1993) 'The churches and economic rationalism'. In Chris James, Chris Jones and Andrew Norton (eds) *A Defence of Economic Rationalism*. Allen and Unwin, Sydney, pp 168–75.

Cleary, Ray (2001) 'A mission of care and justice'. *Age* 14 April.

Cochrane, Allan, Clarke, John and Gewirtz, Sharon (2001) 'Looking for a European welfare state'. In Allan Cochrane, John Clarke and Sharon Gewirtz (eds) *Comparing Welfare States*. Sage, London, pp 261–90.

Cockett, Richard (1994) *Thinking the Unthinkable*. Harper Collins. London.

Coleman, Marie (1968) 'Should social workers go into politics?' *Australian Journal of Social Work* 21(1): 27–28.

Conley, Margaret (1982) 'The undeserving poor: Welfare and labour policy'. In Richard Kennedy (ed) *Australian Welfare History: Critical Essays*. Macmillan, Melbourne, pp 281–302.

Conley, Tom (2001) 'The domestic politics of globalisation'. *Australian Journal of Political Science* 36(2): 223–46.

Considine, Mark (2001) *Enterprising States*. Cambridge University Press, Melbourne.

Costello, Peter (1997) 'Economic Liberalism and the path to prosperity'. In Alan Gregory (ed) *The Menzies Lectures 1978–1998*. Sir Robert Menzies Lecture Trust, Melbourne, pp 328–38.

—— (1998a) *The Australian Taxation System in Need of Reform*. Commonwealth Government, Canberra.

—— (1998b) *Tax Reform: Not a New Tax, a New Tax System*. Commonwealth Government, Canberra.

—— (2002) *Intergenerational Report*. Australian Government, Canberra.

Cox, Eva (1993) 'The economics of mutual support: A feminist approach'. In Stuart Rees, Gordon Rodley and Frank Stilwell (eds) *Beyond the Market*. Pluto Press, Sydney, pp 270–76.

—— (1995) *A Truly Civil Society*. ABC Books, Sydney.

Cox, James (2001) 'The erosion of self-reliance: Welfare dependency and the family'. *Policy* 17(3): 33–36.

Crean, Simon (2001) 'Whose obligation?' *Just Policy, Sound Research, Joint Action: Selected Papers from the 2000 ACOSS Congress*. ACOSS, Sydney, pp 27–33.

Croucher, Richard (1987) *We Refuse to Starve in Silence: A History of the National Unemployed Workers' Movement, 1920–46*. Lawrence and Wishart, London.

Cupper, Les and Hearn, June (1980) 'Australian union involvement in non-industrial issues: The Newport dispute 1971–78'. in GW Ford, June Hearn and Russell Lansbury, (eds) *Australian Labor Relations*. Macmillan, Melbourne, pp 50–75.

Curtain, Richard (2000) *Mutual Obligation: Policy and Practice in Australia Compared with the UK*. Dusseldorp Skills Forum, Sydney.

Davidson, Gay (1988) 'The return of liberal Liberals'. *Australian Society* September: 13–14.

Davidson, Ken (1991) 'Welfare reality versus Hewson and the loony Right'. *Age* 5 October.

Davidson, Peter (1997) 'Directions in tax reform'. *Impact* October: 12.

Davies, Alan and Serle, Geoffrey (1954) *Policies for Progress*. Victorian Fabian Society, Melbourne.

Davis, Edward (1987) *A Comparative Study of Six Unions*. Allen and Unwin, Sydney.

Deacon, Bob, Hulse, Michelle and Stubbs, Paul (1997) *Global Social Policy*. Sage, London.

Deakin, Nicholas (1987) *The Politics of Welfare*. Methuen, London.

Dean, Hartley (1991) *Social Security and Social Control*. Routledge, London.

Denham, Andrew and Garnett, Mark (1996) 'The nature and impact of think tanks in contemporary Britain'. In Michael David Kandiah and Anthony

Seldon (eds) *Ideas and Think Tanks in Contemporary Britain*, volume 1. Frank Cass, London, pp 43–61.

Department of Social Security (1997) *Social Security Compliance Report*. Commonwealth Government, Canberra.

Dickey, Brian (1980) *No Charity There: A Short History of Social Welfare in Australia*. Thomas Nelson, Melbourne.

Downer, Alexander (1994) 'The things that matter'. Address to National Press Club, Canberra, 5 September.

Dullard, Jayne. and Hayward, David (1998) 'The democratic paradox of public choice theory: The case of the Costello cuts'. *Journal of Australian Political Economy* 42: 16–47.

Duncan, Bruce (2000) 'Public theology in a global Catholic perspective'. *Zadok Perspectives* 66: 17–20.

—— (2001) *Crusade Or Conspiracy?: Catholics and the Anti-Communist Struggle in Australia*. UNSW Press, Sydney.

Eardley, Tony and Matheson, George (1999) *Australian Attitudes to Unemployment and Unemployed People*. Social Policy Research Centre, University of NSW, Sydney.

Eardley, Tony, Saunders, Peter and Evans, Ceri (2000) *Community Attitudes Towards Unemployment, Activity Testing and Mutual Obligation*. Social Policy Research Centre, University of NSW, Sydney.

Edgar, Don (2001) *The Patchwork Nation*. Harper Collins, Sydney.

Edwards, Meredith, Howard, Cosmo and Miller, Robin (2001) *Social Policy, Public Policy*. Allen and Unwin, Sydney.

Elliott, Grant (1982) 'The social policy of the New Right'. In Marian Sawer (ed) *Australia and the New Right*. Allen and Unwin, Sydney, pp 120–34.

Elliott, Grant and Graycar, Adam (1979) 'Social welfare'. In Allan Patience and Brian Head (eds) *From Whitlam to Fraser: Reform and Reaction in Australian Politics*. Oxford University Press, Melbourne, pp 88–102.

Emy, Hugh (2001) 'Dancing with wolves: The untenable tenets of the Third Way'. Address to Australian Fabian Society. Melbourne.

Emy, Hugh and Hughes, Owen (1991) *Australian Politics: Realities in Conflict*. Macmillan, Melbourne.

Encel, Sol (1991) 'Defending the welfare state'. In Bede Nairn (ed) *Labor History Essays*, Volume 3. Pluto Press, Sydney, pp 60–68.

Ernst, John and Webber, Michael (1996) 'Ideology and interests: Privatisation in theory and practice'. In Michael Webber and Mary Crooks (eds) *Putting the People Last*. Hyland House, Melbourne, pp 113–40.

Esping-Andersen, Gosta (1990) *The Three Worlds of Welfare Capitalism*. Polity Press, Cambridge.

—— (1996) 'After the golden age? Welfare state dilemmas in a global economy'. In Gosta Esping-Andersen (ed) *Welfare States in Transition*. Sage, London, pp 1–31.

—— (1999) *Social Foundations of Postindustrial Economies*. Oxford University Press, Oxford.

Evatt Foundation (1995) *Unions 2001*. Evatt Foundation, Sydney.

Ewer, Peter, Hampson, Ian, Lloyd, Chris, Rainford, John, Rix, Stephen and Smith, Meg (1991) *Politics and the Accord*. Pluto Press, Sydney.

Fabian Society (2000) *Paying for Progress: A New Politics of Tax for Public Spending*. Fabian Society, London.

Family and Community Services Department (2000) *International Comparison and the International Experience with Welfare Reform.* Canberra (www.facs.gov.au/whatsnew/interwelfare.htm).

Fenna, Alan (1998) *Introduction to Australian Public Policy.* Longman, Melbourne.

Ferguson, John (2000) 'Chewing over welfare'. *Eureka Street* 10(8): 6–7.

Finn, Dan (1997) *Working Nation.* ACOSS, Sydney.

—— (1999) 'Job guarantees for the unemployed: Lessons from Australian welfare reform'. *Journal of Social Policy* 28(1): 53–71.

Fitzpatrick, Tony (1999) 'New welfare associations: An alternative model of well-being'. In Tim Jordan and Adam Lent (eds) *Storming the Millennium: The New Politics of Change.* Lawrence and Wishart, London, pp 156–71.

—— (2002) 'In search of a welfare democracy'. *Social Policy and Society* 1(1): 11–20.

Fox, Charlie (2000) *Fighting Back: The Politics of the Unemployed in Victoria in the Great Depression.* Melbourne University Press, Melbourne.

Frankel, Boris (1992) *From the Prophets Deserts Come.* Arena Publishing, Melbourne.

—— (1997) 'Beyond Labourism and socialism: How the Australian Labor Party developed the model of New Labour'. *New Left Review* 221: 3–33.

—— (2001) *When the Boat Comes in: Transforming Australia in the Age of Globalisation.* Pluto Press, Sydney.

Fraser, Malcolm (1975) 'Government and the people.' Reproduced in Yvonne Thompson, George Brandis and Tom Harley (eds) (1986) *Australian Liberalism: The Continuing Vision.* Liberal Forum, Melbourne, pp 128–34.

Fraser, Nancy and Gordon, Linda (1994) 'A genealogy of dependency: Tracing a keyword of the welfare state'. In Paul James (ed) *Critical Politics: From the Personal to the Global.* Arena Publications, Melbourne, pp 77–109.

Freeland, John (1992) 'The CYSS campaign: An example of collective action against cuts in services'. In Ros Thorpe and Jude Petruchenia (eds) *Community Work or Social Change? An Australian Perspective.* Hale and Iremonger, Sydney, pp 166–79.

Friedman, Milton (1962) *Capitalism and Freedom.* University of Chicago Press, Chicago.

Gager, Owen (1998) 'But they go hungry'. *Arena* 35: 49–50.

Gallop, Geoff (2001) 'Is there a Third Way?' In Paul Nursey-Bray and Carol Lee Bacchi (eds) *Left Directions: Is There a Third Way?* University of Western Australia Press, Perth, pp 32–41.

Gans, Herbert (1995) *The War Against the Poor.* Basic Books, New York.

Garrett, Geoffrey (1998) *Partisan Politics in the Global Economy.* Cambridge University Press, Melbourne.

Garton, Stephen (1990) *Out of Luck: Poor Australians and Social Welfare 1788–1988.* Allen and Unwin, Sydney.

George, Susan (1997) 'How to win the war of ideas'. *Dissent* Summer: 47–53.

George, Vic (1998) 'Political ideology, globalisation and welfare futures in Europe'. *Journal of Social Policy* 27(1): 17–36.

Ghosh, SC (1978) 'The ideological world of Malcolm Fraser'. *Australian Quarterly* 50(3): 6–28.

Gibson, Diane (1990) 'Social policy'. In Christine Jennett and Randal Stewart (eds) *Hawke and Australian Public Policy*. Macmillan, Melbourne, pp 180–203.

Giddens, Anthony (1998) *The Third Way: The Renewal of Social Democracy*. Polity Press, Cambridge.

—— (2000) *The Third Way and its Critics*. Polity Press, Cambridge.

—— (2001) 'Introduction'. In Anthony Giddens (ed) *The Global Third Way Debate*. Polity Press, Cambridge, pp 1–21.

Ginsburg, Norman (2001) 'Globalization and the liberal welfare states'. In Robert Sykes, Bruno Palier and Pauline Prior (eds) *Globalization and European Welfare States*. Palgrave, Basingstoke, pp 173–92.

Goddard, Chris and Liddell, Max (1995) 'Child abuse fatalities and the media: Lessons from a case study'. *Child Abuse Review* 4: 356–64.

Goodin, Robert (1988) *Reasons for Welfare*. Princeton University Press, Princeton.

—— (2000) 'Whither the welfare state?' In Linda Hancock, Brian Howe and Anthony O'Donnell (eds) *Reshaping Australian Social Policy*. Committee for Economic Development of Australia, Melbourne, pp 57–66.

Goodin, Robert, Headey, Bruce, Muffels, Ruud and Dirven, Henk-Jan (1999) *The Real Worlds of Welfare Capitalism*. Cambridge University Press, Melbourne.

Goodin, Robert and Schmidtz, David (1998) *Social Welfare and Individual Responsibility*. Cambridge University Press, Melbourne.

Goodman, James (2000) 'Stopping a juggernaut: The anti-MAI campaign'. In James Goodman and Patricia Ranald (eds) *Stopping the Juggernaut*. Pluto Press, Sydney, pp 33–52.

Gordon, Michael and Gray, Darren (2001) 'Abbott view stirs debate on poverty', *The Age*, 11 July.

Gough, Ian (2001) 'Globalization and regional welfare regimes'. *Global Social Policy* 1(2): 163–89.

Le Grand, Julian (1982) *The Strategy of Equality*. Allen and Unwin, London.

Grattan, Michelle and Gruen, Fred (1993) *Managing Government*. Longman Cheshire, Melbourne.

Gray, Gwen (1995) 'Social policy'. In Scott Prasser, John Nethercote and John Warhurst (eds) *The Menzies Era*. Hale and Iremonger, Sydney, pp 211–27.

Gray, John (1998) *False Dawn: The Delusions of Global Capitalism*. Granta Books, London.

Graycar, Adam (1976) *Social Policy: An Australian Introduction*. Macmillan, Melbourne.

Green, David (1991) *Equalising People: Why Social Justice Threatens Liberty*. Centre for Independent Studies, Sydney.

Gregg, Samuel (1999a) *Christianity and Entrepreneurship*. Centre for Independent Studies, Sydney.

—— (1999b) *Religion and Liberty*. Centre for Independent Studies, Sydney.

Gregory, Bob and Sheehan, Peter (1998) 'The collapse of full employment'. In Ruth Fincher and John Nieuwenhuysen (eds) *Australian Poverty: Then and Now*. Melbourne University Press, Melbourne, pp 103–26.

Grieve Smith, John (1997) *Full Employment: A Pledge Betrayed*. Macmillan, London.

Grimes, Don (1980) 'Security'. In Jane North and Patrick Weller (eds) *Labor: Directions for the Eighties*. Ian Novak, Sydney, pp 144–55.

Gruen, Fred and Grattan, Michelle (1993) *Managing Government: Labor's Achievements and Failures*. Longman Cheshire, Melbourne.

Hannington, Wal (1936) *Unemployed Struggles 1919–1936*. Lawrence and Wishart, London.

Harding, Ann (1999) 'The burdened middle'. In Michael Carman and Ian Rogers (eds) *Out of the Rut: Making Labor a Genuine Alternative*. Allen and Unwin, Sydney pp 71–93.

Harding, Ann and Szukalska (2000) *Financial Disadvantage in Australia: 1999*. Smith Family, Sydney.

Hastings, Graham (2001) 'View from the front-line: An activist perspective on the anti-globalisation movement at the end of 2001'. *Policy, Organisation and Society* 20(2): 44–62.

Hay, Colin (2001) 'Globalization, economic change and the welfare state: The vexatious inquisition of taxation?' In Bruno Sykes, Bruno Palier and Pauline Prior (eds) *Globalization and European Welfare States*. Palgrave, Basingstoke, pp 38–58.

Hayden, Bill (1972) 'New horizons in health and welfare services'. In John McLaren (ed) *Towards a New Australia*. Cheshire, Melbourne, pp 214–43.

Hayek, Friedrich (1944) *The Road to Serfdom*. Routledge and Kegan Paul, London.

Head, Brian (1989) 'Parties and the policy agenda 1978–1988'. In Brian Head and Allan Patience (eds) *From Fraser to Hawke*. Longman Cheshire, Melbourne, pp 486–510.

Healy, Judith (1998) *Welfare Options*. Allen and Unwin, Sydney.

Held, David, McGrew, Anthony, Goldblatt, David and Perraton, Jonathan (1999) *Global Transformations*. Polity Press, Cambridge.

Hemerijck, Anton and Visser, Jelle (2001) 'Dutch lessons in social pragmatism'. In Stuart White (ed) *New Labour*. Palgrave, Basingstoke, pp 190–203.

Henderson, Gerard (1983) 'Fraserism: Myths and realities'. *Quadrant* June: 33–37.

Henderson, Ian (2000) 'Welfare a side issue for business'. *The Australian* 11 September.

Henderson, Ronald (1975) *Australian Government Commission of Inquiry into Poverty. First Main Report*. AGPS, Canberra.

Henderson, Ronald, Harcourt, Alison and Harper, RJA (1970) *People in Poverty: A Melbourne Survey*. Cheshire, Melbourne.

Hewson, John (1991) 'De-regulate the labour market, re-examine service delivery'. *Victorian Council of Social Service Policy Issues Forum* November: 2–8.

—— (1992) 'Hewson fights back'. *Australian Quarterly* Spring: 329–38.

Hill, Michael (1996) *Social Policy: A Comparative Analysis*. Prentice Hall, London.

Hill, Mike (2000) 'Local government as community advocate'. *Just Policy* 19/20: 59–65.

Hinrichs, Karl (2001) 'Ageing and public pension reforms in Western Europe and North America: patterns and politics'. In Jochen Clasen (ed) *What Future for Social Security?* Kluwer Law International, The Hague, pp 157–77.

Hirschman, Albert (1991) *The Rhetoric of Reaction*. Harvard University Press, Cambridge.

Hirst, Paul (1994) *Associative Democracy*. Polity Press, Cambridge.

——l (1997) *From Statism to Pluralism*. UCL Press, London.

Hirst, Paul and Thompson, Grahame (1999) *Globalization in Question*. Polity Press, Cambridge.

Hogan, Michael (1987) *The Sectarian Strand*. Penguin Books, Melbourne.

—— (1990) *Justice Now: Social Justice Statements of the Australian Catholic Bishops*. University of Sydney, Sydney.

—— (1993) *Australian Catholics: The Social Justice Tradition*. Collins Dove, Melbourne.

Hopkinson, Shane (2001) 'Different globalisations'. *Policy, Organisation and Society* 20(2): 63–76.

Horne, Donald (1964) *The Lucky Country*. Penguin Books,Melbourne.

Howard, John (1986) 'The new challenge of liberalism'. *Alfred Deakin Lecture*. Melbourne.

Huber, Evelyne and Stephens, John (2001) 'Welfare state and production regimes in the era of retrenchment'. In Paul Pierson (ed) *The New Politics of the Welfare State*. Oxford University Press, New York, pp 107–45.

Hudson, Robert (1992) 'Privatisation: Who pays? Who profits?' *Victorian Council of Social Service Noticeboard* 5(6).

Hughes, Helen (1960) 'Menzies' millenium'. *Outlook* June: 11–12.

Human Rights and Equal Opportunity Commission (2000) *Avoiding Religious Discrimination in Employment*. HREOC, Sydney (www.hreoc.gov.au).

Humphrey, Michael (2001) 'An Australian Islam? Religion in the multicultural city'. in Abdullah Saeed and Shahram Akbarzadeh (eds) *Muslim Communities in Australia*. UNSW Press, Sydney, pp 33–52.

Ife, Jim (1997) *Rethinking Social Work*. Longman, Melbourne.

—— (2002) *Community Development*. Pearson Education, Sydney.

Imig, Douglas (1996) *Poverty and Power*. University of Nebraska Press, Lincoln.

Industry Commission (1994) *Charitable Organisations in Australia*. Industry Commission, Canberra.

International Monetary Fund (IMF, 2001) *Australia: Staff Report for the 2000 Article IV Consultation*. IMF, Washington D.C.

International Narcotics Control Board (1999) *Annual Report*. INCB, Vienna.

Ironmonger, Duncan (1980) 'The income maintenance policies of the Fraser Government'. *Australian Quarterly* 52(1): 32–39.

Jaensch, Dean (1991) *Parliament, Parties and People: Australian Politics Today*. Longman, Melbourne.

—— (1994) *The Liberals*. Allen and Unwin, Sydney.

James, Michael (1989) 'Introduction'. In Michael James, (ed) *The Welfare State: Foundations and Alternatives*. Centre for Independent Studies, Sydney, pp ix–xi.

Jamrozik, Adam (1991) *Class, Inequality and the State*. Macmillan, Melbourne.

—— (2001) *Social Policy in the Post-Welfare State*. Pearson Education, Sydney.

Johns, Gary (2000) *NGO Way to Go*. Institute of Public Affairs, Melbourne.

—— (2002) 'Why champions of causes need close scrutiny'. *The Australian* 30 January.

Jordan, Bill (1998) *The New Politics of Welfare: Social Justice in a Global Context*. Sage, London.

Jordan, Bill and Jordan, Charlie (2000) *Social Work and the Third Way: Tough Love as Social Policy*. Sage, London.

Jubilee 2000 Website 2000 (www.jubilee2000uk.org).

Jungwirth, Gary (ed) (1997) *Labor Essays: Renewing and Revitalising Labor*. Pluto Press, Sydney.

—— (1998) *Labor Essays: New visions for Government*. Pluto Press, Sydney.

Jupp, James (1959) 'A socialist Australian Labour Party'. *Outlook*, 3(1): 13–14.

Kalisch, David (1991) 'The active society'. *Social Security Journal* August: 3–9.

Kasper, Wolfgang (2000) *Building Prosperity*. Centre for Independent Studies, Sydney.

Keating, Paul (1994) *Working Nation: The White Paper on Employment and Growth*. AGPS, Canberra.

Keen, Susan (1996) *Nonprofit Organisations and Public Policy: Exploring the Research Role of the Brotherhood of St Laurence*. Queensland University of Technology, Brisbane.

Kelly, Bert (1981) *Economics Made Easy*. Brolga Books, Adelaide.

Kelly, Paul (1992) *The End of Certainty: The Story of the 1980s*. Allen and Unwin, Sydney.

Kerr, Duncan (2001) *Elect the Ambassador*. Pluto Press, Sydney.

van Kersbergen, Kees (2000) 'The declining resistance of welfare states to change?' In Stein Kuhnle (ed) *Survival of the European Welfare State*. Routledge, London, pp 19–36.

Kewley, Thomas (1969) *Australia's Welfare State*. Macmillan, Melbourne.

Kinnear, Pamela (2000) *Mutual Obligation: Ethical and Social Implications*. Australia Institute, Canberra.

—— (2001) *Population Ageing: Crisis or Transition?* Australia Institute, Canberra.

Klein, Angela (1998) 'Germany's unemployed take to the streets'. *International Viewpoint* 298: 3.

Koivusalo, Meri and Ollila, Eeva (1997) *Making a Healthy World: Agencies, Actors and Policies in International Health*. Zed Books, London.

Kuhne, Stein and Alestalo, Matti (2000) 'Growth, adjustments and survival of European welfare states'. In Stein Kuhnle (ed) *Survival of the European Welfare State*. Routledge, London, pp 3–18.

Kusuma, Rosemary (1998) 'Local action on unemployment'. *ACOSS Impact* October: 4.

Lackner, Susan (1998) 'Listen, I don't want to work: Young people and unemployment, a preliminary report'. In Judith Bessant and Sandy Cook (eds) *Against The Odds: Young People and Work*. Australian Clearinghouse for Youth Studies, Hobart, pp 220–27.

Lambert, Suzanne (1994) 'Sole parent income support: Cause or cure of sole parent poverty'. *Australian Journal of Social Issues* 29(1): 75–97.

Langmore, John (2000) 'Some background context to the origins of the Accord'. In Kenneth Wilson, Joanne Bradford and Maree Fitzpatrick (eds) *Australia in Accord*. South Pacific Publishing, Melbourne, pp 19–28.

Langmore, John and Quiggin, John (1994) *Work for All*. Melbourne University Press, Melbourne.

Latham, Mark (1998) *Civilising Global Capital*. Allen and Unwin, Sydney.

—— (1999) 'Why it is vital to break the cycle of welfare dependency'. *Australian Financial Review* 9 August.

—— (2001a) 'Making welfare work'. In Peter Botsman, and Mark Latham (eds) *The Enabling State*. Pluto Press, Sydney, pp 115–31.

—— (2001b) 'Stakeholder welfare'. *Quadrant* March: 14–21.

—— (2001c) 'The new economy and the new politics'. In Peter Botsman and Mark Latham (eds) *The Enabling State*. Pluto Press, Sydney, pp 13–35.

Lawrence, Carmen (2000) 'Rebuild a true social contract'. *Access* 2(6): 17–20.

Lawrence, Glenda, Bammer, Gabriele and Chapman, Simon (2000) 'Sending the wrong signal: Analysis of print media coverage of the ACT heroin prescription trial proposal, August 1997'. *Australian and New Zealand Journal of Public Health* 24(3): 254–64.

Lawrence, John (1965) *Professional Social Work in Australia*. Australian National University, Canberra.

Leisering, Lutz (2001) 'Germany: Reform from within'. In Pete Alcock and Gary Craig (eds) *International Social Policy*. Palgrave, Basingstoke, pp 161–82.

Lennie, Ian and Skenridge, Pat (1978) 'Social work: The wolf in sheep's clothing'. *Arena* 51: 47–92.

Leonard, Peter (1997) *Postmodern Welfare*. Sage, London.

Liberal Party of Australia (1977) 'Our aims: The Liberal perspective'. In Graeme Starr (ed) *The Liberal Party of Australia: A Documentary History*. Drummond/Heinemann, Melbourne, pp 357–59.

—— (1983) *Report of the Committee of Review: Facing the Facts*. Liberal Party, Canberra.

Link, Rosemary, Bibus, Anthony and Lyons, Karen (2000) *When Children Pay: US Welfare Reform and its Implications for UK Policy*. Child Poverty Action Group, London.

Lister, Ruth (1997) *Citizenship: Feminist Perspectives*. New York University Press, New York.

Louis, Les (1968) *Trade Unions and the Depression: A Study of Victoria, 1930–1932*. ANU Press, Canberra.

Lowenstein, Wendy (1997) *Weevils at Work*. Catalyst Press, Sydney.

Lubove, Roy (1972) *The Professional Altruist*. Atheneum, New York.

Lynch, Phillip (1973) Social Services Bill. Hansard, 7 March, 343–44.

Lyons, Karen (1999) *International Social Work: Themes and Perspectives*. Ashgate, Aldershot, Hampshire.

Lyons, Mark (1988) 'A view from the community'. In Newton Daddow (ed) *Report on the National Churches Consultation on Poverty in Australia*. Victorian Council of Christian Education, Melbourne, pp 85–90.

—— (1995) 'Advocacy for low income Australians: The ACOSS experience'. Paper presented to 1995 Independent Sector Spring Research Forum, Alexandria (Virginia).

—— (2001) *Third Sector*. Allen and Unwin, Sydney.

Macintyre, Clement (1999) 'From entitlement to obligation in the Australian welfare state'. *Australian Journal of Social Issues* 34(2): 103–18.

—— (2001) 'Welfare, citizenship and the Third Way'. In Paul Nursey-Bray and Carol Lee Bacchi (eds) *Left Directions: Is There a Third Way?* University of Western Australia Press, Perth, pp 83–94.

Macintyre, Stuart (1986) 'The short history of social democracy in Australia'. in Don Rawson (ed) *Blast, Budge or Bypass: Towards a Social Democratic Australia*. Academy of the Social Sciences, Canberra, pp 133–45.

Mackay, Hugh (2001) 'Snapshot of a nation'. *Age* 8 October.

Maddox, Graeme and Battin, Tim (1991) 'Australian Labor and the socialist tradition'. *Australian Journal of Political Science* 26: 181–96.

Marsh, Ian (1995) *Beyond the Two Party System*. Cambridge University Press, Melbourne.

—— (2000) 'Gaps in policy-making capacities: Interest groups, social movements, think tanks and the media'. In Michael Keating, John Wanna and Patrick Weller (eds) *Institutions on the Edge?* Allen and Unwin, Sydney, 178–204.

Martin, Hans-Peter and Schumann, Harald (1997) *The Global Trap*. Pluto Press, Sydney.

Massaro, Thomas (1998) *Catholic Social Teaching and United States Welfare Reform*. Liturgical Press, Minnesota.

—— (2000) *Living Justice: Catholic Social Teaching in Action*. Sheed and Ward, Franklin (Wisconsin).

Masterman-Smith, Helen (2000) 'Latham's sacramental wine of work: Some possible implications for working-class women in Western Sydney'. In Jock Collins and Scott Poynting (eds) *The Other Sydney*. Common Ground, Melbourne, pp 242–48.

Matthews, Trevor (1989) 'Interest groups'. In Rodney Smith and Lex Watson (eds) *Politics in Australia*. Allen and Unwin, Sydney, pp 211–27.

May, John (1996) 'The role of peak bodies in a civil society'. In Adam Farrar and Jane Inglis (eds) *Keeping it Together*. Pluto Press, Sydney, pp 245–72.

—— (2001) 'The challenge of poverty: The case of ACOSS'. In Marian Sawer and Gianni Zappala (eds) *Speaking for the People*. Melbourne University Press, Melbourne, pp 246–71.

McBride, Stephen and Williams, Russell (2001) 'Globalization, the restructuring of labour markets and policy convergence'. *Global Social Policy* 1(3): 281–309.

McCormack, Vince (2001) *Dead Man's Shoes*. Tasmanian Council of Social Service, Hobart.

Mead, Lawrence (1997) 'The rise of paternalism'. In L Mead (ed) *The New Paternalism*. Brookings Institution, Washington DC, pp 1–38.

Mendelsohn, Ronald (1954) *Social Security in the British Commonwealth*. Athlone Press, London.

Mendes, Philip (1993) 'The New Right and the anti-welfare state'. *Victorian Council of Social Service Policy Issues Forum* Summer: 2–11.

—— (1996) Welfare politics in Australia: A history of the Australian Council of Social Service. PhD thesis, La Trobe University, Melbourne.

—— (1997a) 'Blaming the victim: The new assault on the welfare state'. *Journal of Economic and Social Policy* 2(1): 41–53.

—— (1997b) 'Economic rationalism, the churches and the politics of welfare'. *Melbourne Journal of Politics* 24: 141–65.

—— (1997c) 'The ideology and politics of Howard's Work for the Dole Scheme'. *Australian Association of Social Workers National Bulletin* 7(2): 15–19.

—— (1998a) 'From Keynes to Hayek: The social welfare philosophy of the Liberal Party of Australia, 1983–1997'. *Policy, Organisation and Society* 15: 65–87.

—— (1998b) 'Social workers, professional associations and social justice'. *Northern Radius* 5(1): 11–14.

—— (1998c) 'The Australian Trade Union Movement and the welfare sector: A natural alliance?' *Journal of Australian Political Economy* 42: 106–28.

—— (1998d) 'The social policy of the ALP: Past, present and future'. *Social Alternatives* 17(3): 34–37.

—— (1998e) 'The times they are a-taxing'. *Australian Quarterly* 70(5): 48–52.

—— (1999a) 'From protest to acquiescence: Political movements of the unemployed'. *Social Alternatives* 18(4): 44–50.

—— (1999b) 'From the wage earners welfare state to the targeted welfare state: The social welfare policies of the Australian Labor Party, 1983–99'. Australian Social Work 52(4): 33–38.

—— (2000a) 'Economic rationalism vs social justice: The relationship between the Federal Liberal Party and the Australian Council of Social Service 1983–2000'. *Journal of Australian Political Economy* 46: 103–25.

—— (2000b) 'Eliminating welfare dependency not poverty: A critical analysis of the Howard Government's Welfare Reform Review'. *Policy, Organisation and Society* 19(2): 23–38.

—— (2000c) 'Reconstituting the public as the private: John Howard on the welfare state'. *Journal of Economic and Social Policy* 4(2): 33–47.

—— (2000d) 'Social conservatism vs social justice: The portrayal of child abuse in the press in Victoria, Australia'. *Child Abuse Review* 9: 49–61.

—— (2001a) 'Hardline or moderate? Peter Costello on the welfare state'. *Australian Quarterly* 73(2): 32–33.

—— (2001b) 'Mark Latham, the Third Way and the Australian welfare state'. *Melbourne Journal of Politics* 27: 86–101.

—— (2001c) 'Nimbyism vs social inclusion: Local communities and illicit drugs'. *Youth Studies Australia* 20(2): 17–22.

—— (2001d) 'Public attacks on social work in Australia: The two *Bulletin* affairs'. *Australian Social Work* 53(3): 55–62.

—— (2001e) 'Public choice theory and the de-funding of community welfare groups'. *Social Alternatives* 20(3): 50–55.

—— (2002a) 'Drug wars Down Under: The illfated struggle for safe injecting facilities in Victoria, Australia'. *International Journal of Social Welfare* 11(2): 140–49.

—— (2002b) 'Setting a conservative policy agenda: The Victorian print media, young people in care and chroming'. *Children Australia* 27(1): 10–14.

—— (2003) 'Social workers and social action: A case study of the AASW Victorian branch'. *Australian Social Work*, in press.

Menzies, Robert (1942a) 'The four freedoms: Freedom from want'. Reprinted in Yvonne Thompson, George Brandis and Tom Harley (eds) (1986) *Australian Liberalism: The Continuing Vision*. Liberal Forum, Melbourne, pp 24–25.

—— (1942b) 'The forgotten people'. Reprinted in Yvonne Thompson, George Brandis and Tom Harley (eds) (1986) *Australian Liberalism: The Continuing Vision*. Liberal Forum, Melbourne, pp 16–21.

—— (1970) *The Measure of the Years*. Cassell, London.

Midgley, James (2001) 'The United States: Welfare, work and development'. *International Journal of Social Welfare* 10(4): 284–93.

Milburn, Caroline (1993) 'Looking for jobless answers'. *Age* 18 February.

Millar, Jane (2001) 'Establishing family policy in Britain'. *Family Matters* 58: 28–33.

Mishra, Ramesh (1984) *The Welfare State in Crisis*. Harvester Press, Brighton.

—— (1989) 'Riding the new wave: social work and the neo-conservative challenge'. *International Social Work* 32: 171–82.

—— (1999) *Globalization and the Welfare State*. Edward Elgar, Cheltenham, UK.

Mission Australia (2002) *There's something different about this place*. Mission Australia, Sydney.

Mitchell, Deborah (1997) 'The sustainability of the welfare state: Debates, myths, agendas'. *Just Policy* 9: 53–57.

—— (2001) 'Managing the new social risks'. In Christopher Sheil (ed) *Globalisation: Australian Impacts*. UNSW Press, Sydney, pp 236–48.

Moore, Andrew (1995) *The Right Road: A History of Right-Wing Politics in Australia*. Oxford University Press, Melbourne.

Moore, Des (1998) *The Case for Further Deregulation of the Labour Market*. Commonwealth of Australia, Canberra.

Mowbray, Martin (1980) 'Non-government welfare: State roles of the Councils of Social Service'. *Australia/New Zealand Journal of Sociology* November: 52–60.

Mullaly, Robert (1997) *Structural Social Work*, second edn. Oxford University Press, Ontario.

Murphy, John (1987) 'Labor and the Right'. *Thesis Eleven* 18/19: 179–86.

Murphy, John and Thomas, Barrie (2000) 'Developing social capital: A new role for business'. In Ian Winter (ed) *Social Capital and Public Policy in Australia*. AIFS, Melbourne, pp 136–64.

Murphy, John, Thomas, Barrie and Glazebrook, Mark (2002) *Partnerships with Business*. Triple A Foundation, Melbourne.

Murray, Charles (1984) *Losing Ground: American Social Policy, 1950–1980*. Basic Books, New York.

Nahan, Mike and Warby, Michael (1998) *From Workfare State to Transfer State*. Institute of Public Affairs, Melbourne.

National Coalition Against Poverty (2001) *Australia Fair*. Uniting Church, Melbourne.

Newman, Jocelyn (1999) *The Challenge of Welfare Dependency in the 21st Century*. Department of Family and Community Services, Canberra.

Newman, Jocelyn (2000) *Welfare Reform: A Stronger, Fairer Australia*. Department of Family and Community Services, Canberra.

Newton, Maxwell (1980) 'Bunny of the welfare state'. *Australian* 24 May.

Nicholas, Alistair and Goodman, John (1990) *Voluntary Welfare: A Greater Role for Private Charities*. Centre for Independent Studies, Sydney.

Norton, Andrew (2000) 'Liberalism and the Liberal Party of Australia' In Paul Boreham, Geoffrey Stokes and Richard Hall (eds) *The Politics of Australian Society*. Longman, Sydney, pp 22–37.

O'Connor, Brendon (1999) American liberalism, conservatism and the attack on welfare: From the great society to the end of welfare as we know it. PhD thesis, La Trobe University, Melbourne.

—— (2001) 'The intellectual origins of welfare dependency'. *Australian Journal of Social Issues* 36(3): 221–36.

O'Connor, Ian, Wilson, Jill and Setterlund, Deborah (1999) *Social Work and Welfare Practice*. Pearson Education, Sydney.

O'Donnell, Anthony (1999) 'Redistribution and risk in the Australian welfare state'. In Glenn Patmore and Dennis Glover (eds) *New Voices for Social Democracy: Labor Essays 1999–2000*. Pluto Press, Sydney, pp 129–40.

OECD (2001) *Taxing Wages*. OECD, Paris.

Officer, Bob (1996) *National Commission of Audit*. AGPS, Canberra.

van Oorschot, Wim (2001) 'Popular support for social security: A sociological perspective'. In Jochen Clasen (ed) *What Future for Social Security?* Kluwer Law International, The Hague, pp 33–52.

Oppenheim, Carey (2001) 'Enabling participation? New Labour's welfare-to-work policies'. In Stuart White (ed) *New Labour: The Progressive Future*. Palgrave, Basingstoke, pp 77–92.

Oxfam International (1999) *The IMF: Wrong Diagnosis, Wrong Medicine*. Oxfam, Washington DC.

Ozanne, Elizabeth (2000) 'Constructing and reconstructing old age: The evolution of aged policy in Australia'. In Anthony McMahon, Jane Thomson, and Christopher Williams (eds) *Understanding the Australian Welfare State*. Tertiary Press, Melbourne, pp 185–98.

Palier, Bruno and Sykes, Robert (2001) 'Challenges and change: Issues and perspectives in the analysis of globalization and the European welfare states'. In Robert Sykes, Bruno Palier and Pauline Prior (eds) *Globalization and European Welfare States*. Palgrave, Basingstoke, pp 1–16.

Peacock, Andrew (1983) 'The Liberal approach to change'. Reprinted in Yvonne Thompson, George Brandis and Tom Harley (eds) (1986) *Australian Liberalism: The Continuing Vision*. Liberal Forum, Melbourne, pp 174–80.

Pearce, Dennis, Ridout, Heather and Disney, Julian (2002) *Independent Review of Breaches and Penalties in the Social Security System*. ACOSS, Sydney.

Pemberton, Alec (1980) 'Doing something about nothing: A note on the Australian Government's response to dole fraud'. *Australian and New Zealand Journal of Sociology* 16(3): 72–76.

Penington, David (2000) 'Illicit drugs: The difficulties in achieving rational public policy'. La Trobe Politics Society Annual Lecture, 11 September.

Petras, James (2002) 'Unemployed workers' movement in Argentina'. *Social Policy* 32(3): 10–15.

Pierson, Christopher (1991) *Beyond the Welfare State?* Polity Press, London.

—— (2001) 'Globalisation and the end of social democracy'. *Australian Journal of Politics and History* 47(4): 459–74.

Pierson, Paul (1994) *Dismantling the Welfare State?* Cambridge University Press, New York.

—— (1996) 'The new politics of the welfare state'. *World Politics* 48(2): 143–79.

—— (2001) 'Coping with permanent austerity'. In Paul Pierson (ed) *The New Politics of the Welfare State*. Oxford University Press, New York, pp 410–56.

Piven, Frances Fox and Cloward, Richard (1972) *Poor People's Movements*. Pantheon Books, New York.

Pixley, Jocelyn (1996) 'Economic democracy: Beyond wage earners' welfare?' In John Wilson, Jane Thomson and Anthony McMahon (eds) *The Australian Welfare State: Key Documents and Themes*. Macmillan, Melbourne, pp 38–61.

Pratt, Alan (2002) 'Universalism or selectivism? The provision of services in the modern welfare state'. In Michael Lavalette and Alan Pratt (eds) *Social Policy*. Sage, London, pp 256–74.

Preece, Gordon (2002) 'An age of sewn lips'. *Arena Magazine* 58: 41–43.

Pusey, Michael (1991) *Economic Rationalism in Canberra*. Cambridge University Press, Cambridge.

Putnis, Peter (2001) 'Popular discourses and images of poverty and welfare in the news media'. In Ruth Fincher and Peter Saunders (eds) *Creating Unequal Futures?* Allen and Unwin, Sydney, pp 70–101.

Quiggin, John (1991) 'The private interest theory of politics: Liberal or authoritarian'. *Policy* Autumn: 51–54.

—— (1998) *Taxing Times*. UNSW Press, Sydney.

Ramia, Gaby (1995) 'The boss knows best: Judith Sloan, industrial relations reform and social protection in Australia'. *Just Policy* 2: 44–48.

Ranald, Patricia (2002) 'Resisting the IMF: Korean unions and economic crisis'. In James Goodman (ed) *Protest and Globalisation*. Pluto Press, Sydney, pp 185–202.

Raskall, Phil (1993) 'Widening income disparities in Australia'. In Stuart Rees, Gordon Rodley and Frank Stilwell (eds) *Beyond the Market: Alternatives to Economic Rationalism*. Pluto Press, Sydney, pp 38–52.

Reference Group on Welfare Reform (2000) *Participation Support for a More Equitable Society*. Department of Family and Community Services, Canberra.

Rhodes, Martin (2001) 'The political economy of social pacts: Competitive corporatism and European welfare reform'. In Paul Pierson (ed) *The New Politics of the Welfare State*. Oxford University Press, New York, pp 165–96.

Richardson, Graeme (1991) Implications of the Liberals' proposal to privatise the Department of Social Security. Unpublished paper, Canberra.

Rodger, John (2000) *From a Welfare State to a Welfare Society*. Macmillan, London.

Roe, Jill (1985) 'Social science, social policy and the slump in Britain'. In Jill Roe (ed) *Unemployment: Are There Lessons from History?* Hale and Iremonger, Sydney, pp 36–57.

Room, Graham (1999) 'Social exclusion, solidarity and the challenge of globalization'. *International Journal of Social Welfare* 8(3): 166–74.

Roskam, John (2001) 'Liberalism and social welfare.' In John Nethercote (ed) *Liberalism and the Australian Federation*. Federation Press, Sydney, pp 267–86.

Rundle, Guy (2002) 'Commonsense and the ALP', *Arena Magazine*, 57: 21–26.

Salvation Army (2001) *Stepping into the Breach: A Report on Centrelink Breaching and Emergency Relief.* Salvation Army Australia Southern Territory, Melbourne.

Samuel, Peter (1973) 'Some people really do believe in economic common sense'. *Bulletin* 24 February: 66.

Saunders, Peter (1998) *Global Pressures, National Responses: The Australian Welfare State in Context.* Social Policy Research Centre, University of NSW, Sydney.

Saunders, Peter (1999) 'Families, welfare and social policy'. *Family Matters* 54: 4–11.

—— (2002) *Poor Statistics: Getting the Facts Right About Poverty in Australia.* Centre for Independent Studies, Sydney.

Scalmer, Sean (1997) 'Being practical in early and contemporary Labor politics: A Labourist critique'. *Australian Journal of Politics and History* 43(3): 301–11.

Scott, Andrew (2000) *Running on Empty.* Pluto Press, Sydney.

Scott, David (1981) *Don't Mourn for Me — Organise: The Social and Political Uses of Voluntary Organisations.* Allen and Unwin, Sydney.

Self, Peter (1993) *Government by the Market? The Politics of Public Choice.* Macmillan, London.

Shamsullah, Ardel (1990) 'The Australian welfare state under Coalition Government: Remembering the forgotten people'. In Russell Ross (ed) *Social Policy in Australia: What Future for the Welfare State?* Volume 4. Social Policy Research Centre, University of NSW, Sydney, pp 105–109.

Shaver, Sheila (1987) 'Design for a welfare state: The Joint Parliamentary Committee on Social Security'. *Historical Studies* 88: 411–31.

—— (1993) 'The post-pension transition'. *Social Policy Research Centre Newsletter* 49: 6–7.

Sheehan, Peter (2001) 'The causes of increased earnings inequality: The international literature'. In Jeff Borland, Bob Gregory and Peter Sheehan (eds) *Work Rich, Work Poor.* Victoria University, Melbourne, pp 40–59.

Sheen, Veronica and Trethewey, Jenny (1990) *Unemployment in the Recession: Policies for Reform.* Brotherhood of St Laurence, Melbourne.

Sherraden, Michael (1991) *Assets and the Poor.* Sharpe, New York.

Shin, Dong-Myeon (2000) 'Economic policy and social policy: Policy-linkages in an era of globalisation'. *International Journal of Social Welfare* 9(1): 17–30.

Simons, Robert (1995) *Competing Gospels: Public Theology and Economic Theory.* EJ Dwyer, Sydney.

Singleton, Gwynneth (1990) *The Accord and the Australian Labour Movement.* Melbourne University Press, Melbourne.

—— (1997) 'Government–business relations'. In Gwynneth Singleton (ed) *The Second Keating Government.* University of Canberra, Canberra, pp 143–51.

Singleton, John (1977) *Rip Van Australia.* Cassell Australia, Melbourne.

Smith, Martin (1993) *Pressure, Power and Policy.* Harvester Wheatsheaf, New York.

Smith, Rodney (1993) 'Australian attitudes to employment and unemployment'. In Paul Smyth (ed) *The Employment White Paper: A New Social Charter?* Uniya Publications, Sydney, pp 42–58.

—— (1994) 'The major party competition: Social welfare since 1972'. In Michael Wearing and Rosemary Berreen (eds) *Welfare and Social Policy in Australia*. Harcourt Brace, Sydney, pp 57–79.

—— (1995) 'Dislocating citizens: The young unemployed'. In Michael Hogan and Kathy Dempsey (eds) *Equity and Citizenship Under Keating*. Public Affairs Research Centre, University of Sydney, Sydney, pp 141–63.

Smyth, Paul (1995a) *Australian Social Policy: The Keynesian Chapter*. UNSW Press, Sydney.

—— (1995b) 'Review essay'. *Just Policy* 3: 51–54.

Social Welfare Commission (1975) *Annual Report*. AGPS, Canberra.

Solas, John (2000) 'A poor state of affairs'. *Australian Quarterly* 72(2): 24–30.

Squires, Peter (1990) *Anti-Social Policy: Welfare, Ideology and the Disciplinary State*. Harvester Wheatsheaf, Hemel Hempstead (Hertfordshire).

St Vincent de Paul Society (2001) *Two Australias: Addressing Inequality and Poverty*. St Vincent de Paul Society, Sydney.

Steketee, Mike (1985) 'The Howard way to better welfare'. *Sydney Morning Herald* 24 May.

Stilwell, Frank (2000) *Changing Track*. Pluto Press, Sydney.

Stokes, Geoff (1994) 'Australian political thought: Editorial introduction'. In Geoff Stokes (ed) *Australian Political Ideas*. UNSW Press, Sydney, pp 1–18.

Stone, Diane (1991) 'Old guard versus new partisans: think tanks in transition'. *Australian Journal of Political Science* 26: 197–215.

—— (1996) *Capturing the Political Imagination: Think Tanks and the Policy Process*. Frank Cass, London.

Stone, John (1991) 'Restoring trust by speaking your mind'. *Financial Review* 10 October.

Strangio, Paul (2001) *No Toxic Dump*. Pluto Press, Sydney.

Stretton, Hugh and Orchard, Lionel (1994) *Public Goods, Public Enterprise, Public Choice*. St Martin's Press, London.

Stubbs, John (1966) *The Hidden People: Poverty in Australia*. Cheshire-Lansdown, London.

Sullivan, Lucy (2000) *Behavioural Poverty*. Centre for Independent Studies, Sydney.

Swan, Wayne (1995) 'Facilitating Australia's transition to lower employment'. In Richard Hicks, Peter Creed, Wendy Patton and John Tomlinson (eds) *Unemployment: Developments and Transitions*. Australian Academic Press, Brisbane, pp 1–10.

Swank, Duane (1998) 'Funding the welfare state: Globalization and the taxation of business in advanced market economies'. *Political Studies* 46: 671–92.

Tanner, Lindsay (1999) *Open Australia*. Pluto Press, Sydney.

Taylor-Gooby, Peter (2001a) 'Polity, policy-making and welfare futures'. In Peter Taylor-Gooby (ed) *Welfare States Under Pressure*. Sage, London, pp 171–88.

—— (2001b) 'The politics of welfare in Europe'. In Peter Taylor-Gooby (ed) *Welfare States under Pressure*. Sage, London, pp 1–28.

Teeple, Gary (2000) *Globalization and the Decline of Social Reform*. Garamond Press, Ontario.

Theophanous, Andrew (1993) *Understanding Social Justice: An Australian Perspective*. Elikia Books, Melbourne.

Tiver, Peter (1979) 'Liberals' ideas on social policy'. In Cameron Hazlehurst (ed) *Australian Conservatism*. ANU Press, Canberra, pp 311–30.

Tomlinson, John (1982) *Betrayed by Bureaucracy*. Wobbly Press, Darwin.

Tulloch, Patricia (1979) *Poor Policies: Australian Income Security 1972–77*. Crook Helm, London.

Turner, Adair (2001) *Just Capital*. Macmillan, London.

Twentyman, Les (2000) *The Les Twentyman Story*. Hardie Grant Books, Melbourne.

Unemployed Workers' Union (UWU, 1982–89) *UWU Newsletter*. UWU, Melbourne.

—— (1991) *Policy, Aims and Objectives*. UWU, Melbourne.

United Nations Development Programme (1999) *Human Development Report*. United Nations, Geneva (www.undp.org/hdro/report.html).

Uniting Care Australia (2001) *Principles for a Fair and Equitable Social Security System in Australia*. Uniting Care Australia, Canberra.

Uniting Church (1996) *Theological and Philosophical Foundation Document*. Community Services Australia, Melbourne.

Vandenbroucke, Frank (2001) 'Active welfare'. *Policy Network* 1: 136–46.

Visser, Jelle and Hemerijck, Anton (1997) *A Dutch Miracle*. Amsterdam University Press, Amsterdam.

Vorspan, Albert and Saperstein, David (1992) *Tough Choices: Jewish Perspectives on Social Justice*. UAHC Press, New York.

Wagner, David (2000) *What's Love Got To Do With It? A Critical Look at American Charity*. New Press, New York.

Warhurst, John (1997) 'Changing relationships between governments and interest groups'. In Scott Prasser and Graeme Starr (eds) *Policy and Change: The Howard Mandate*. Hale and Iremonger, Sydney, pp 111–25.

Warhurst, John, Brown, Jerome and Higgins, Rohan (2000) 'Tax groupings: The group politics of taxation reform'. In Marion Simms and John Warhurst (eds) *Howard's Agenda: The 1998 Australian Election*. University of Queensland Press, Brisbane, pp 167–73.

Watts, Rob (1987) *The Foundations of the National Welfare State*. Allen and Unwin, Sydney.

—— (1989) 'In fractured times: The accord and social policy under Hawke, 1983–87'. In Richard Kennedy (ed) *Australian Welfare: Historical Sociology*. Macmillan, Melbourne, pp 104–31.

—— (2000a) 'Australia's welfare policy and Latham's Third Way'. *Southern Review* 33(2): 143–64.

—— (2000b) 'The persistence of unemployment is the work of economists: Australian unemployment policy, 1983–1996'. *Journal of Economic and Social Policy* 4(2): 48–70.

Wearing, Michael (2000) *Working in Community Services*. Allen and Unwin, Sydney.

Weatherley, Richard (1993) *Compliance Policies in Social Security*. Urban Research Program, Australian National University, Canberra.

Weeks, Wendy (2000) 'Reflections on social work and human service theory and practice with families and communities'. In Wendy Weeks and Margaret Quinn (eds) *Issues Facing Australian Families*. Longman, Sydney, pp 119–36.

Weiss, Linda (1998) *The Myth of the Powerless State*. Polity Press, Cambridge.

Wentworth, William (1969) 'Social services and poverty'. In GG Masterman (ed) *Poverty in Australia*. Angus and Robertson, Sydney, pp 1–18.

Westfield, Mark (1999) 'The business of balance'. In Paul Kelly (ed) *Future Tense*. Allen and Unwin, Sydney, pp 67–76.

White, Stuart (2001) 'The ambiguities of the Third Way'. In Stuart White (ed) *New Labour: The Progressive Future?* Palgrave, Basingstoke, pp 3–17.

Whiteford, Peter (1994) 'Income distribution and social policy under a reformist government: The Australian experience'. *Policy and Politics* 22(4): 239–55.

—— (1998) 'Is Australia particularly unequal?' In Paul Smyth and Bettina Cass (eds) *Contesting the Way*. Cambridge University Press, Melbourne, pp 197–214.

Whitfield, Dexter (2001) *Public Services or Corporate Welfare*. Pluto Press, London.

Whitlam, Gough (1985) *The Whitlam Government 1972–1975*. Viking, Sydney.

Wilby, Peter (2001) 'The end of an era'. *New Statesman* 3 December: 6–7.

Williams, John (1988) 'Getting the New Right right'. *National Outlook* October: 8–11.

Wilson, Shaun and Turnbull, Nick (2001) 'Wedge politics and welfare reform in Australia'. *Australian Journal of Politics and History* 47(3): 384–402.

Windschuttle, Keith (1979) *Unemployment*. Penguin Books, Melbourne.

—— (1988) *The Media*, 3rd edn. Penguin Books, Melbourne.

Wiseman, John (1996) 'A kinder road to hell? Labor and the politics of progressive competitiveness in Australia'. In Leo Panitch (ed) *Socialist Register 1996*. Merlin Press, London, pp 93–110.

—— (1998) *Global Nation?* Cambridge University Press, Melbourne.

Woolfe, Therese (1988) Witness and teacher: The Catholic Commission for Justice and Peace 1968–1987. PhD thesis, University of Sydney, Sydney.

Yeates, Nicole (2001) *Globalization and Social Policy*. Sage, London.

—— (2002) 'Globalization and social policy: From global neoliberal hegemony to global political pluralism'. *Global Social Policy* 2(1): 69–91.

Yencken, David and Porter, Libby (2001) *A Just and Sustainable Australia*. ACOSS, Sydney.

Ziguras, Steve (2001) 'Social entrepreneurs conference'. *Brotherhood Comment* April: 12–13.

INDEX